# ACT AS A FEMINIST

*Act as a Feminist* maps a female genealogy of UK actor training practices from 1970 to 2020 as an alternative to traditional male lineages. It re-orientates thinking about acting through its intersections with feminisms and positions it as a critical pedagogy, fit for purpose in the twenty-first century.

The book draws attention to the pioneering contributions women have made to actor training, highlights the importance of recognising the political potential of acting, and problematises the inequities for a female majority inspired to work in an industry where they remain a minority. Part One opens up the epistemic scope, shaping a methodology to evaluate the critical potential of pedagogic practice. It argues that feminist approaches offer an alternative affirmative position for training, a *via positiva* and a way to *re-make* mimesis. In Part Two, the methodology is applied to the work of UK women practitioners through analysis of the pedagogic exchange in training grounds. Each chapter focuses on how the broad curriculum of acting intersects with gender as technique to produce a hidden curriculum, with case studies on Jane Boston and Nadine George (voice), Niamh Dowling and Vanessa Ewan (movement), Alison Hodge and Kristine Landon-Smith (acting) and Katie Mitchell and Emma Rice (directing). The book concludes with a feminist manifesto for change in acting.

Written for students, actors, directors, teachers of acting, voice and movement, and anyone with an interest in feminisms and critical pedagogies, *Act as a Feminist* offers new ways of thinking and approaches to practice.

**Lisa Peck** is Lecturer in Theatre Practice at University of Sussex and Associate Tutor at Royal Central School of Speech and Drama. She has worked in drama education for over twenty-five years as a teacher educator in universities and drama schools and as a consultant for The National Theatre and Digital Theatre Plus. She researches pedagogic practices in actor training in relation with feminisms, working at the intersection between social science and humanities.

# ACT AS A FEMINIST

## Towards a Critical Acting Pedagogy

Lisa Peck

NEW YORK AND LONDON

First published 2021
by Routledge
52 Vanderbilt Avenue, New York, NY 10017

and by Routledge
2 Park Square, Milton Park, Abingdon, Oxon, OX14 4RN

*Routledge is an imprint of the Taylor & Francis Group, an informa business*

© 2021 Lisa Peck

The right of Lisa Peck to be identified as author of this work has been asserted by her in accordance with sections 77 and 78 of the Copyright, Designs and Patents Act 1988.

All rights reserved. No part of this book may be reprinted or reproduced or utilised in any form or by any electronic, mechanical, or other means, now known or hereafter invented, including photocopying and recording, or in any information storage or retrieval system, without permission in writing from the publishers.

*Trademark notice*: Product or corporate names may be trademarks or registered trademarks, and are used only for identification and explanation without intent to infringe.

*Library of Congress Cataloging-in-Publication Data*
A catalog record for this title has been requested

ISBN: 978-0-8153-5235-8 (hbk)
ISBN: 978-0-8153-5236-5 (pbk)
ISBN: 978-1-351-13051-6 (ebk)

Typeset in Bembo
by MPS Limited, Dehradun

This book is dedicated to the memory of Alison Hodge (1959–2019)

# CONTENTS

*Acknowledgements* x
*Preface* xii

**Introduction** 1

*Acting   1*
  *Where to learn?   1*
  *How to learn?   3*
  *What to learn?   3*
*Pedagogy   6*
  *Anti-pedagogical prejudice   6*
  *Disembody, disempower, 'disembrain'   8*
*Feminism   10*
  *Where are the women?   11*
  *'Being' female   11*
  *Post-feminist equality?   13*
*Overview of chapters   14*

**PART I**
**Shaping a Methodology** 23

1   **Feminist Underpinnings in Acting:**
    **Re-Making Mimesis** 25

    *Unlearning and the hidden curriculum of acting   26*

*The female ontology of acting: The matter of doubling, vision and vulnerability*  29
   *The matter of doubling: Being like a girl*  30
   *The matter of vision: Seeing like a girl*  33
   *The matter of vulnerability: Feeling like a girl*  35
   *Re-making mimesis: New feminist materialisms and acting*  37

**2  Feminist Interventions: *Via Positiva* and Critical Acting Pedagogy**     45

*Acting and pedagogical frameworks*  46
   *Foundational pedagogies: Play and the 'via negativa'*  49
   *Feminist interventions: Power, affirmativity and the 'via positiva'*  53
*Towards a Critical Acting Pedagogy: Difference, the critical position and feminist acting approaches*  57
   *Difference*  57
   *The critical position*  58
   *Feminist acting approaches*  61

# PART II
# Considering Practice    71

**3  Women and the Matter of Voice**     73

*Jane Boston: Thinking through voice*  76
   *Becoming voice*  79
   *The second text*  83
*Nadine George: The healing voice*  86
   *Touching feeling in voice*  89
   *Queering voice*  91

**4  Women and the Matter of Movement**     100

*Feminist ways and movement teaching*  104
*Vanessa Ewan: The cultural body*  108
   *Foundational practices: Learning 'to see' through keys and codes*  109
   *'Doing' gender: Gender as technique*  111
   *'Doing' intimacy: Intimacy as technique*  114
*Niamh Dowling: The ecological body*  116
   *Foundational practices: Towards a nomadic pedagogy*  117
   *Mattering language*  122

## 5  Women and the Matter of Acting — 134

*Kristine Landon-Smith: Intra-cultural acting   137*
  *'All these little parts of yourself'   140*
  *'Doing' race   143*
*Alison Hodge: The relational actor   145*
  *Foundational practices: Sensuality, touch and feeling   149*
  *Queering acting   153*

## 6  Women and the Matter of Directing — 162

*Katie Mitchell: Schooling actors   165*
  *Feminist director pedagogue   167*
  *Re-making mimesis: Vital materialism   173*
  *Agential realism and cyborgs   176*
*Emma Rice: A school for wise children   178*
  *Pedagogy for the collective imagination   181*
  *Vital materialism and the 'feminine masquerade'   186*
  *Bric-a-brac, thing-ness and agential realism   188*

## Conclusion — 198

*Changing the culture: A feminist manifesto for acting   200*
  *A Feminist Manifesto for Acting   200*
*Theoretical underpinnings: A Critical Acting Pedagogy   203*
*Pedagogical practices: Implementing a Critical Acting Pedagogy   207*

*Index*   215

# ACKNOWLEDGEMENTS

I stand on the shoulders of others.

The work of inspiring women is at the heart of this book, and I am forever grateful to the practitioners who taught me, who allowed me into their workshops and rehearsal rooms and who shared their practice so generously: Jane Boston, Nadine George, Vanessa Ewan, Niamh Dowling, Kristine Landon-Smith, Alison Hodge, Katie Mitchell and Emma Rice. It has been a privilege.

Capturing the learning exchange would not have been possible without the voices of actors training and/or working with these women: Ysmahane Yaqini, David Walshe, Imogen Hale, Antonio Harris, Jackie Le, Tania Bre, Daniela Casilda, Sandy McDade, Nick Fletcher, Kate Duchêne, Mike Shepherd, Tristan Sturrock, Lizzie Walker. I am indebted to the practitioners who have contributed to the discussion through interviews: Di Trevis, Deborah Warner, Fiona Shaw, Bella Merlin, Sarah-Davey Hull, Shona Morris, Catherine Alexander and Jeanette Nelson. I also thank all those scholars and practitioners working across the disciplines of feminism, movement, voice and acting who offered feedback to drafts of chapters: Elaine Aston, Frank Camilleri, Tara McAllister-Veil, Rockford Sansom, Shona Morris, Libby Worth, Mark Evans, Benjamin Fowler, Sarah Davey-Hull and Gill Lamden. Particular thanks to Talia Rogers for encouragement, advice and feedback throughout the process. Thanks to Chris Hurford for sharing Alison Hodge's photographic archive and to Chiara D'Anna for the cover photo of Daniela Garcia.

Thanks to my colleagues in University of Sussex: Sara Jane Bailes, whose academic guidance started me on my way; Jason Price for his steadfast support; Ben Fowler for being a writing buddy; William McEvoy, Arabella Stanger and Augusto Corrieri for their encouragement. Thanks to Hannah Vincent for support with writing. Thanks to my students past and present for their questions, their imagination, bravery and belief in the possibility of change. You continue to teach me.

Thank you to Stacie Walker, Lucia Accorsi and Mayank Sharma at Routledge.

Finally, thanks to my friends (you know who you are) and to my family who have supported me over the last ten years on a road I never expected to travel. To my parents, whose love and support has enabled me to embrace academia later in life; to my wonderful daughters Ella, Olive and Isobel, who inspire me; and finally, to Simon, my anchor in life.

Thank you for the love.

# PREFACE

This book is a call to arms. To *Act as a Feminist* we need to re-consider acting in its broadest terms, beyond the patriarchal structures that limit how the field is understood and experienced. The practitioners I write about include women working in fields that constitute a UK actor training curriculum: Jane Boston and Nadine George (voice); Vanessa Ewan and Niamh Dowling (movement); Kristine Landon-Smith and Alison Hodge (acting); and, recognising the life-long learning of the actor, Katie Mitchell and Emma Rice (director pedagogues). Whilst these women do not necessarily identify as feminist, or work with approaches consciously formed by their gendered position, I assess the potential of their pedagogies through a feminist methodology. Working at the intersection between feminist critical theory and education, I re-conceptualise the knowledges of acting to propose a Critical Acting Pedagogy (CAP), informed by the work of women whose perspectives have been marginalised in actor training.

I have worked in the UK for three decades as a theatre-maker and educator in a range of contexts: secondary and further education, drama teacher education, drama school and university theatre and performance programmes. I apply my expertise as a feminist teacher educator to actor training practices and my position of 'between-ness', with one foot in social science and the other in humanities, offers a particular vantage point. I'm driven by Eve Sedgwick's provocation that 'thinking beside' might be a more productive way to ignite change than 'thinking beyond'.[1] My 'beside' investigation resists the faultlines that maneuver thinking into one or other camp – social science *or* humanities. I intersect new feminist materialisms *with* acting pedagogies to propose new paradigms for training.[2]

This enquiry began over ten years ago when I undertook post-graduate study at a UK drama school. I was provoked by a number of silences heard loudly in the field.

The first was the absence of women in the recognised lineages of actor training.³ My aim is to draw attention to the important contributions of women and to highlight the inequities for a female majority inspired to become actors in an industry where, in terms of employment, they remain a minority. Working from the premise that women navigate a marginal space, I speculate on what this position might enable in acting by starting to map an alternative female genealogy of training. The second silence concerns the pedagogy of acting, the processes of teaching and learning, where *how* an actor learns is eclipsed by methodology or methods of practice; in other words, *what* an actor does.⁴ I'm particularly interested in the personal and social knowledges of an acting curriculum that come into being through the interactions between actor and teacher/pedagogue. Although previous studies have examined acting pedagogies, few offer specific examples of practice to analyse the teaching and learning.⁵ The third silence is the voice of the actor reflecting on her/his/their learning; wherever possible I give space to hear the actor's voice. The fourth is the neutering of gender in the discourse of pedagogy in acting and theatre-making. I problematise assumptions of the 'neutral' acting body by pointing to frameworks in theory and practice where techniques of acting and gender converge.⁶ Collectively, attending to these four silences opens up the epistemic scope of actor training through the innovative pedagogic practices of women.

## Notes

1 Eve Sedgwick offers us a different way of thinking. She states, '"Beside" permits a spacious agnosticism about several of the linear logics that enforce dualistic thinking: non-contradiction or the law of the excluded middle, cause versus effect, subject versus object', in *Touching Feeling: Affect, Pedagogy, Performativity* (Durham: Duke University Press, 2003) 8.
2 Frank Camilleri identifies four approaches to writing about performance training: essentialist perspectives, which offer methods (as opposed to paradigms) such as practitioner focused studies; cross-sectional perspectives, which are conceptual, such as genre/discipline-based studies; performers' unique perspectives; and post-human perspectives, which look for models at the crossroads of psycho-physicality. To some extent my hybrid project slips and slides among all of these, but its ambition is to reconceptualise acting pedagogies in relation to new feminist materialisms.
Frank Camilleri, *Performer Training Reconfigured: Post-Psychophysical Perspectives for the 21st Century* (London & New York: Methuen, 2019) 13–20.
3 Jonathan Pitches, *The Actor Training Reader,* ed. Mark Evans (London & New York: Routledge, 2015) 56.
4 Here I am thinking of the tendency to document actor training as a series of exercises or approaches.

5 When using the term 'pedagogy' I refer to the changing consciousness between the person controlling the learning environment (in this case the teacher/director) and the learner (in this case the actor), and the changing knowledge that they produce together. I adopt this understanding of the term, as it neither privileges one agency over the other, nor denies the teacher/director as a neutral transmitter or the student as a passive receiver. In this way pedagogy is a fruitful site for uniting research, methodology and praxis as through pedagogical practices new paradigms for training are produced. The recent collection of essays in *Approaches to Actor Training: International Perspectives*, ed. John Freeman (London & New York: Macmillan International Higher Education, 2019), offers examples of pedagogy in practice. Scholars working to develop this enquiry in the UK include, but are not limited to: Maria Kapsali, 'Editorial', 'Training Politics and Ideology', *Theatre, Dance and Performance Training* 5(2), (2014): 104; Evi Stamatio, 'A Materialist Feminist Perspective on Time in Actor Training: The Commodity of Illusion' in *Time and Performer Training* (London & New York: Routledge, 2019) 50–62; Sherrill Gow, 'Queering Brechtian Feminism: Breaking Down Gender Binaries in Musical Theatre Pedagogical Practices', *Studies in Musical Theatre* 12 (3), (2018): 343–353.

6 In this way my project responds to Ben Spatz, *What a Body Can Do: Technique as Knowledge. Practice as Research* (London & New York: Routledge, 2015) 157.

# INTRODUCTION

I hope that the title of this book, *Act as a Feminist: Towards a Critical Acting Pedagogy* immediately provokes the reader with questions about terms of reference. Why acting? Why pedagogy? Why feminism? What are the contexts, constraints and complexities in choosing these words? How do they shape this book's topographies? Forms of pedagogy and feminism, in relation to the development of UK acting since the 1970s, are the layers of sediment that run throughout.[1] Both are produced by the mechanisms of power that shape the parameters of the field. In marking the boundaries in the discourse of acting and noting what is absent, we can question what is and what isn't valued to push against closed systems. In setting up the context for UK actor training I start with the questions facing an aspiring actor: Where to learn? How to learn? What to learn? This draws attention to the seismic ruptures which have shaped the fault lines in acting over the last five decades.

## Acting

### *Where to learn?*

In the context of this study it is important to note that many of the original London drama schools, flourishing in the 1900s and in the post-war years, were started by pioneering women.[2] Drama schools offered vocational actor training, were accredited by the Conference of Drama Schools (CDS)[3] and funded differently from universities. The first opportunity to study Drama at a university was at Bristol in 1948. During the 1950s, 1960s and 1970s more people aspired to act, and market forces responded with a growing number of training opportunities. In 1975, the Gulbenkian Report, *Going on The Stage,* was commissioned in response to concern about the growth of various acting courses in Higher Education (HE), where the distinction between vocational training providers was blurred. This raised difficulties for local authorities when students applied for grants to train at an accredited drama school when they had access to a drama course locally and, whilst recognising the inevitable crossover in teaching a practice-based subject, the report recommended that distinction should be maintained between the vocational training provided in drama schools and universities.[4] In 1975, there were seven universities in England and Wales offering drama degrees, either as single or joint honours, described as falling within the 'Liberal Arts – Humanistic' category.[5] This number swelled during the next fifteen years at undergraduate and postgraduate levels, in part due to the expansion of universities and the proliferation of courses reflecting the growth of Performance Studies as an academic discipline, which radically changed the field of study and research. By the 1990s, students in the UK could do a three-year Bachelor of Arts degree at University in a wide variety of related subjects: acting, drama, theatre studies, performance studies, performing arts, applied theatre, devised and collaborative theatre, musical theatre, theatre-in-education and community theatre. The market was saturated and fault lines in the landscape between drama school training and university education were threatened.

During the following decade, the shifts in funding strategies at HE, in particular the loss of student discretionary awards, altered the terrain completely and the clear distinction between institutions became blurred. In 2002, drama schools affiliated with universities to secure their funding systems and acting diplomas changed currency to become acting degree courses in line with national benchmarks and abiding with assessment requirements set by the then regulator Higher Education Funding Council of England (HEFCE), with written assignments, agreed assessment criteria and graded degree classifications. In 2002, 15 out of 21 CDS drama schools were offering degrees and by 2012 all the UK drama schools (not including private institutions), were attached to universities. For example, East 15 is part of The University of Essex, Guilford School of Acting is part of The University of Surrey and The Royal Birmingham Conservatoire is part of Birmingham City University. The 2012 economic change to student fees significantly transformed the HE landscape, with parity between the cost of an acting degree at drama school and a degree at university and grants available for both. Employability became a success criteria for 'multiversities', where vocational training became a necessary part of education.[6] In blurring its distinction through affiliation with the University of London, Royal Central School of Speech and Drama (RCSSD), one of the UK's oldest conservatoires, proclaimed its hybridity, 'Central is a unity of opposites; it is the entire ethos around the conservatoire delivery on one hand, and the entire ethos around HE delivery on the other hand. And we see this as a productive tension'.[7] Currently, there are over 2,500 undergraduate degree options, which include either/or/a combination of acting, drama, theatre, performance in their titles.[8] The obfuscation has moved to a new level, with an increasing number of independent Acting degrees now offered by universities: on the south coast you can do an Acting BA at Falmouth, Bournemouth and Chichester Universities. More students currently undertake vocational actor training at universities than at drama schools, and it is easy to see why confusion abounds.[9]

## How to learn?

Whilst drama schools might proclaim 'unity' with universities, there remains a number of practical and pragmatic differences: how you get accepted into a course, how you learn and how you are assessed. Firstly, the entry criteria. All acting degrees require an audition, which in the case of the most revered drama schools, remains fiercely competitive with only one in seven applicants successful.[10] To attend an audition you must pay a fee and your previous qualifications will not determine your offer. In comparison, if you want to study Drama, Theatre and Performance at university you are unlikely to be required to audition but you may be offered an interview or a workshop. There is no direct fee and your offer will depend on achieving certain grades in order to secure your place. Secondly, the contact time. Drama schools, still funded differently due to their vocational status, offer a minimum of 30 hours tuition a week, whilst most universities offer around 10–12.[11] Thirdly, there are no industry showcases at the end of a drama degree at university, which many lecturers see as a welcome emancipation from serving a conservative and defunct notion of 'industry'. Fourthly, a university degree tends to place more onus on the assessment of academic research and writing, whilst the purpose of drama schools remains to train actors for the profession through practice. Inevitably, when two very different institutions (the academy and the conservatoire) attempt to unite, tensions and hierarchies emerge: academic versus vocational, theory versus practice, radicalism versus conservatism. Whilst over the last twenty years drama schools and universities have found ways to make these tensions productive, different perceptions around actor training – *what* it is, *how* it should be taught, *who* should have access to it and, in an industry with 90% unemployment, *if* such numbers *should* be taught – remain engrained for many. Indeed, 'acting' itself has become a contested term, re-understood and re-defined through the emergence of Performance Studies.

## What to learn?

Through the 1980s and 1990s the development of Performance Studies, originating in U.S. scholarship, changed the drama/theatre curricular at UK universities. In 1992, Richard Schechner called for 'A New Paradigm for Theatre in the Academy' with a move away from 'outmoded' theatre studies and the potential blurring of boundaries between vocational and academic theatre education, towards a Performance Studies curriculum.[12] This interdisciplinary approach, which intersected anthropology, sociology and ecology, interrogated performance as a form of every-day meaning making and, in its engagement with critical theory, served an academic curriculum. Performance Studies, both theoretically and through the experimental performance of the time, drew a distinction between 'performance', seen to be kinetic and politicised, and 'acting', which many viewed as tied to mimesis and industry expectations of representation, implicitly inscribing oppressive structures. As boundaries were drawn around the discourses of Theatre Studies and acting, Performance Studies and performing, the possible cross-fertilisation of knowledge, in particular the intersection of pedagogical practices, was closed down and territories were marked.

Certain texts instill these divisions. U.S. scholar and practitioner Michael Kirby, in his 1972 essay 'Acting and Not Acting', draws distinctions between different types of performing, where 'Acting means to feign, to simulate, to re-present, to impersonate'.[13] Kirby's continuum moves from 'non matrixed' performance, such as stage-hands moving scenery, to, at the other end of the scale, 'simple acting', where 'one element or dimension of acting is used';[14] then to 'complex acting', where there is an onus on emotional embodiment. This much-cited essay, whilst acknowledging the matrix as a continuum where one category might bleed into another, reduces acting in attempting to categorise it. Whilst recognising that acting changes depending on style, Kirby places it firmly in the realm of pretense, built on the premise that the actor is 'other' than themselves, 'feigning' when 'being' in character or expressing an emotion.[15] In contrast to acting, performance is task based, kinetic and behavioural, 'doing' as opposed to 'being'. In this case, the performer is not 'in' character but is seen to be 'themselves'. Whilst Kirby maintains that the only value system applied to his matrix should be one of personal taste, to my mind a value system is inherent and a number of problems emerge:[16] his consideration of acting and performing is orientated towards the receiver/audience/critic, rather than the actor/performer themselves, focusing more on the product than the process, with little distinction made between technique and style; I find his explanations about 'simple' or 'complex' acting to be generalised, with the suggestion that the more business involved the more 'complex' the acting; through its re-production of emotion, which reflects the dominant U.S. method acting tradition at the time, acting is orientated towards the representative and the mimetic, inherently cultivating homogeneity and conformity. Consequently, the actor necessarily 'disappears herself', which is met with suspicion and skepticism in a post-modern context and implicitly de-politicises acting. This perspective has infiltrated contemporary attitudes; a performer in Anglo-German performance collective Gob Squad states:

> I was offered a place at the Royal Academy of Dramatic Art to learn to act like Kate Winslet and Laurence Olivier but I never went. During an

audition they said to me: 'Have you ever actually been in a theatre? Because what you are doing here has nothing to do with acting – you're just playing yourself!'[17]

Opinions like this perpetuate the idea that acting is tied to division from self, whilst performing supports agency. Consequentially, acting is inextricably linked to the historical figure of Stanislavski and the naturalistic demands of the early twentieth century text-based acting, with an assumption of what that means. So, why have perceptions of what acting is and what an acting curriculum might enable been reduced in this way?

The post-structuralist rejection of psychology spurred a movement away from states of being to doing. Freudian and Lacanian psychoanalytic theories, with their linear deterministic narratives, are problematic when searching for self-actualisation and our capacity for change. In 1997, theatre and performance scholar Phillip Auslander mapped this shift in *From Acting to Performance: Essays in Modernism and Post-Modernism*, interrogating the shift to performance through a variety of post-structuralist positions.[18] The title immediately places acting in a historicised position. Whilst examining the acting/performing of Willem Defoe, Auslander, like Kirby, considers the subject from the position of performance scholar/spectator and lacks the perspective of the acting process. It's important to note that when Defoe himself examines his own practice he points to the lack of distinction for him between acting and performing, as both are intrinsically structured through task. Referring to the three roles he played in the three parts of The Wooster Group's *L.S.D* (himself, the character of John Proctor, and himself rehearsing John Proctor), Defoe reflects that '"he" is me because "John Proctor" means nothing to me. There's no real pretending, there's no transformation ... Just different action is required of him'.[19] Unfortunately, we rarely get insights like this from actors exploring the complex embodied experience of acting and the lack of clean categorisations. The field of performance can seem to divorce itself from acting lineages when, as Yana Meerzon identifies in her discussion on the Wooster Group, training and onstage behaviour 'can be traced back to the major twentieth-century pedagogical schools in acting.[20] Stanislavski's method of physical acting with its focus on discovering a logical score of actions and Grotowski's staging of the actor's self through psychophysical impulses can be recognised in the Wooster Group's performance approaches. Stanislavski scholar Sharon Karnicke critiques the way that performance scholars 'advance alternative performance theories and techniques that inadvertently seem to reinvent Stanislavski'.[21] In the hands of performance scholars, acting tends to be reduced to a historicised style, which forecloses the process itself and the experience of the actor. Consequently, whilst performing is seen to enable agency and be committed to questions of 'otherness' and identity, the reductive re-presentation of acting negates agency and perpetuates oppressive structures. In this way, the political potential that the acting curriculum offers is closed down and perceptions about what is and is not acting are locked in outmoded traditions. When we attend to the personal and social knowledges of acting that are taught *beside* technique we can open up its epistemic scope and release it from these fetters. This knowledge has been referred to variously as 'dispositional attitudes',[22] 'transferable skills'[23] and 'the invisible dimension' of a 'bigger life project'.[24] I'm interested in how these knowledges of acting, which are difficult to qualify, come into being as embodied knowing.

## Pedagogy

### *Anti-pedagogical prejudice*

How is pedagogy positioned in the field of acting and what does this disclose? Whilst acting practitioners offer methodologies to enable a remote dissemination of practical knowledge, few studies focus on the learning partnership between the actor and the teacher. We have to look to early twentieth-century accounts to find such examples. Stanislavski's *An Actor Prepares,* published in 1936, arguably the most seminal book on learning to act because it was the first to systematically narrate a technique, is structured around the reciprocal dialogue between teacher/director and actor.[25] The split persona of learner and teacher allows for a pedagogical enquiry that moves beyond methodology to focus on the learning exchange. Another pedagogical process, this one infused with a gendered position of power, is Boleslavski's *Acting the First Six Lessons,* first published in 1933, between the teacher (referred to as 'I') and a young female actor, shockingly referred to as 'the Creature'.[26] Recently, performers have documented their own process of learning, but I have yet to find a text that offers a similar exchange.[27] In order to change the ways we think about acting we need to look *through* methods of practice to focus on *how* learning happens.

This is necessary as the stakes are high. In 2013, theatre critic Lyn Gardner asked the question 'Are Actors Just Puppets?' suggesting that by listing actors as 'cast', separate from the 'creatives', the actor's agency was diminished.[28] In 2014, The Standing Conference of University Drama Departments (SCUDD), which represents the interests of Drama, Theatre and Performance in the UK Higher Education sector, generated an online thread in response to the question, 'Are we experiencing the death of the professional actor?'[29] In recognition that ideas about what constitutes acting have changed, the SCUDD thread cautioned that traditional perceptions about training urgently needed review. Accordingly, the July 2014 edition of the journal *Theatre, Dance and Performance Training,* entitled 'Training, Politics and Ideology', called for a political turn, where the actor might be reconsidered as a 'cultural worker'. The key concern was that pedagogies reaffirm existing conditions when they should offer resistance.[30]

Part of the ongoing challenge for scholarship is that the ways of learning in acting are too diverse to suggest a common pedagogy. Actors work in highly idiosyncratic ways, drawing on the modes of performance and types of training they have experienced to address specific problems in particular contexts.[31] Lifelong learning is contingent on the communities of practice and the form and aesthetic of the work. There is limited access for researchers to rehearsal rooms and training grounds as directors and teachers are rarely comfortable having an observer in the room as it changes the dynamic. Moreover, there is an underlying sense that theatre/acting/stagecraft is a practical magic that cannot be articulated and should guard its mystique. Consequently, until recently, the majority of studies on processes have tended to rely on interviews without the added perspective of observer or participant.[32] By continuing to avoid these challenges pedagogy is sidelined and the development of alternative approaches is shut down. In its broader context, the possibility for cross-fertilisation of knowledge is denied.

Ross Prior's 2012 study, *Teaching Actors,* highlights the resistance to notions of pedagogy in UK and Australian conservatoire training.[33] According to Prior there is a lack of value placed on articulating teaching and learning processes in a vocational setting where 'professionals do their job, they don't define it'.[34] He critiques the prevailing view that learning to act happens by osmosis and that acting cannot be taught, only coached. The idea that actor training is 'completely organic' replaces explicit pedagogic language with words such as 'passion' and 'inspiration' to describe the learning process.[35] The trainers rarely had specific educational knowledge, as their capital came from their experience of working in the industry. As a result there was no acknowledged division between *what* they taught and *how* they taught and their pedagogy was 'the methodology of particular acting processes employed, which adhered to heroes or idols'.[36] The actor trainers talked about their practice synoptically, replicating their own experience of learning so that tacit meanings prevailed, which were metaphorical and anecdotal rather than theoretically discursive or critically evaluative.

When teaching and learning approaches are tacit it is impossible to critically examine, develop or efficiently pass on a body of teaching knowledge, resulting in practices that are vulnerable to hit-and-miss approaches. Over the last two decades a number of international and national organisations have been set up to share perspectives on training. These include, but are not limited to: The International Platform for Performer Training, The Standing Conference of Drama Departments, Practice as Research in Performance, and Performing Arts Learning and Teaching Innovation Network. The journal, *Theatre Dance and Performance Training,* started in 2010, has been a vital contributor to sharing and developing networks of pedagogic research. Recently, scholarship has examined acting pedagogies more explicitly with Ellen Margolis and Lisa Tyler Renard's edited collection, *The Politics of American Actor Training,*[37] Camilleri's *Performer Training Reconfigured*[38] and *Approaches to Actor Training: International Perspectives*[39] reclaiming the politics of acting in thinking through training practices. There is a movement to explore the *how* and *why* of acting and progressive pedagogies are starting to emerge.⁴⁰ In 2019, a roundtable discussion at RCSSD brought together course leaders of one-year MA actor training programmes from across conservatoires in the UK to discuss the future of training.⁴¹ A common goal emerged: to facilitate the creative artist through inclusive curriculums that challenge outmoded notions of industry with a willingness to share pedagogical approaches. There is recognition that the lack of attention given to pedagogy stifles development in the field and the capital of the actor suffers the legacy of this neglect. At worst, this perpetuates oppressive power structures that can disempower, disembody and 'disembrain' (or de-intellectualise) the actor.

## *Disembody, disempower, 'disembrain'*

Empowerment can be seen to be something one undertakes for oneself; it is not done 'to' or 'for' someone. Education should enable us to consider our own power in relation to our contexts. As such, if we don't make the processes of learning explicit for actors we can be seen to disempower them. Brazilian educationalist Paulo Freire theorised the construct of empowerment in *Pedagogy of the Oppressed,* to offer a critical pedagogy for education.⁴² His consideration of power recognises that certain forms of knowledge and ways of knowing are privileged by the dominant economic imperatives, which ensure that education functions to serve the needs of those in power. Consequently, pedagogy is always political.⁴³ Without explicit engagement with and awareness of pedagogy, actors are depoliticised and disempowered. Historically, theatre-making required that the actor serve the text, the writer, the director, the company, the industry with her/his/their body, emotions and vulnerabilities. The relegation of pedagogy maintains an acceptance of this service to the industry. Kapsali notes that, 'by following the guidelines of the industry, training reinforces the status quo by preparing artists that are disciplined and passionate enough to accept the working conditions'.⁴⁴ In the UK, where there is a surplus of actors and twice as many male to female roles, actors remain economically vulnerable to mechanisms of control.⁴⁵ In a field where unemployment is seen as a matter of course, the concept of servitude becomes a professional trait. Actor and director Fiona Shaw observes, 'Where I've worked in various theatres the passivity of actors shocks me [...] there's a lot in the culture of actors that needs to be run in a different way'.⁴⁶ The idea of the 'passive actor' recalls the 'docile bodies' of Foucault's critique of the mechanisms of power.⁴⁷ Applying a Foucauldian lens, the actor's body is the site of complex inscriptions of power, a phenomenological and hermeneutic embodiment of knowledge, technique and attitudes.

Roanna Mitchell, in problematising acting as aesthetic labour, cites Cressida Hayes' use of the term 'aspectal captivity' to describe the way that power operates on the actor's body through surveillance.⁴⁸ The body, as primary capital, is objectified and the expectation to embody the idealised image disembodies the actor.⁴⁹ Mitchell's research positions the 'Body as Servant' and points to a culture of servitude and captivity inherent in the field, citing common sayings such as the 'show must go on' and 'no pain no gain'.[50] If the actor is not 'suffering for the art' then they are not evidencing the necessary qualities of sacrifice and this acting mythology is borne out through the psychological exposure of the American Method system[51] or Eastern traditions of durational physical stamina.[52] These traditions have grown from guru-type male lineages, which neuter the actor's body.

The gendered implications of this perception of training are difficult to measure. However, taking for example the circumstances of entry into UK drama schools (where the female is immediately at a disadvantage, with a 2:1 female/male ratio at audition), women are marginalised in an environment where the power of the trainer/auditioner/viewer is pervasive. The actor is produced as a commodity within the industry and these conditions become exaggerated for the female due to the phallogocentric systems of control.[53]

Mark Seton's research into the ethics of embodiment in acting exposes how, in a teaching environment where the teacher/student 'profoundly form each other and are formed by each other', vital ethical training practices are neglected.[54] One of the expectations of actors is that they demonstrate their vulnerability physically and emotionally, learning to be 'accessible', 'porous' or more 'truthful'. There is a dangerous risk of an abuse of power in a climate where fostering vulnerability is a condition of success. As one trainer in Prior's study expressed, 'You've got to look out for the person and try not to destroy them. That's my pedagogy really'.[55] This questionable reading of pedagogy and the vocabulary of violence is worrying. The notion of being 'destroyed' was also present in Seton's study where one female trainer asserted that the training experience at her institution would 'seduce' rather than 'rape' the students.[56] Learning to act has been mythologised as a 'painful' and 'penetrative' process, suggesting violent acts of abuse. The idea that actors must supplicate themselves, both physically and psychologically, is seen as part of the legitimised knowledge of the profession and appears to sanction painful experience within acting pedagogy.

It is encouraging that in the last few years, responding to actors' complaints about inequality and oppression, a number of initiatives have emerged that seem to herald change: in 2017, 'Acting Up', a government strategy, presented recommendations to address the lack of diversity in training grounds;[57] in 2018, Equity's 'Manifesto for Casting' prompted a new code of conduct for casting directors, which acknowledged potentially exploitative structures and inequality in casting and audition practices;[58] in 2018, the Federation of Drama Schools confronted issues of consent in training, prompting drama schools to agree to a critical code for consent. This recognised 'the complexities of permission, ethical caring, appropriate physical contact and personal integrity in and out of classes, and the rehearsal room, particularly in circumstances where there is a power imbalance';[59] in 2020, responding to the consciousness raising of the Black Lives Matter movement, UK drama schools were forced to openly acknowledge ongoing issues of systemic racism and commit to change in structural practices and behaviours.[60] These initiatives demonstrate that disempowerment and disembodiment in training will no longer be tolerated.

Finally, the repeated trope to 'Get out of your head!' or 'Don't think about it, just do it!' alluding to the inhibition of impulses where the actor becomes frozen in thinking about what to do, perpetuates a discourse of outmoded dualisms. Playing on the term 'disembodied', such directions 'dis-embrain' the actor. The Cartesian separation of the body and the mind relegates the brain/mind/intelligence as an obstacle to somatic knowledge. In his critique of training practices, Kent Sjostrom argues that by rejecting the value of theorising or questioning pedagogy, new ways of learning are closed down. He suggests that instead of telling actors not to think about it, it might be more useful to guide them towards what they should think about.[61]

Whilst some point to the damaging ethical neglect in actor training and agitate for institutions to improve their policies, I propose that a more explicit understanding and sharing of pedagogy can empower, embody and 'embrain' the actor. The feminist potential in the practices of women points to a Critical Acting Pedagogy as a vital antidote to patriarchal systems, which reduce acting to 'another branch of study of the dead white males'.[62]

## Feminism

Why is taking a feminist position so important in this context and how do I understand this term? Sarah Ahmed explains feminism as, 'how we pick each other up. So much history in a word; so much it too has picked up'.[63] The word itself is contextual and contingent, an adhesive surface sticking to the unique particles of personal experience. My understanding of feminism is material, produced through actions and attitudes with a common intention, to resist oppression and exploitation of *all* people. The troubling notion of 'post feminism', which came to the fore in cultural studies discourse in the mid-1980s, deemed feminism redundant within the neoliberal ideology of personal success, where gender equality was falsely seen to be happening. However, whilst some Western women have certainly benefited from a perceived culture shift, the vast majority of women across the world continue to be discriminated against because of their sex/gender.[64] How can the actor's training enable her/him/them as cultural agent, to challenge prejudice? Rather than seeing training as re-inscribing oppressive norms I'm interested in its ability to transform culture. How might training be re-imagined for the future? I use gender difference as my primary lens with a particular commitment to address inequalities affecting women in the field, but I'm attentive to all differences including race, age, sexuality, class and able-ism. For me, acting as a feminist agitates beyond notions of equality and idealistic intentions. Indeed, it thinks beyond humans. It is an ecological, ethical and epistemic shift in thinking about being in the world. A way to navigate, make sense of things and to keep our balance. Following Ahmed, in my attempt to map an alternative female genealogy of actor training, I'm picking up what has been sidelined, marginalised and hushed up.

## *Where are the women?*

The absence of women in actor training lineages is striking. Jonathan Pitches, recognising this gap in *The Actor Training Reader*, where Kristine Linklater is the only female to be represented amongst thirteen international practitioners, notes how issues of gender in training are too often overlooked.[65] Pitches observes that in Alison Hodge's first edition of *Twentieth Century Actor Training* two out of fourteen practitioners were female, which subsequently increased to six in the second edition with the inclusion of: Monika Pagneux, Stella Adler, Anne Bogart, Joan Littlewood, Maria Knebel and Arianne Mnouchkine.[66] Hodge's mapping of a more equally gendered landscape offers an alternative to the dominant male lineages of established gurus and acolytes: Stanislavski, Chekhov, Meyerhold, Grotowski, Strasberg, Meisner, Lecoq and Gaulier. Indeed, until recently, some UK drama schools continued to refer to teachers as 'Masters'. The male domain of training can be seen to espouse a guru tradition, built on the premise that the master holds all the answers and that the student is in their thrall, dependent on their instruction. This gendered power dynamic and the expectation that practitioners reproduce rather than challenge received knowledge stifles pedagogical development and infantalises acting. Actor trainers bemoan the androcentric, heterocentric, ableist and Eurocentric traditions of training curriculums.[67] A gendered reframing of the landscape, its foundations, fault lines and genealogies can re-focus perspectives.

One way of addressing the relative absence of women's practice is to document their histories, which, as Susan Bassnett argues, ensures that the traces will not disappear altogether.[68] There are a number of organisations in the UK that document women's work: The Women's Library housed at the London School of Economics; The Women's Theatre Collection at The University of Bristol; and The Magdelena Project, an international body based in Wales, which represents the work of women in theatre.[69] Sue Parrish, Artistic Director of pioneering UK feminist theatre company *Sphinx,* draws attention to what is lost when women are 'hidden from history'.[70] Without these histories the cultural struggles of women's work are marginalised and important developmental pedagogies are lost. Through witnessing the teaching/learning exchange this book gives space to document the formative contributions of women's pedagogic practices.

## *'Being' female*

Of course, when it comes to gender, terms of reference are particularly slippery, described by Spatz as 'riddled with danger'.[71] In deciding to focus on the work of women it is not my intention to homogenise or to mythologise women as more emotionally intelligent, better listeners, more maternal, more instinctive, more generous, more emotional or more corporeal. However, I am interested in how qualities or states situated as female, or feminine, operate and are produced within the developing pedagogies of acting. Naturally, being a feminist is not a 'women only' domain and a feminist lens can be applied to the work of men, but my particular concern is to foreground women's practices, under-represented in training lineages. In doing so, I work from an intersectional feminism, recognising the multiple expressions and preoccupations that the term 'woman' includes and the differences *between* women, as opposed to reducing 'woman' to sameness.[72] Some scholars have cautioned that intersectionality fixes identity and presumes stable categories.[73] Rosi Braidotti looks towards a post-intersectional position when she cautions that we don't just consider differences *between* women but recognize the differences *within* 'woman', which challenges notions of the fixed self.[74] In this way 'woman' signals the contingent nature of the term.

One challenge to the gender specificity of this book is that it will ghettoise practice into some sort of essentialist women-only domain. Elaine Aston and Geraldine Harris place [Women] in square brackets in the title of their study: *Performance Practice and Process. Contemporary [Women] Practitioners*, to present the term as an expansive category.[75] Whilst, to my mind, the use of brackets seems to entrap, more than liberate; it points to how gender fluidity and gender re-alignment have significantly shifted our assumptions about gender/sex normativity and binaries. What does 'being' female mean in an LGBT+ society? Cis females, might be in transition to becoming trans males; they might be gender neutral, or gender fluid, identifying with the plural pronoun 'they' as opposed to 'she' or 'he' and vice-a-versa for cis men. As such, twenty-first-century cultural and social assumptions about who is included and, most importantly, excluded from this category are expanded to recognise hybrid identities and the body in its fluid states of becoming. Therefore, I use the term female to include all those who identify with 'being' female.

A key concern is to attend to the neutering of gender in the discourse of acting pedagogy, looking at the ways that teachers teach, directors direct and actors learn through a gendered lens. The neutering of the 'actor' is addressed in the re-orientated title of Rosemary Malague's important feminist study of American acting, *An Actress Prepares*.[76] However, unlike Malague, my project is not solely concerned with the female condition in training, but relates to *all* those in a marginal position, focusing as much on difference – difference in bodies, difference in pedagogies – as sameness in women's approaches. In a symposium in 2016, Malague, referring to her ongoing project, 'Act like a feminist: empowering strategies for actresses and their teachers' provoked me to question what it means to act *as* a feminist in the field of acting?[77] In this book, I'm not so much seeking feminist acting techniques as I am pursuing a feminist methodology to assess the feminist potential of pedagogies – thinking through how we might act *as* a feminist within a Critical Acting Pedagogy.

## *Post-feminist equality?*

A feminist re-thinking of actor training seems particularly timely. The post-feminist claim can be viewed as an unhelpful smoke screen, obscuring the degrees of sexism experienced on a daily basis by women in all areas of life. At this cultural moment feminism seems to have become mainstream through popular culture and social media: Laura Bates leads the *Everyday Sexism Project* on Twitter inviting women to share stories of their daily encounters with sexism. The *Me Too* or #Me Too movement, started by Alyssa Milano in 2006, a global campaign to speak out about sexual violence, which garnered huge attention in 2017, was prompted by the public accusations from many high-profile female actors of sexual harassment and assault by Harvey Weinstein, an influential U.S. film producer, who by 2020 was convicted. It appears that misogyny and sexual exploitation, viewed by some to be a professional condition of the acting industry, will no longer be hushed up. This movement has no doubt propelled the previously mentioned codes of conduct for casting and issues of consent in UK acting. The idea of 'the casting couch', where a female actor will offer a male director/producer sexual favours to secure employment, reifies the unspoken contract whereby women are exchanged as goods in the hands of men. One must question the extent to which there are ingrained assumptions around the sexual permissiveness of female actors, harking back to the seventeenth century when acting and prostitution were conflated. The British idiom, 'said the actress to the bishop', is a double entendre, producing sexual innuendo from an innocent remark. The equivalent American expression is 'that's what she said'. The assumptions inherent in these expressions require consideration in relation to contemporary perceptions around acting. To what extent have training practices in the twenty-first century redefined perceptions of acting for women?

At this time the acting profession offers little post-feminist equality for the aspiring female actor. Let us consider this narrative in light of the data. When a young woman decides that she wants to enter the profession and train she will be competing with over twice as many females to males for a place.[78] This inequity will continue should she enter the profession in any field (writer, director, producer, actor), where her male peer is twice as likely to gain employment. Purple Seven's 'Gender and Theatre' report considered 6000 plays across 159 UK venues between 2012 and 2015; during this time there has been a slow increase in female directors (34%–39%) and female writers (27%–32%) but casting has remained static (39%).[79] If she does get work, it will be unlikely that she will perform in a play written by a woman and she is almost three times as likely to be directed by a male. As her career progresses she may find it difficult to balance the possibility of a family life with the working structures of performing. If she is able to continue working through her forties she will struggle to maintain a career, as the number of female parts become increasingly limited. It may be that, at some point, she considers teaching as an option, or directing. Finding more secure employment allows for greater stability of family life and the possibility for more control over her work. In the case of teaching, she is most likely to work in the fields of voice or movement. If she does teach acting, it is unlikely that she will become course leader and affect changes to the curriculum.[80] As a director, she will be a more risky proposition for theatres and if she does achieve early success, it will be a challenge to maintain her career through her later years. She will earn less than her male peers doing exactly the same job.[81] Although, undoubtedly, during the last decade there have been improvements, the stubborn disparity of this picture remains.

And to what extent might her work as a female actor confront and challenge discrimination? The field of cultural reproduction produces and solidifies meanings in the cultural consciousness through its representations. When most of the stories we see on our screens and stages are about white, young, able-bodied cis male protagonists what are we being told about the world? How do the stories we are given access to represent and help us to understand our experiences? When the majority of the audience are female why do we continue to accept that theatre and film will prioritise men's stories, situations and dilemmas? Vicky Featherstone, artistic director of the Royal Court Theatre in London, points to a gendered cultural psyche. She asks:

> Do we know how to write and watch plays that have complex, flawed female characters? Is there something in our cultural DNA that makes us respond differently when a play has a central male character?[82]

When what is popular continues to reproduce the 'logic of the same' the hegemony grows stronger.[83] For feminists, be they men or women, the powerful potentiality of theatre and performance to affect change can't be underestimated; indeed it is an urgent responsibility. Responding to this, I turn to 'mattering feminisms' (feminist theories that interrogate the body as matter) intersecting with acting pedagogies, in order to foreground the positivity of difference in actor training.[84]

## Overview of chapters

You can encounter this book from many entrances. You might want to jump straight to Part Two and the practice that most interests you or meet the practice through the critical feminist framings that are explained in Part One. Each chapter has been conceived as a discrete entity and so speaks to a distinct set of challenges, a particular type of knowledge and practices.

The first two chapters, which form Part One, set up the theoretical groundwork that underpins how I think about practice. Chapter 1, 'Feminist Underpinnings in Acting: *Re-Making Mimesis*', overviews particular shifts in feminist critical and performance theories over the last three decades to consider how this has impacted the changing knowledges of acting, re-conceptualising the anti-pedagogical stance through feminist epistemologies. I open up ideas of technique to point to the hidden curriculum of acting, the personal and social knowledge which foregrounds the in-between, relational space of becoming. Returning to feminist constructs of visibility and doubling allows me to speculate on ideas of female knowledge in relation to acting. Taking performativity as my tool, I consider gender technique *beside* acting technique to explain how feminist new materialisms, which re-conceptualise the body as matter, offer ways to 're-make' mimesis.[85] In Chapter 2, 'Feminist Interventions: *Via Positiva* and Critical Acting Pedagogy', I consider how pleasure and discipline operate beside each other in feminist pedagogies, to re-think endurance and sustainability in positive ways. In 'Acting and Pedagogical Frameworks' I identify two foundational pedagogies in acting – 'play' and the *via negativa*. Re-orientating these constructs from a feminist position enables a liberatory practice that, drawing on Braidotti's affirmative politics, produces a *via positiva*.[86] Finally, I foreground the 'positivity of difference' to reconsider acting as a critical pedagogy, with the actor as cultural worker.[87] Part One works to open up the epistemic field in order to advance pedagogical perspectives; it constructs a methodology to assess the feminist potential of pedagogic practices, which I apply in Part Two.

Part Two turns to practice, to overview the field of actor training in its broadest sense, with chapters on women working in voice, movement and acting, including text and devising practices in rehearsal with directors. I acknowledge that this structure appears to re-affirm the separatist divide in the curriculum of actor training. A feminist position would be more likely to pursue the integrated nature of these fields.[88] However, as I overview each discipline I consider what may be lost and/or gained around this separatist approach, questioning why certain fields have become gendered. Each chapter addresses the hidden histories of women with two case studies from different contexts, training grounds and industry practice, focusing on particular aspects of pedagogy through the lens of new feminist materialisms. Collectively, these chapters map a female genealogy of actor training which shows the potential of a Critical Acting Pedagogy.

I have selected practitioners whose significant body of work and contribution to UK training or theatre-making has been recognised professionally and in scholarship and whose practice seems particularly pertinent to developing personal and social knowledge *beside* technique. Most of these women are positioned within traditional training/theatre settings and, as such, can be seen to be part of the status quo, needing to bend to institutional pressures at the expense of radicalism. However, through their pedagogies they enact feminisms which enable actors to make politicised choices. The process of selection has been organic – over the last decade I have bumped into their work, as opposed to seeking it out. Each encounter has stayed with me and called me to return again and again: I was taught by Ali Hodge and Nadine George; first observed the work of Vanessa

Ewan, Katie Mitchell and Jane Boston as part of my MA thesis; first came to the work of Kristine Landon-Smith and Emma Rice through symposiums. I am greatly indebted to these women for generously opening up their studios and rehearsal rooms to me as I progressed this study. I must stress that I am not necessarily expressing their views, as some do not position their work as feminist. The position I take, the lens I apply and analysis I work with enables me to be in conversation with and writing *through* their practices, thinking about the ways that their pedagogies enact feminisms. Inevitably, within the parameters of this book, I have had to be selective and will have missed important initiatives and contributions.[89] A particular regret is that I have only been able to include the work of one BAME (Black, Asian and Minority Ethnic) practitioner. This illuminates another gaping absence in the training landscape – the distinct lack of diversity. Ahmed talks of 'diversity work' as pushing through walls – walls that are only obstacles for *some* bodies.[90] As we illuminate one absence we shine a light on another; as we push through one wall another appears. Recent accounts of systemic racism in UK drama schools expose structures and practices which will no longer be tolerated and there is a commitment to improve diversity amongst staff and students and to decolonise the curriculum.[91] I hope that my efforts might act as a spur for others to confront this challenge in future research; moreover, that a critical acting pedagogy might sharpen perspectives for all minoritarian positions in the politics of acting.

In Chapter 3, 'Women and The Matter of Voice', I overview the field of voice training in the UK to speculate on why this is a female domain. Voice teaching emerges as deeply politicised and potentially radical in its liberatory potential. Jane Boston, Head of the International Centre of Voice at RSCCD, uses her feminism to shape her pedagogy. Nadine George, founder of Voice Studio International, implements a gendered architecture to queer the voice, harnessing its potential for holistic self-development. Chapter 4: 'Woman and the Matter of Movement' points to the ways that feminist articulations of the body emerge in movement for actors. Vanessa Ewan has developed a training process which helps the actor discover the expression of the physical being through the cultural body.[92] Considering Ewan's practice, I focus on the way she teaches actors how to 'see' through movement with a particular focus on gender and intimacy. Niamh Dowling has developed international training collaborations which foreground choice for the actor through a nomadic pedagogy that enables the ecological body. Chapter 5, 'Women and the Matter of Acting', draws on the work of two practitioners working in different contexts in UK actor training. Kristine Landon-Smith has developed an intra-cultural practice, which tackles the particular problem of enabling the actor to work with the multiplicity of the self, to access their culture operating from the positivity of difference. She developed her approach through her education work with Tamasha, a UK company working with British Asian artists. I focus on how she liberates the actor by accessing each individual's multiple cultural identity. Alison Hodge, to whose memory I dedicate this book, worked for most of her career teaching in universities and drama schools in the UK. Her scholarship has made a major contribution to the understanding of actor training approaches and her practice, *Core Training for the Relational Actor,* builds an actor's relational awareness.[93] Here I consider how she develops the 'feeling', or emotional accessibility of the actor through different forms of touch. Chapter 6, 'Women and the Matter of Directing' considers the work of Katie Mitchell and Emma Rice, two self-proclaimed feminist UK directors who have made a significant impact on the way that theatre is made and the way that actors learn to act. The pedagogic exchange with certain directors can be formative to the life-long learning of the actor and consequently I position Mitchell and Rice as director/pedagogues. Through observations and interviews, I unpick the foundational pedagogic features of their practice to identify emergent feminist acting approaches.

A call to arms demands a manifesto – a declaration, statement of principle or mission statement. According to Ahmed, 'A manifesto not only causes a disturbance, it aims to cause this disturbance',[94] In the Conclusion I offer a feminist manifesto for acting in the twenty-first century that challenges institutions to reconsider their positions. Speculating on what a re-imagined critical acting curriculum might look like I ask a series of 'what if's'. What if we did things differently? How might learning objectives, curriculum content, pedagogical approaches and scaffolding structures meet the demands of acting for the future, whatever challenges that presents us with? Underpinning a Critical ActingPedagogy' is an affirmative politics, that confronts patriarchal systems to propose a different way of thinking about being with each other in the world.

## Notes

1 I confine my focus to the UK, which at the time of writing includes England, Scotland, Wales and Northern Ireland, where actor training is acknowledged to be world class and yet, until recently, there has been a lack of research interrogating the politics and implications of its pedagogy.
2 For example: Elsie Fogerty (1865–1945) founded the Central School of Speech and Drama in 1906 in the Albert Hall. Ruth Conti (1874–1936) founded the Italia Conti Academy of Theatre Arts in 1911 at the Savoy Theatre. In 1950, Rose Bruford, a female actor and voice and speech teacher who taught at the Royal Academy of Music, founded Rose Bruford in Kent. Margaret Bury and Jean Newlove founded East 15 in 1961 in Essex.
3 The Conference of Drama Schools represented the top 21 accredited UK Drama schools, and it ran between 1969 and 2012. In was succeeded by Drama UK, 2012–2106 and currently by The Federation of Drama Schools.
4 Fundação Calouste Gulbenkian, *Going on the Stage: A Report to the Calouste Gulbenkian Foundation on Professional Training for Drama* (Calouste Gulbenkian Foundation, 1975).
5 Ben Francombe, 'Falling Off a Wall: Degrees of Change in British Actor Training', *Studies in Theatre and Performance,* 21(3), (2002): 176–187.
6 Ross Prior, workshop for actor trainers at Royal Central School of Speech and Drama (06.10.13).
7 Simon Sheppard, from a talk at Birkbeck with Drama UK (18.04.13).

8  This was in the years 2019–2020 https://www.ucas.com/explore/subjects/creative-arts [accessed 20.06.20].
9  John Freeman (ed.), *Approaches to Actor Training: International Perspectives*, (London & New York: Macmillan International Higher Education, 2019) 3.
10  Alistair Smith, 'Competition Fiercer for Drama Schools than for Oxbridge', *The Stage* (26.06.07) https://www.thestage.co.uk/news/2007/competition-fiercer-for-drama-schools-than-fo [accessed 17.09.10].
11  Some Acting BAs at university are starting to offer more hours' contact time. For example, Falmouth University offers 15–18 hours a week.
12  Richard Schechner, 'A New Paradigm for Theatre in the Academy', *TDR (1988–)* (Winter, 1992), 36(4): 7–10.
13  Michael Kirby, 'On Acting and Not-Acting', *The Drama Review: TDR*, (1972), 16(1): 3–15, 3.
14  Ibid, 8.
15  Geraldine Harris, writing about contemporary performance, explains that it is the extent to which the quotation marks are shown that determines playing styles. Geraldine Harris, *Staging Femininities: Performance and Performativity* (Manchester and New York: University Press, 1999) 77.
16  Ibid, 15.
17  'We Are Gob Squad and So Are You' [Adventures in Remote Lecturing] https://www.gobsquad.com/projects/we-are-gob-squad-and-so-are-you/ [accessed 12.06.20].
18  Phillip Auslander, *From Acting to Performance: Essays in Modernism and Postmodernism* (London & New York: Routledge, 1997) 39–45.
19  Ibid, 43.
20  Yana Meerzon, 'Taming the Impulse': On The Wooster Group's Acting Techniques and Methodologies', *Theatre Dance and Performance Training*, 4(3): 381–398, 382.
21  Sharon Carnicke, 'Active Analysis for Twenty-First Century Actors', https://www-digitaltheatreplus-com.ezproxy.sussex.ac.uk/education/collections/digital-theatre/active-analysis-for-twenty-first- [accessed 12.06.20].
22  Simon Murray cited by Maria Kapsali, 'Training for a Cold Climate: Edited Transcript of Roundtable Discussion', in *Theatre, Dance and Performance Training*, 5(2), (2014): 2019–2231.
23  Stephen Wangh, *The Heart of Teaching. Empowering Students in the Performing Arts.* (London & New York: Routledge, 2013) 139.
24  Camilleri, op.cit. 105.
25  Konstantin Stanislavki, *An Actor's Work* (New York & London: Routledge, 2008).
26  Rhonda Blair considers the problem of overt sexism in her editorial introduction to Richard Boleslavsky, *Acting: The First Six Lessons. Documents from the American Laboratory Theatre* (London & New York: Routledge, 2010) xi. This edition documents the influence of Maria Ouspenskaya on Boleslavsky's method.
27  An example is Bella Merlin, *The Psycho-Physical Approach to Actor Training* (London & New York: Routledge, 2002).
28  Lyn Gardner, 'Are Actors Just Puppets'? *The Guardian*, 1.05.13 https://www.theguardian.com/stage/theatreblog/2013/may/01/are-actors-ju [accessed 11.04.20].
29  SCUDD online thread, *Re: The Death of the Professional Actor* <http://www.scudd.org.uk> [accessed 06.05.14 – 09.05.14].
30  Kapsali, 104.
31  Phillip Zarrilli, Jerri Daboo and Rebecca Loukes, *Acting: Psychophysical Phenomenon and Process* (Basingstoke: Palgrave Macmillan, 2013) 6.
32  The inaccessibility of observing directors is acknowledged by Helen Manfull, *Taking Stage: Women Directors on Directing* (London: Methuen, 1999) 61. Like Prior's study, her book relied on interviews with directors as opposed to observation of practice in

rehearsals. For recent examples exploring pedagogy in practice I refer the reader to John Freeman (ed.), *Approaches to Actor Training: International Perspectives* (London & New York: Macmillan International Higher Education, 2019).
33 Ross Prior, *Teaching Actors: Knowledge Transfer in Actor Training* (Bristol: Intellect, 2012) 172–174.
34 Donald Schön focused on the training of professionals in a number of areas, most usefully for this study in the field of music training. Donald Schön, *Educating the Reflective Practitioner* (San Francisco: Jossey-Bass, 1987) 12.
35 Prior, 172–174.
36 Ibid., 161.
37 Ellen Margolis, Lissa Tyler Renaud (eds), *The Politics of American Actor Training*, (London & New York: Routledge, 2010).
38 Camilleri, op. cit.
39 Freeman, op cit.
40 During the last decade a number of conferences have opened up this debate. The Reflective Conservatoire Conference at Guildhall in 2018, 'Artists as Citizens' considered the social responsibility of the artist. https://www.gsmd.ac.uk/about_the_school/research/events_researchworks/reflective_conservatoire_conference/ [accessed 19.12.19]. In 2018, the working group for performer training at the Theatre and Performance Research Association (TAPRA) conference in Aberystwyth considered 'Who are we training for'? with questions such as: 'Can training respect and work through marginality or does its very process and logic cultivate homogeneity and conformity'? http://tapra.org/call-participation/tapra-2018-aberystwyth-performer-training-wg-who-are-we-training-for/ [05.06.19].
41 Actor Training Roundtable, Royal Central School of Speech and Drama, 18.07.19.
42 Paulo Freire, *Pedagogy of the Oppressed* (New York & Great Britain: Continuum, 2000).
43 Paulo Freire, *Education for Critical Consciousness* (London & New York: Continuum, 1974) 44.
44 Kapsali, 161.
45 Charlotte Higgins, 'Women in Theatre: Why Do So Few Make It To the Top?', *The Guardian* http://www.theguardian.com/stage/2012/dec/10/women-in-theatre-glass-ceiling [accessed 11.11.13].
46 Interview with Fiona Shaw. Glyndebourne, East Sussex (24.09.13).
47 Foucault argues that disciplinary forces subjugate the body as a malleable object, which can be used, transformed and improved to best serve the new forms of economic, political and military organisations. Michel Foucault, *Power: Essential works of Michel Foucault 1954–1984. Volume 3* (London: Penguin, 1984) 323–340.
48 Cressida Heyes, *Self-Transformations: Foucault, Ethics and Normalised Bodies* (New York: Oxford University Press, 2007), 18, cited in Roanna Mitchell, 'Seen But Not Heard: An Embodied Account of the (Student) Actor's Aesthetic Labour', *Theatre, Dance and Performance Training* (2014), 5(1): 66.
49 Mitchell, 59–73.
50 Roanna Mitchell, 'The Actor's Body: Identity and Image', Royal Central School of Speech and Drama (15.10.13).
51 Ellen Mergolis and Lissa Tyler Renaud, *The Politics of American Actor Training* (London & New York: Routledge, 2009).
52 Jerzy Grotowski, *Towards a Poor Theatre: Statement of Principles* (London & New York: Routledge, 2002), 211–218.
53 Geoff Coleman, Head of Acting at RCSSD at the time of writing, acknowledged the need for a training programme to address the female experience at drama school. He comments, 'We have nearly 5,000 people applying to our course each year and there are about 11,000 people applying to be actors in the sector each year. Two thirds of them

are women. If when they arrive they are not given the same opportunities and challenging narratives they can develop worries about their own gender and their approach to their own gender as required by the industry [...] This pressure has to stop'. Geoffrey Coleman, 'Creating the Roles and Expanding the Boundaries', *Vamps, Vixens and Feminists Fighting the Backlash*. Sphinx Theatre Company. Young Vic (29.10.10), 17–29 http://www.sphinxtheatre.co.uk/resource.html [accessed 12.06.14].
54 Ibid., 5.
55 Prior, 169.
56 Mark Seton, 'The Ethics of Embodiment: Actor Training and Habitual Vulnerability', *Performing Ethos*, 1(1), (2010): 5–18, 9.
57 Tracy Brabin, Gloria De Piero and Sarah Coombes (2017), 'Acting Up Report: Labour's Inquiry into Access and Diversity in the Performing Arts', https://d3n8a8pro7vhmx.cloudfront.net/campaigncountdown/pages/1157/attachm [accessed 15.04.20].
58 Equity 'Manifesto for Casting' https://www.equity.org.uk/getting-involved/campaigns/manifesto-for-casting/ [accessed 15.04.20].
59 Georgia Snow, 'Drama Schools Commit to Ethical Guidelines to Tackle Sexual Harassment', *The Stage* (19.04.18) https://www.thestage.co.uk/news/2018/drama-schools-commit-ethical-guidelines-tack [accessed 15.04.20].
60 Black Lives Matter was founded in 2013 in response to the acquittal of Trayvon Martin's murder. Black Lives Matter Foundation, Inc. is a global organization in the U.S., UK and Canada, whose mission is to eradicate white supremacy and to intervene in violence inflicted on Black communities by the state and vigilantes. The murder of George Floyd by a white policeman on 25.05.20 ignited global support. UK Drama schools were publicly accused of systemic racism:Lanre Bakara, 'Drama Schools Accused of Hypocrisy over Anti-Racism Statements' *The Guardian* (09.06.20) https://www.theguardian.com/stage/2020/jun/06/drama-schools-accused-of-hypocrisy-over-anti-racism-statements [accessed 17.06.20].
61 Kent Sjostrom, 'Reflection, Lore and Acting: The Practitioner's Approach', *Nordic Theatre Studies*, 20 (2008): 61–68.
62 Maria Kapsali, 'Training for a Cold Climate. Edited Transcript of Roundtable Discussion', *Theatre, Dance and Performance Training*, 5(2), (2014): 231.
63 Sarah Ahmed, *Living a Feminist Life* (Duke University Press Books, 2017) 1.
64 Kim Solga, *Theatre and Feminism* (London & New York: Palgrave Macmillan, 2016).
65 Jonathan Pitches, *The Actor Training Reader,* ed. Mark Evans (London & New York: Routledge, 2015) 56.
66 Pitches, citing Alison Hodge, *Twentieth Century Actor Training* (London: Routledge, 2010) 57.
67 Actor Training Roundtable, Royal Central School of Speech and Drama, 18.07.19.
68 Susan Bassnett, 'The Changing Status of Women in Theatre', in *The Routledge Reader in Gender and Performance*, ed. Lizbeth Goodman (London & New York: Routledge,1998) 88.
69 The Women's Theatre collection was established in 1990 to provide a centre for playscripts by women. The Magdelena Project was founded in 1983 and provides an international forum for women performers and researchers. More information at http://www.themagdalenaproject.org/en/content/magdalena-project [accessed 11.11.13].
70 Sue Parrish, 'Gender Equality Requires Context', *The Stage* (24.10.13) http://www.thestage.co.uk/features/analysis-opinion/2013/10/letters-october-24–2013 [accessed on 01.10.13].
71 Spatz (2015) 178.
72 The term 'intersectional' was used by Kimberlé Crenshaw to problematise the differentiation between gender and race in the lived experience of women of colour. See Kimberlé Crenshaw, 'Mapping the Margins: Intersectionality, Identity Politics and Violence against Women of Colour', *Stanford Law Review* 46(3): 1241–1299.

73 Jennifer C. Nash, 'Practicing Love: Black Feminism, Love-Politics, and Post-Intersectionality', *Meridians*, 11(2), (2011): 1–24.
74 Rosi Braidotti, *Nomadic Theory: The Portable Rosi Braidotti* (New York & Chichester: Colombia University Press, 2011) 148.
75 Elaine Aston and Geraldine Harris, *Performance Practice and Process: Contemporary [Women] Practitioners* (Basingstoke: Palgrave Macmillan, 2008) 1.
76 Rosemary Malague, *An Actress Prepares: Women and 'The Method'*. (London & New York: Routledge, 2011).
77 Rosemary Malague, 'Act Like A Feminist: Empowering Strategies for Actresses and Their Teachers', RCSSD (15.03.16).
78 Higher Education Statistics Agency – the official source of data for UK universities and HE colleges. http://www.hesa.ac.uk [accessed 20.07.20]. Figures taken from 'UCAS Conservatoires End of Cycle Report 2019' identify a 7.1% rise in applications with 6920 women and 3990 men. This translates to 1600 admissions for women and 1225 men. https://www.ucas.com/data-and-analysis/ucas-conservatoires-releases/ucas-conservatoires-end-cycle-2019-data-resources [accessed 20.07.20].
79 Purple Seven (2015) 'Gender in Theatre' http://purpleseven.com/media.ashx/gender- thought-leadership.pdf [accessed 16.06.16].
80 Through the gender breakdowns of the seventeen drama schools in Drama UK, I was able to consider the gender breakdown across curriculum areas. http://www.dramauk.co.uk [accessed 11.10.13].
81 Tonic Theatre. http://www.tonictheatre.co.uk [accessed 12.08.15].
82 Sarah Compton, 'Sexism on the Stage – Meet the Women Tearing Up the Script', *The Guardian* (17.01.16) https://www.theguardian.com/stage/2016/jan/17/sexism-stage-female-playwrights-royal-court-theatre [accessed 22.02.16].
83 Charlotte Higgins, 'Women in Theatre: Why Do So Few Make It to the Top?' *The Guardian* (910.12.120) http://www.theguardian.com/satge/2012/dec/10/women-in-theatre-glass-ceiling [accessed 11.11.13].
84 'Mattering feminisms' refer to materialist approaches that recognise the body as matter inscribed by social constructs. In particular, I look to the work of Rosi Braidotti and new feminist materialists, such as Karen Barad who are concerned with the bio-politics of the body and its possibility to change culture. These ideas are considered in Part One.
85 This references Elin Diamond, *Unmaking Mimesis: Essays on Feminism and Theatre* (London & New York: Routledge, 1997).
86 Braidotti, 315.
87 Braidotti, 161.
88 For more on this see Experience Bryon, *Integrative Performance Practice: Practice and Theory for the Interdisciplinary Performer* (London and New York: Routledge, 2014).
89 I acknowledge that, other than discussion of Katie Mitchell's 'cyborg pedagogy' in Chapter 6, there is no examination of progressive technological practices, which I recognise as essential in training for the future.
90 Sarah Ahmed, *Living a Feminist Life* (Durham and London: Duke University Press, 2017) 136.
91 I'm aware that terms such as 'diversity', 'inclusivity' and 'decolonisation' are contested in this context. See Eve Tuck and K. Wayne Yang, 'Decolonization is not a metaphor', *Decolonization: Indigeneity, Education and Society* (2012), 1(1): 1–40.
92 Vanessa Ewan and Debbie Green, *Actor Movement: Expression of the Physical Being* (London & New York: Bloomsbury Methuen Drama, 2015).
93 Alison Hodge, *Core Training for the Relational Actor* (London: Routledge, 2013).
94 Ahmed, 251.

# PART I
# Shaping a Methodology

# 1
# FEMINIST UNDERPINNINGS IN ACTING

*Re-Making Mimesis*

What matters in the matter of acting? This chapter, alongside Chapter 2, constructs a methodology to assess the feminist potential of pedagogic practices in Part Two. Recent studies point to new paradigms for acting that re-conceptualise its epistemic scope and foreground materiality in moving towards a post-psychophysical practice.[1] Responding to these provocations, I consider the epistemologies and ontologies of acting in relation with feminist critical theories since the 1970s, in particular feminist materialisms.[2] When discourse in training tends to neuter gender and assumes the male 'I' it seems vital to position acting, alongside gender as technique. Working from the premise that actors and people identifying as female both experience a minoritarian position within patriarchal structures, being female, a disadvantage in terms of employment, becomes an advantage in approaching acting as a critical practice.

Drawing on a range of feminist critical thinking, from philosophy, education, science and performance studies three central tenets can be plaited together to construct a female genealogy of acting as an alternative to male lineages and frameworks of learning. Here, I reference a Foucauldian genealogy that questions 'the constitution of knowledges, discourses and domains'.[3] In agitating for this change, it is expedient to adopt a 'strategic essentialism' and to consider certain ideas around female-ness.[4] Whilst this is my focus, it's important to reiterate that the constructs examined here are not exclusive to those identifying as female but speak to any individual in a minoritarian position.[5] The first strand outlines how the knowledges of acting intersect with feminist epistemologies that challenge hierarchies, and question ways of knowing. Knowledge is not acquired through a linear acquisitive process but is cyclical and repetitive, enabling a *knowing how* and then a *realised knowing*, where learning happens through misunderstanding. Dualisms, so dominant in acting discourse (inner/outer, body/mind, self/other, presence/absence, being/seeing), are dismantled to assert non-hierarchical ways of understanding, reflecting Eve Sedgwick's view that ideas can operate *beside* each other as opposed to being structured in dualistic narratives.[6] From this perspective, feminist epistemologies allow us to re-think the ideological foundations of acting and to foreground its personal and social knowledge, which I term 'the hidden curriculum'.[7] The second strand re-considers acting as a female ontology, with ways of knowing located in a female domain. I re-think notions of doubling, visuality and vulnerability, well trodden paths in feminist performance theory, in relation to acting knowledges.[8] The third strand focusses on the recent bio-political turn to consider how new feminist materialisms can sharpen the tool of performativity and broaden our perspectives when thinking through feminist acting pedagogies. Collectively, these three strands underpin the feminist foundations on which to build an architecture for pedagogic interventions in Chapter 2.

## Unlearning and the hidden curriculum of acting

There is synergy between feminist epistemologies and acting as both resist Western male theories of knowledge and give value to different ways of coming to learn.[9] A feminist position sees knowledge construction as relational and situated, formed within the community as opposed to within the individual struggling for epistemic autonomy.[10] It foregrounds the matter of individual particularity, recognising that gender, race, class, sexuality, culture, age and ableism affect understanding. It resists the linear ways that history is remembered and critiques the contextual power structures that make meaning and create systems of subordination. Looking at feminist theories of knowledge helps us to understand the anti-pedagogical prejudice in acting outlined in the Introduction to this book.[11]

I have noted that directors and acting teachers become uncomfortable with the idea of their practice being categorised, as this pins down a creative process, which they would rather view as organic and evolutionary. This reflects an orientation in the field towards *knowing that* as opposed to *knowing how* and a concern to avoid generic descriptions of practice.[12] Acting pedagogy resists the modes of value and educational structures that have come to define how knowledge can be measured. Similarly, a feminist paradigm locates the rational structures of scientific or objective knowledge in the masculine hegemony of universal truth. Feminist readings of the Enlightenment identify woman with the fall from grace, therefore inherently unstable and man with logic, reason and stability. Binary opposites (nature/reason, rational/irrational, subject/object, mind/body, masculine/feminine) produce what Luce Irigaray terms the 'Logic of the Same', and have come to define phallocentricism.[13] The actor trainers in Prior's study *Teaching Actors: Knowledge Transfer in Actor Training* can be seen to take a feminist position in their resistance to structures which attempt to rationalise ways of learning in acting, which are somatic, non-linear, at times chaotic, processual and transitory.[14] The desire for order, stability and empirical outcomes can be seen as a more cerebral position, whilst the actor's learning is embodied, accessing the irrational such as: emotion, instinct, instability, vulnerability and impulse. From this perspective, it is not unreasonable to suggest that the knowledge of acting is located within a female domain and that resistance to articulating pedagogies may indicate an unwillingness to impose structures or linear processes onto learning, which is intangible and unpredictable.

Feminist epistemologies are built on the gaps and distortions of knowledge that challenge constructs of 'ownership' to focus on the experiential and notions of difference.[15] It's important to note that Western 'difference' is often reduced to *one* difference (gender, sexuality, class, race, age, ableism), where difference is marked against its antithesis or lack. I conceptualise difference as polyvalence – difference *within* as well as *between* – maintaining a positive economy, where differences can be mined for their potential. In mapping an alternative female genealogy of training, these gaps, spaces between and differences offer alternatives to the dualistic frameworks that dominate acting discourse. Actors use notions of inside/outside, individual/ensemble, external/internal, objective/subjective, self/other, representing/presenting to make sense of the double nature of the experience of acting. Feminist epistemologies of difference invite us to think in the gaps between. Sedgwick's 'beside thinking', which allows for flux and possibility, supports my thinking throughout this book.[16] These alternative topographies draw attention to the knowledges of acting that develop *beside*, *in between* and *through* technique or skill. This 'hidden curriculum' facilitates a critical practice that enables the actor to act as a feminist.

Educationalist Vic Kelley explains the hidden curriculum as learning that is not explicitly identified in the examined curricula, which can include attitudes or qualities.[17] In acting, the task of nurturing the personal and social consciousness of the actor is acknowledged by trainers in Prior's study. He explains personal and social knowledge as 'ethics, interpersonal skills, community responsibility and environmental awareness'.[18] The actor trainers viewed this knowledge as politically productive in its potential to 'produce better human beings' who 'understand humanity not judge it'.[19] This type of knowledge, which has been described as 'dispositional attitudes',[20] 'transferable skills'[21] and 'the invisible dimension'[22] is key to politicising acting pedagogies. It enables relational understanding and the reflexive space of meta-learning to develop beside each other, producing a heutagogy, where the actor learns to become her/his/their own teacher.[23] Whilst these knowledges are foundational, they can remain tacit within the curriculum and side-lined in the discourse of training.

Turning to educational theory, we can see how subjugated knowledge, overlooked or hidden in the value economy of a field, can be the unseen pivot on which an oppressive learning practice balances. Paulo Freire developed a critical 'pedagogy of the oppressed', where individuals from predominantly marginalised groups were empowered to take control in the processes of their learning.[24] Developing this approach, Henry Giroux drew attention to what he termed 'naïve knowledges, located low down in the hierarchy', but which functioned as a politically empowered pedagogy for marginal groups.[25] Camilleri, referencing Calvin Taylor, picks up this idea when he points to the difference between material and immaterial labour in relation to acting knowledge; immaterial labour includes techniques of collaboration, interaction and creative embodiment.[26] In addition, and recognising that this list is not exhaustive, I identify the transferable skills of the actor as: imagination, emotional intelligence, being-in-the-moment, impulse, intuition, flow, emotional availability, trust, respect, generosity, inner listening, bodily care, polyphonic awareness, empathy, altruism, collaboration, reflection, reflexivity, learning through mistakes, playfulness, knowing the value of fear, self-discipline and resilience. I am particularly concerned with knowledge that enables the actor to critically reconsider her/himself in the world: generosity, empathy, altruism, reflexivity, collaboration, respect. Capturing *how* these subjectively experienced knowledges are produced through the interaction between learner and teacher/director is hard to describe and almost impossible to quantify but, in order to develop a better understanding of the political potential of acting pedagogy, it seems vital. Such knowledges do not fit into any easily structured or measurable system of learning. However, this hidden curriculum equips actors to manage the complex challenges of acting, to operate in a state of 'habitual vulnerability' and to enable heutagogy.[27]

Feminist approaches to knowledge construction embrace the knowledges of the hidden curriculum. As an embodied practice, acting immediately takes its reference from a bodily knowledge and a 'felt sense', which operates beyond the limits of cerebral reasoning. Hence the trope, 'Get out of your head!' might be explained as a rejection of hegemony, which shuts down the possibility of an embodied wholeness. This points towards a more female somatic knowledge where the capacity of the body to work with the qualities of instinct, impulse and emotional becoming are nurtured.[28] This phenomenological position, which underpins psychophysical acting paradigms, harnesses the bodymind to recognise that the body thinks. In moving towards post-psychophysical approaches, the phenomenological works *beside* the materialist, looking to the inner and outer in relation to exterior forces, which Camilleri describes as the *bodyworld*.[29] This relational thinking characterises feminist epistemologies.

The value placed on acquisitive knowledge and 'knowing that' is challenged by a feminist position that argues for the value of *not* knowing. Peggy Phelan gives value to that which is not really 'there' within the boundaries of the real and argues that meaning exists in the space between. She asks: 'How can one invent a pedagogy for disappearance and loss and not for acquisition and control? How can one teach the generative power of misunderstanding?'[30] Phelan calls for value to be placed on subjectivity and identity rather than representational visibility, 'to find a way of knowing that doesn't start with what you see' and points to the liberating possibilities of a performative pedagogy, which I consider in Chapter 2.[31] Feminist approaches recognise the value gained by inhabiting the space of not knowing, where knowing is always relational. Phelan's call for 'disappearance' and 'loss' presents learning as a fluid, processual state of becoming. This coming to understand through misunderstanding, like seeing presence through absence, is a form of dialectical pedagogy adopted in both psychotherapy and in holistic somatic practice where learning happens through the whole body.[32] I propose that constructs of feminist epistemologies underpin acting pedagogies, where teaching/learning is relational, somatic and the chaos of not knowing can be transformative and productive.

In thinking through feminist intersections with acting knowledges perhaps a more radical provocation is that ways of knowing in acting should be re-evaluated through a sexed and gendered lens. When we unpick the hidden curriculum is this immaterial labour particularly associated with matters of female-ness and, if so, what might this thinking offer acting pedagogies?

## The female ontology of acting: The matter of doubling, vision and vulnerability

> In the creative process there is the father, the author of the play; the mother, the actor pregnant with the part; and the child, the role to be born.[33]

Stanislavski's familial metaphor for the creative process of acting provides an appropriate starting point to consider the aspects of acting associated with notions of female-ness. When psychophysical acting discourse fails to acknowledge the particularity of bodies it seems necessary to foreground the matter of the female body to pose the question: what if acting is a female way of knowing?

Stanislavski's metaphor for acting situates the actor as female, labouring in the production of phallocentric truth. Other male twentieth-century acting pedagogues have similarly alluded to acting as a female domain. The Artistic Director of Polish company Gardzienice, Wlodimir Staniewski, asserts,

> Real 'acting out' occurs when the man is able to break through the limitations of his male conditions and assumptions to reach the secret and the enigma of the female body. Of course you cannot get it without identifying with the female soul and vice versa.[34]

We can presume that 'real acting out' means finding some form of liberation. Staniewski attributes this 'old' knowledge to ancient Greek and Eastern theatre traditions where, by playing a woman, the (male) actor acquires 'knowledge about what you have broken through'.[35] Apart from the normative male 'I' and problematic suggestion of penetration assumed in this statement, Staniewski's provocation prompts the questions: What specific knowledge has a man 'broken through' when he plays a female? What is the 'secret' or the 'enigma' of the female body? How do we identify with the 'female soul'? Why should a male performing female be more revelatory than a female performing female? Surely any woman asked to perform female would ask 'What female?' Erica Munk, responding to the International School of Theatre Anthropology (ISTA) conference, 'The Female Role and Its Representation on Stage in Various Cultures', asks similar questions.[36] Her frustration centers on the way in which constructs of 'female' were used as a vehicle for exploring technique for male actors. At the conference, Eugenio Barba called on the actor to harness both animus and anima energy, without any discussion of what anima energy might be, or due consideration given to the implications of codified female representation. Munk concludes, 'When men are securely in their power they will play woman's roles, create the very idea of womanhood and, smugly tap into feminine energy whilst refusing to ask women to use it'.[37] Ben Spatz, in his study of technique as knowledge, makes important comparisons between acting and gender and points to feminine techniques, 'even (or perhaps especially) when this is practiced by individuals classified as male'.[38] Unlike Staniewski, Spatz starts to consider *what* constitutes feminine techniques, looking to sport, cooking and pregnancy for examples.

In considering what the 'secret' or the 'enigma' of the female body might be, or what 'feminine techniques' might refer to in an acting practice, it seems appropriate to examine these terms via feminist critical theories. This approach is necessary in order to redress the balance and find appropriate mechanisms to understand Staniewski's perspective from a female position. What does it mean to be, to see, to feel like a girl? Ideas around the matter of doubling, vision and vulnerability – three constructs pertinent to acting and to female-ness – are a good place to start in order to locate specific synergies. These features appear repeatedly in the practices of the practitioners working across voice, movement, text and devising approaches examined in Part Two.

## *The matter of doubling: Being like a girl*

Constructs of doubling and duplicity, acquiring presence through absence and existing with a double consciousness of being and being seen, tropes pertinent to acting knowledge, are embedded in notions of female identity where twentieth-century psychoanalysis has situated the female self as 'other'. What emerges when we consider the doubling condition of acting in relation to the doubling associated with a female state of being?

Since the 1970s, feminist theory, in resisting patriarchal structures, has presented different notions of the female self, focusing on biological difference to intersect with psychoanalytic and post-structuralist theories of identity.[39] Of course, any overview inevitably reduces the complex and particular to generalisms and I suggest that readers use these references as a springboard for investigation. Broadly speaking, the feminism emerging through the 1970s and 1980s, second wave feminism, tended to fall into two camps. The first, the 'gynocentric' camp, celebrated biological difference and pointed to essential female traits, a characteristic of French feminist scholarship and the work of Luce Irigaray, Hélène Cixous and Simone de Beauvoir.[40] The second, 'cultural materialist', moved from the sexed term 'female' to 'feminine', which assumed that women operate in categories of sexual difference as seen in the work of Judith Butler from the late 1980s onwards, where gender is a type of performative technique.

The psychoanalytic theory of Jacques Lacan proved provocative to the French feminists who had rejected Freud's biological determinism and found Lacan's reading of gender formation as a socio-psychological construction a more productive concept to work with. Lacan famously remarked, 'There is no such thing as woman'.[41] Feminist readings of Lacan, in particular his constructs of 'the real', 'the imaginary' and 'the symbolic', can be usefully applied to examinations of the double consciousness of acting in relation to the female condition. In order to appreciate this shift in feminist thinking we need to briefly set out Lacan's key ideas.

Lacan reworked Freud's ideas about castration and the Oedipal complex to propose a difference between the penis as an organ, and the phallus as a signifier of power. The gendered subject is determined by the 'lack of the phallus', which defines sex and imposes the symbolic. The phallus signifies power, which the female is seen to lack. Lacan's mirror stage highlights how development is based on specular (visual) rather than spoken relationships.[42] During the mirror stage a child looks in the mirror and misrecognises the image of themselves as themself, structuring all further images as a projected reality, which Lacan terms – 'the imaginary'. The ego is created through the narcissistic recognition of one's own appearance to others. Key to visual culture, this specular awareness and sense of otherness provokes the child to miss the feeling of oneness with the mother and to desire the '*jouissance*' of sexual gratification.[43] Language formation, which is termed 'the symbolic', is the way for the child to communicate their desire for the phallus and their recognition of female as lack – the lack of the phallus and the anxiety of losing '*jouissance*'. Therefore, Lacan's comment 'There is no such thing as woman' expresses the way that 'woman' is constructed through lack.[44] The Lacanian term 'the real' is the final state of being; it refers to a sort of primordial unconscious – a waiting to become. Any sense of difference, or 'other', only exists within the hierarchy of values that produce it, and woman is constructed purely through the negative economies of *not* being a man and what has been lost.

Feminist theorists look for ways to destabilise Lacan's gender construction, to problematise the female in the subjective construction of self.[45] Elizabeth Gotz sees in the construction of women as 'lack of the lack',[46] a foundational state of femaleness. She asks the question: 'Are women not partly the unconscious?' and presents Freud's and Lacan's unconscious as a metaphor for the female, as what is repressed and intolerable to the social order.[47] From this perspective women, like actors, are seen to be potentially dangerous through their essential duplicity. In 1929, psychologist Joan Riviere articulated the doubling state in relation to the performance of femininity in 'Womanliness as a Masquerade'.[48] Riviere put forward the idea that intellectual women were driven by Oedipal rivalry and castration fantasies and had to hide their masculinity in order to protect themselves and perform their womanliness with flirtation. She explained, 'Womanliness could be therefore assumed and worn as a mask, both to hide the possession of masculinity and to hide the reprisals expected if she were found to possess it'.[49] In 1949, Simone de Beauvoir presented the female as doubled, 'instead of coinciding exactly with herself, she now begins to exist *outside*'.[50] This idea that the female condition necessitates doubling, masking, disguising, or hiding, perpetuates the notion of female-ness as an act. Steven Heath makes a direct connection between the female and acting, citing Nietzsche, '[D]o they [women] not have to be first of all and above all else actresses? ... they "put on something" even when they take off everything ... woman is so artistic'.[51] We are reminded here of the Lacanian idea of 'woman' appearing through disappearing and only coming into being as the negative referent. Woman is always lacking what she desires (the phallus), and always wanting, so division is the condition of her subjectivity and therefore her identity is uncertain. In Lacanian terms, the subject's division in the symbolic means that they are subjectively alienated, which becomes a feature of the female consciousness. Moira Gatens makes another connection between 'acting' and being female:

> If woman, for example, speaks from this body, she is limited in what she can say. If she lives by this reason and this ethic, she still lives from the body of another: an actress, still a body bit, a mouthpiece'.[52]

She questions why it is that women seem to be complicit in their own reductive self determination. In a chapter entitled 'Women and her doubles' Gatens calls for a state of polyvalence (the positivity of difference) as a necessary antidote to resist limiting notions of doubling which maintain a binary status quo of lack and absence rendering females as passive others. When viewed with the 'positivity of difference'[53] constructs of doubling and female alienation might be reconsidered as a valuable knowledge, which Julia Kristeva describes as a kind of 'separate vigilance'.[54] This allows for a heightened reflexive awareness and a double consciousness as both object and subject – a necessary way of knowing in acting. This ideological position paves the way for the affirmative politics of a feminist acting pedagogy, which I consider in Chapter 2.

If both acting and the state of being female are produced through states of doubling then it seems important for developing knowledge in the field to look to the ways that feminisms have re-defined this knowledge from a positive position. I suggest that this female knowledge becomes an asset for the actor and it points to the female 'enigma', or feminine technique so compelling to Staniewski, Barba and Spatz. Of course, the idea of doubling is relational and is produced through an aspectual exchange. Feminist theory, in particular performance scholarship, has problematised 'looking-at-being looked-at-ness' to disrupt specular regimes which maintain women-as-object. These ideas, which conflate gender and acting as technique, help to reify a female ontology of acting and are seen in a number of the practices explored in Part Two: Vanessa Ewan's movement work gives space for actors to explore the movement between the doubled state of self and actor; Kristine-Landon Smith's acting approach reveals the positivity of difference, working from the doubled cultural self.

### *The matter of vision: Seeing like a girl*

> A Woman must continually watch herself. She is almost continually accompanied by her own image of herself ... From earliest childhood she has been taught and persuaded to survey herself continually.[55]

John Berger proposes that ways of seeing yourself operate from a position of unequal visuality. Sherry Shapiro develops this idea to position the notion of 'seeing' as 'knowing' within a male economy, linking the idea of seeing to a masculine form of ownership.[56] Returning to a Lacanian position, one is unable to see oneself as one exists through the eyes of the other and so the imaginary vision of ourselves, as we are perceived by the other, constructs our sense of subjective self. The representational self is unequal in terms of power and dependent on sex, age, class, ethnicity and able-ism.[57] When the self only comes into being through being seen and that visuality is unequal, feminist thinking necessarily works to challenge this. Phelan presents the unequal position of the performer as essentially female:

> As a description of the power relationships operative in many forms of performance Foucault's observations suggest the degree to which the silent spectator dominates and controls the exchange. (As Dustin Hoffman made so clear in *Tootsie*, the performer is always in the female position in relation to power). Women and performers, more often than not, are 'scripted' to 'sell' or 'confess' something to someone who is in the position to buy or to forgive.[58]

Phelan's observation is another example of converging the state of female-ness with the actor. Staniewski may be referring to the actor 'breaking through' these aspectual power structures when he alludes to the 'female enigma'.[59] The breaking through is a movement from the privileged male position to the female position. Only by becoming minoritarian can the male actor gain the insight and experience of the marginal political position and, as the female always occupies this space, one can conclude that her sex enables the positivity of difference.[60] In other words, she necessarily acquires an awareness of how to exist and, at best, negotiate with mechanisms of power in the performance of the everyday.

Drawing on Lacan, Phelan suggests that one way to resist the female degradation of self as the 'social I' of the symbolic, is by paying attention to the 'imaginary I'. If identity is relationally constructed through the specular, we have the potential to make ourselves into the image that we believe the other wants to see, where there *is* no distinction made between us. In this way, we can move beyond theorising the masculine gaze, to pursue what Phelan refers to as a 'reciprocal gaze'.[61] Looking at and for the other, we seek to represent ourselves to ourselves, as a social form of self-reproduction. As such, the reciprocal gaze is a politically productive way of resisting phallocentric structures. In acting, working with a reciprocal gaze, where one is accurately observing the ways in which power is exchanged, renegotiated and passed between moment to moment can disrupt scopic regimes. As we will see in Part Two, Niamh Dowling's movement work, Alison Hodge's relational acting and Nadine George's voice work, all enable a reciprocal gaze. This then, is at the forefront of feminist acting pedagogies.

In the 1980s and 1990s feminist critical theories, in particular materialist thinking around the performativity of gender shifted the ways that feminist theatre scholars thought about visuality and the female body. This came to the fore in the landmark year 1988–1989, and the works of: Sue Ellen Case, *Feminism and Theatre;* Jill Dolan, *The Feminist Spectator as Critic;* and Lynda Hart's edited collection *Making a Spectacle: Feminist Essays on Contemporary Women's Theatre.*[62] The number of texts responding to this subject, which can be seen as a first wave of pioneering feminist theatre theory, was testament to a shifting cultural moment where there was a renewed focus on female activism.[63] Feminist materialist scholarship cautioned against the female actor essentialising ideas of femaleness when, in order to recognise gender as technique, she should apply a reflexive double consciousness. In her seminal interrogation of feminist performance, *Unmaking Mimesis*, Elin Diamond considers the possibility of reclaiming acting for feminist action through a materialist approach, where through her authorship of the playing, the actor draws attention to the irreducibility of notions of truth. She states:

> A feminist mimesis, if there is such a thing, would take the relation to the real as productive, not referential, geared to change, not to reproducing the same. It would explore the tendency to tyrannical modeling (subjective/ideological projections masquerading as universal truths), even in its own operations.[64]

From this position the actor is not serving and perpetuating hegemony when s/he/they act but, as 'the other' being 'the other', s/he/they have the potential to challenge, de-rail and transform. Diamond outlines how reflexive approaches might help the actor to rethink visuality and enable a critical perspective. In a chapter titled 'Spectator, author, gestus', she explains that by working with gestic feminist criticism, 'the historical actor, the character, the spectator (and) the author, enter and disrupt the scopic regime of realist representation'.[65] One way of achieving this in practice is to utilise the Brechtian 'not but' approach,[66] where the dialectic is made explicit to employ a double gesture. The actor takes authorship of her action by showing her/his/their attitude to it in the playing. Diamond's thesis presents mimesis as an ethical accounting, realism as revealing and concealing assumptions and Brechtian theatre as attempting to historicise. She concludes that feminist work will do all three to enable a double vision, which she explains as not 'to-be-looked-at-ness' but 'looking at being-looked-at-ness' or even 'just looking-ness'.[67] This marks an important shift in the 1990s for feminist acting approaches, where actors and teachers/directors consciously alter the aspectual exchange as seen in the work of Rhonda Blair and Katie Mitchell in Part Two.[68] In sketching the final section of this female ontology of acting I turn to feelings, particularly associated with female-ness.

## *The matter of vulnerability: Feeling like a girl*

Acting necessitates what Mark Seton refers to as a 'habitual vulnerability',[69] where developing psychophysical and emotional accessibility is a professional trait. Turning to feminist theory, one is able to reconsider the value of vulnerability within a female domain of acting. Women have been oppressed as victims of their bodies through male-constructed notions of hysteria and loss of control. Such constructions have rendered (and continue to render) the female body vulnerable, but within the discipline of acting, vulnerability acquires a positive value. Whilst I recognise that this can be only a cursory overview, it is important to recall how representations of vulnerability have been produced through the female body.

If we look to Greek theatre (550 BC–220 BC) we can find many examples of the female body depicted as out-of-control, wracked with the pangs of childbirth and/or the torment of sexual desire: Euripides' *Medea* (431 BC) or Clytemnestra in Aeschylus' *Agamemnon* (458 BC). In Seneca's *Phaedra* (54 AD), drawing on Ancient Greek myths, the chorus speaks in generic terms about the body of a woman, calling it '*dustropos harmonia*' an 'ill-tuned harmony'.[70] The female body experiences pregnancy, birth and menstruation, which render her powerless in the face of physical pain, whilst simultaneously the victim of objectification. The psychophysical connection between emotion or passionate excess and the female body is evidenced in female humours, where physicians attributed certain features of emotional distress to the menstrual cycle. Joseph Roach maps how developments in medical science affected the way that actors approached acting emotion, and he cites the dominant fifteenth-century belief that the passions were symptomatic of psychophysical maladies. The humours, or fluids in the body, were thought to rise up and attack the brain and heart thus rendering the victim hysterical, 'Hysteria drives the womb or entrails, *the mother*, upwards in the body, suffocating and poisoning the vital organs'.[71] When we overview historical readings of hysteria we can recognise the paradox of the female body, which claims power through its vulnerability. Anna Furse's feminist theatre scholarship and practice has made important inroads to advance this debate.[72]

By the eighteenth century, hysteria was no longer seen as a visceral disorder but as a nervous condition now known as 'the Hyp', or 'The English malady' and as a specifically female disease, with the treatment of hysterical women well documented. In the nineteenth century a new kind of social realism saw drama concerned with, '[t]he object (hysteria/the fallen woman), the claim to truth (the discovery of her secret) and a common genealogy (nineteenth century melodramatic and clinical spectacles)'.[73] Freud's clinical spectacles attempted to find a cure for hysteria, which he explained as symptomatic of a woman's bisexuality, 'An hysterical symptom is the expression of both a masculine and a feminine unconscious sexual fantasy'.[74] For Freud, the female's repression of homosexual impulses as a child and her consequent desire to be male, results in masochistic impulses as symptoms of the hysterical woman.

In feminist discourse, hysteria becomes a significant manifestation of social oppression and an enabling fiction within patriarchy that justifies female oppression. Juliet Mitchell, framing hysteria in the nineteenth century, explains it as 'the pre-political manifestation of feminism. If femininity is by definition hysterical, feminism is the demand for the right to be hysterical'.[75] This position has synergy with valued ways of knowing in acting where a mark of an actor's skill is her ability to access heightened emotion and work with habitual vulnerability.

Erinn Gilson applies feminist critique to open up positive readings of vulnerability and to consider its ethical merits.[76] She considers how Hélène Cixous presents vulnerability as both a strength and a female disposition in her essay 'Sorties', where she draws a picture of her own experiences of vulnerability. Gilson reads Cixous' vulnerability as feminine in its open way of relating to others and sharing emotional fragility, without judging relationships on a scale of profit and return. This stands in contrast to a masculine economy, which is characterised by hiding emotional weakness in the desire to achieve mastery and control and judging interactions for their potential gain. Cixous describes vulnerability in terms of fragility, receptivity and self-dispossession. This is seen in the way that a feminine economy doesn't immediately presume that others pose a threat to the self and so is more open to a posture of 'non closure that is not submission but confidence and comprehension'.[77] A woman admits otherness to herself to a greater extent, without expecting a transactional return on the investment and, in opening up herself to others, she is able to alter herself in relation as a 'gift of changeability'.[78] In this vulnerability comes strength, which Gilson explains as 'force in fragility'.[79] When we apply this idea to the knowledges of acting we can find a correlation in Seton's 'habitual vulnerability', which he describes not so much as an attribute, but as an ongoing personal accomplishment in the actor's capacity to be affected and to affect others.[80] As such, constructs of female vulnerability offer valuable ways of knowing for the actor. In Part Two, the practices of Alison Hodge, Emma Rice and Nadine George can be seen to enable force in fragility with actors.

Whilst I speculate here on a female ontology of acting, where understanding how to be, how to see, how to feel, might be reconsidered as feminine technique, I am mindful that these states of being might equally apply to any human who is marginalised for the sake of another. Whilst acting discourse increasingly turns to science to better understand its complexities, in looking to feminisms we can shift thinking around the paradigms of acting. It seems vital that in an aspectual profession we look beyond the psychophysical to give critical consideration to the material contexts, which produce constructs of representation. In the twenty-first century, socio-materialist theories, the post-phenomenological, techno-science, post humanisms and new materialisms seek to redefine questions of deep materiality.[81] Culture is no longer the most determining factor in the ways that bodies are seen, but the body itself has its own knowledge and ability to transform culture. Consequently, techniques of acting and gender have the potential to re-conceptualise representational norms.

## Re-making mimesis: New feminist materialisms and acting

How can feminist materialisms shift our way of thinking about the knowledges of acting? Throughout the 1980s and 1990s, constructionist feminists, speaking back to the corporeal turn in social theory, situated the body as material and used performativity as a tool to challenge and disrupt linguistic and scopic regimes. Feminist thinking about the operational body offers us alternative constructs to re-consider its doubling. Ben Spatz, referencing Judith Butler's construct of gender performativity, connects acting and gender technique as both produce bodies inscribed with repeated actions within imposed social structures.[82] Butler points to this when she states:

> Actors are always already on the stage, within the terms of the performance. Just as a script may be enacted in various ways, and just as a play requires both text and interpretation, so the gendered body acts its part in a culturally restricted corporeal space and enacts its interpretations within the confines of already existing directives.[83]

She challenges the normative readings of 'woman as other' and 'man as subject' as missing the point that these categories are effects of institutions and practices, with multiple and diffuse points of origin. For her, gender is relational and contextual and is understood differently depending on how power is articulated. Women can't *be* because they are the relation of difference, neither subject nor other, but exist simultaneously as both. Materialist feminism recognises that humans and the material world affect each other but as humans shape the material world their very shaping returns to shape them. As such, rather like the dual circularity of a mobüs strip, matter consolidates political, social relations that determine its state of being. However, successful political action shows that human beings have the power to transform the conditions that inscribe their bodies. Whilst Butler recognises that through repetition we can change the shape of this mobüs strip, her application of performativity, like Diamond's un-making of mimesis, relies on constructs of causation and reflection, which privilege the cultural/social over nature and/or the body itself.

Over the last two decades feminist ideas about the relational construction of identity consider phenomenological theory of embodiment *beside* Marxist and post-structuralist re-elaborations of the intersection between bodies and power. In other words, they employ a *thinking-beside* paradigm, where the body and the social conditions are mutually informing and neither is privileged. The idea that identity is created through relational interaction opens up a politically empowering space for female bodies to move beyond ideas of 'being as lack' or 'in relation *to*' towards a positivity of difference, constantly in a state of becoming and 'in relation *with*'. This allows for a non-unitary image of a multi-layered subject. For Rosi Braidotti, 'the re-location of difference and of the self-other relation' is central to her nomadic theory, which applies ideas associated with nomadism to states of becoming and locates the in-between space as one of potential empowerment.[84] In 'Feminist Transpositions' she elaborates on the way that postmodern theories of feminism stress the state of becoming, its hybridity, its transitional nature and its nomadic process.[85] In order to cope with the effects of advanced capitalism we need to focus on *processes* as opposed to *products*, as only by doing this can we manage the habitual conditions of instability. My focus on pedagogies is fueled by this imperative. When we look through methodologies to pay attention to the processes of coming to learn we can shift dominant and oppressive structures. Braidotti looks towards the post-human and calls for feminist theory to move beyond the limitations of poststructuralist linguistic critique to return to the body in what she terms 'a vital materialism'.[86] Her nomadic theory speaks strongly to the knowledges and ways of being in acting and is particularly evident in the movement practice of Niamh Dowling, examined in Part Two.

New feminist materialism sees bio-literate feminists, such as Donna Haraway,[87] Fausto Sterling,[88] Karen Barad,[89] Elizabeth Grosz[90] and Jane Bennet,[91] fight matter with matter to think about new kinds of bodies and gender systems that are being constructed.[92] From this perspective, the body and the self are always in motion, changing moment to moment in relation to others and, internally, in relation to their own material components. Whilst some feminists will be skeptical that this biological imperative might be reductive, new materialism shifts the balance away from power affecting bodies to a framework where culture and bodies have reciprocal effects on each other. It's not a case of *either* culture *or* nature affecting a body, but a recognition that these are entangled and, recalling Sedgewick, work *beside* each other.[93] Applying this premise to acting allows us to look beyond the psychophysical bodymind towards what Camilleri terms the *bodyworld*, the capacities of bodies, organisms and objects to work in relation with social inscriptions and constraints.[94] In this way we might better understand how the body's materiality itself can have an active role in the dissemination of power and look towards what Sandra Reeve terms, the ecological body, 'a-body-in-movement-in-a-changing-environment'.[95]

Karen Barad's work interrogates the co-constitutive intra-activity between human and non-human agents. She offers an alternative to the linguistic turn of post-structural materialism and shifts ideas about realism through her construct of 'agential realism':[96] agential in the way it gives agency to that which lacks agency – in this case, things. Her ideas are persuasive when thinking about acting pedagogies. Indeed, they offer educational research new analytical tools to help re-think the entanglements among knowledge domains, subjects, objects and practices.[97]

Barad's theory responds to Niels Bohr, an atomic physicist who considers philosophy in relation to science. Bohr repositioned the body itself as a mass of atoms in constant states of becoming. When meaning is made relationally and the body is seen as plastic rather than a fixed state of being, we can re-think how we come into being. Barad critiques Foucault's and Butler's constructs of performativity, which reinforce a hierarchy, placing culture above nature. She resists this, positioning all processes as intra-actions, 'diffractions' as opposed to 'reflections', which read insights *through* one another.[98] This effectively shifts feminist theories, which consider reflection, and consequently mimesis, as the essential condition of coming into being *in relation to* the other, and it undermines the anthropocentric paradigms of twentieth-century psychoanalysis. When we start to see meaning created through every aspect of *being in relation with* and measurement as always relational, we dissolve dualist thinking and the continual privileging of culture, which as many feminists argue, reinforces appropriation and precludes the possibility of change. When what is happening *within* an actor's body and *how* it is operating is viewed to be as important as *what* the body is doing; when the prop, costume, space or technology that an actor is working with is seen to be as important and necessary in meaning-making as the body itself, a new type of reality is encountered, an agential reality, which holds radical possibility for feminists in the ways it asserts a relational ontology that shifts the status quo. In Part Two, I consider the ways that objects are used within the pedagogic practices of Jane Boston, Vanessa Ewan, Alison Hodge, Emma Rice and Katie Mitchell.

Moving on from Diamond's strategy for 'un-making mimesis', where realism is reflexively deconstructed through Brechtian strategies, Barad's agential realism offers feminist theatre-makers new tactics to change thinking around mimesis in praxis. The interpretation of realism shifts its focus from human agency to flatten hierarchies and recognise the influence of non-human agents. Mimesis can then be re-imagined, not as a reflection of reality – with bodies inscribed on, but as a diffractive *process*, a way of playfully exploring identity through the inscribing body as a formative and potentially transformative technique. When we reconfigure mimesis as a process, experienced by the actor and by spectators in performance, always in a state of flux and possibility, we can release acting technique from its representational fetters and recognise its radical potential to refigure constructs of identity. This *re-makes* mimesis, recognising its productive and liberatory potential. I pick this up in Chapter 2, thinking through mimesis-as-play as a foundational pedagogy in actor training and in Chapter 6 through the work of Katie Mitchell.

At this cultural moment, it seems vital to push against the ethical and ecological boundaries that confine notions of acting and actor training. Thinking through feminisms allows us to reconceptualise its epistemic scope, in other words, the nature of knowledge in acting, to foreground the ecological body, rooted in a respect for the vitality of all matter. Since the 1970s, feminist critical and performance theories have questioned what might constitute female-ness; how the mechanisms of power inscribe bodies, and how we might move beyond cultural representations of mimesis to see the body as inscribing through an agential realism. When we turn to new feminist materialisms, looking beyond the dialogic agency of human beings and the bodymind to consider ways that alternative apparatus operate in the bodyworld, power is re-constituted. In this way the pedagogic exchange can enable an ethical and ecological accounting.

## Notes

1 Frank Camilleri, *Performer Training Reconfigured: Post-Psychophysical Perspectives for the Twenty-First Century* (London & New York: Methuen, 2019).
2 Materialist theories recognise that historical, social and cultural contexts impact human consciousness and bodies. New materialist feminisms, a term coined in the 1990s and seen in the scholarship of Rosi Braidotti, Karen Barad, Jane Bennett and Elizabeth Grosz amongst others, considers how materiality, in the form of spaces, conditions and the non-human contribute to human subjectivity.
3 Michel Foucault, *The Essential Foucault: Selections from Essential Works of Foucault, 1954–1984* (New York: The New Press, 2003) 306.
4 Gayatri Spivak, 'Can the Subaltern Speak?' in Nelson, C. and Grossberg, L. *Marxism and the Interpretation of Culture* (Basingstoke: Macmillan Education, 1988) 271–313.
5 In the Introduction to this book I explain, 'I use gender difference as my primary lens with a particular commitment to address inequalities affecting women in the field, but I'm attentive to all differences including ethnicity, age, class and able-ism. For me, acting as a feminist agitates beyond notions of equality and idealistic intentions. Indeed, it thinks beyond humans. It is an ecological, ethical and epistemic shift in thinking

about being in the world. A way to navigate, make sense of things and to keep our balance'.
6 Eve Sedgwick, *Touching Feeling: Affect, Pedagogy, Performativity* (Durham: Duke University Press, 2003) 8.
7 This term is used by educationalist Henry Giroux to describe types of knowledges that are seen to hold less value in a capitalist economy. Henry Giroux, *Schooling for a Democracy: Critical Pedagogy in the Modern Age* (London: Routledge, 1989). My contention is that the personal and social knowledges of acting are given less value than technique. I develop my thinking around this in Chapter 2.
8 Kim Solga, *Theatre and Feminism* (London & New York: Palgrave Macmillan, 2016).
9 Linda Alcroff and Elizabeth Potter, *Feminist Epsistemologies* (London & New York: Routledge, 1993).
10 Antonia Cavarrero, *For More Than One Voice: Towards a Philosophy of Vocal Expression* (USA: Stanford University Press, 2005).
11 Ross Prior, *Teaching Actors: Knowledge Transfer in Actor Training* (Bristol, UK, Chicago, USA: Intellect, 2012).
12 Donald Schön, *The Reflective Practitioner: How Professionals Think in Action* (London: Temple Smith, 1983).
13 Liz Stanley, 'The Knowing Because Experiencing Subject: Narratives, Lives and Autobiography' in Kathleen Lennon and Margaret Whitford, *Knowing the Difference. Feminist Perspectives in Epistemology* (London: Routledge, 1994) 164.
14 Prior, op.cit.
15 Sue Jackson, 'Crossing Borders and Changing Pedagogies: From Giroux and Freire to Feminist Theories of Education', *Gender and Education*, 9(4), (1997): 457–468.
16 Sedgewick, op.cit.
17 Vic Kelly, *The Curriculum: Theory and Practice* (London: Paul Chapman, 1999).
18 Prior, 164.
19 Prior, 164–168.
20 Simon Murray cited by Maria Kapsali, 'Training for a Cold Climate: Edited Transcript of Roundtable Discussion', in *Theatre, Dance and Performance Training*, 5(2), (2014): 231.
21 Stephen Wangh, *The Heart of Teaching. Empowering Students in the Performing Arts* (London & New York: Routledge, 2013) 139.
22 Camilleri points to a similar aspect of training, which he refers to as the 'invisible dimension'. He positions this within the ethical dimension of training, which is wholly relational and exists in human experience, where *how* you do something is more important than *what* you do. Whilst Camilleri sees this as different from transferable skills, because they are located firmly in relation to artistic technique, he acknowledges the amorphous nature of this knowledge to 'extend the parameters of aesthetic performance to certain (but not all) aspects of one's life. On the other hand, the invisible dimension potentially affects one's life 'in its totality'. Frank Camilleri, *Performer Training Reconfigured: Post-Psychophysical Perspectives for the Twenty-First Century* (London & New York: Methuen, 2019) 105.
23 Wangh, 144.
24 Paulo Freire, *Education for Critical Consciousness* (London & New York: Continuum, 1974).
25 Henry Giroux, *Schooling for a Democracy: Critical Pedagogy in the Modern Age*. (London & New York: Routledge, 1989) 47.
26 Camilleri, 214.
27 Mark Seton, 'The Ethics of Embodiment: Actor Training and Habitual Vulnerability', *Performing Ethos*, 1(1), (2010): 5–18.
28 Luce Irigaray posits that 'Women are concerned with a corporeal geography whereas men establish new linguistic territories' in *Sexes and Genealogies* (New York: Columbia University Press, 1993) 175.

29 Camilleri, 218.
30 Peggy Phelan, *Unmarked: The Politics of Performance* (London & New York: Routledge, 1993)173.
31 Actor trainer Matt Hargraves applies this same position to acting when he calls for a pedagogy that celebrates 'failing to finish' and 'not knowing', where 'the call for definitive answers should be continually suspended'. Hargraves cited by Kapsali, op.cit. 227.
32 I am particularly thinking here about the holistic practices employed by actors regularly such as Feldenkrais, Alexander Technique, Yoga.
33 Konstantin Stanislavski, *An Actor Prepares*, trans. Elizabeth Hapgood (London & Tonbridge: Geoffrey Bles, 1937) 312.
34 Wlodimir Staniewski and Alison Hodge, *Hidden Territories: The Theatre of Gardzienice* (London & New York: Routledge, 2004) 97.
35 Ibid.
36 Erica Munk, 'The Rights of Women', *Performing Arts Journal*, 10(2), (1986), 35–42.
37 Ibid. 42.
38 Ben Spatz, *What a Body Can Do: Technique as Knowledge. Practice as Research.* (Routledge, London & New York, 2015) 189.
39 Sarah Edge, *Images and the Self: Semiotic Chora in Recent Postfeminist Theory* (2000) Formations seminar paper [accessed 20.11.13].
40 I'm thinking of the seminal texts: Luce Irigaray, *Speculum of the Other Woman* (Ithaca, New York: Cornell University Press, 1983); Simone de Beauvoir, *The Second Sex* (London: Vintage Books, 1997); Hélène Cixous, 'The Laugh of the Medusa', *Signs*, 1(4): 875–893.
41 Jacque Lacan, 'Télévision' (1973) in *Television: A Challenge to the Psychoanalytic Establishment*, ed. Joan Copjec, trans. Denis Hollier, Rosalind Krauss and Annette Michelson (New York: Norton, 1990) 60.
42 Jacques Lacan, 'Mirror Stage as Formative of the I Function, as Revealed in Psychoanalytical Experience' (1949) in *Ecrits: A Selection*, trans. Bruce Fink (New York: W.W. Norton, 2002).
43 In Chapter 4 "Women and the Matter of Movement' I think about the way that the construct of *jouissance* can be used as a feminist material.
44 Lacan, op.cit.
45 For example, in *Speculum of the Other Woman*, Luce Irigaray transforms the mirror into a political weapon and denounces the specular reflection status imposed on women by men.
46 Elizabeth Gotz, *Jacques Lacan: A Feminist Introduction* (London & New York: Routledge, 1990) 55.
47 Ibid. 171.
48 Joan Riviere, 'Womanliness as a Masquerade' in *Formations of Fantasy*, ed. Victor Burgin, James Donald, Cora Kaplan (London & New York: Routledge, 1986).
49 Ibid. 37.
50 de Beauvoir, 373.
51 Steven Heath, 'Joan Riviere and The Masquerade' in *Formations of Fantasy*, ed. Victor Burgin, James Donald, Cora Kaplan (London & New York: Routledge, 1986) 45–61.
52 Moira Gatens, *Imaginary Bodies: Ethics, Power and Corporeality* (London & New York, 1996) 25.
53 Braidotti, op.cit.
54 Kristeva, op.cit.
55 John Berger, *Ways of Seeing* (London: British Broadcasting Corporation and Penguin Books, 1972) 46.
56 Sherry Shapiro, *Pedagogy and the Politics of the Body: A Critical Praxis* (London & New York: Routledge, 1999).

57 As Phelan notes, 'The proposition that one sees oneself in terms of the other and the other in terms of oneself is itself differently marked according to men and women'. In *Unmarked: The Politics of Performance* (London & New York: Routledge, 1993) 17.
58 Ibid. 163
59 Staniewski, op.cit.
60 Rosi Braidotti, *Nomadic Theory: The Portable Rosi Braidotti* (New York & Chichester: Columbia University Press, 2011) 148.
61 Ibid. 17.
62 Sue Ellen Case, *Feminism and Theatre* (London: Routledge, 1988); Jill Dolan, *The Feminist Spectator as Critic* (Ann Arbor: University of Michigan Press, 1988); Lynda Hart, ed., *Making a Spectacle: Feminist Essays on Contemporary Women's Theatre* (Ann Arbor: University of Michigan Press, 1989), referenced by Solga, op.cit. 16.
63 In 1989, Kimberlé Williams introduced the idea of intersectionality.
64 Elin Diamond, *Un-Making Mimesis* (London & New York: Routledge, 1997) xvi.
65 Ibid. 54.
66 Bertolt Brecht, *Brecht on Theatre: The Development of an Aesthetic* (London: Methuen, 1964) 137.
67 Diamond, 52.
68 Rhonda Blair, 'Liberating the Young Actor: Feminist Pedagogy and Performance'. *Theatre Topics,* 2(1), 1995, 13–23. Katie Mitchell's work forms one of the case studies in Chapter 6.
69 Seton, op.cit.
70 Seton, 346.
71 Joseph Roach, *The Player's Passion: Studies in the Science of Acting* (The University of Michigan Press, 1993) 48.
72 Anna Furse, *Augustine (Big Hysteria)* (London & New York: Routledge, 1997), Anna Furse, *Performing Nerves: Four Plays, Four Essays on Hysteria* (London & New York: Routledge, 2020).
73 Diamond, xiii.
74 Siegmund Freud cited by Penny Farfan, *Women, Modernism, and Performance* (United Kingdom, Cambridge: University Press, 2004).
75 Juliet Mitchell in Elaine Showalter, *The Female Malady: Women, Madness and English Culture 1830–1980* (Harmondsworth & New York: Penguin Books, 1987) 333–334.
76 Erinn Gilson, *The Ethics of Vulnerability: A Feminist Analysis of Social Life and Practice* (London & New York: Routledge, 2014).
77 Ibid. 86.
78 Ibid. 88.
79 Ibid. 95.
80 Seton, op.cit.
81 Camilleri, xii.
82 Spatz, op.cit.
83 Judith Butler, 'Performative Acts and Gender Construction: An Essay in Phenomenology and Feminist Theory' in Sue-Ellen Case, *Performing Feminisms: Feminist Critical Theory and Theatre* (London & USA: John Hopkins University Press, 1990) 277.
84 Braidotti, 15.
85 Ibid. 13–16.
86 Ibid. 16.
87 Donna Haraway, *Simians, Cyborgs and Women: The Reinvention of Nature* (London & New York: Routledge, 1991) 127–149.
88 Anne Fausto-Sterling, *Sexing the Body: Gender Politics and the Construction of Sexuality* (New York: Basic Books, 2000).

89 Karen Barad, 'Posthumanist Performativity: Toward an Understanding of How Matter Comes to Matter', *Signs*, 28(3), (Spring, 2003): 801–831.
90 Elizabeth Grosz, *Volatile Bodies: Towards a Corporeal Feminism* (Indiana University Press, 1994).
91 Jane Bennet, *Vibrant Matter: A Political Ecology of Things* (Duke University Press, 2010).
92 Braidotti, 65.
93 My contention is that arguments about essentialism in 2020 are rendered redundant in light of the developed scientific understanding of the vital materialism of bodies. Biological materialism has moved beyond the historical materialism of Simone de Beauvoir to recognise that bodies are not only embedded and embodied, but are self organising and vital. If one's sexualised body determines one's power and the brain is part of the body, then the brain is also sexed. Thus, the sexed body/brain experiences and interacts with others from its particular position. This does not mean that female experience can be generalised, or that the female body has somehow moved beyond social inscription. Notions of sexuality and gender are always in a state of becoming, as all experience is relationally constructed and impossible to predict or pin down. In this way all bodies have the potential to resist foreclosing structures as bodily components are in constant flux. There are differences *between* women and *within* every woman. However, looking to the specificity of the female sexed state allows us to mine its alternative knowledge.
94 Camilleri, op. cit.
95 Sandra Reeve, *New Ways of Seeing a Body* (Devon: Triarchy Press, 2011) 48.
96 Barad, 820.
97 Carol A. Taylor, Gabrielle Ivinson, 'Material Feminisms: New Directions for Education', *Gender in Education*, 25(6), (2013): 666–670.
98 Ibid. 668.

# 2

# FEMINIST INTERVENTIONS

*Via Positiva* and Critical Acting Pedagogy

The anti-pedagogic prejudice in acting stymies the political potential of learning to act.[1] Looking behind *what* an actor does to focus on *how* an actor learns dispels some of the mysticism of acting that perpetuates closed models of learning. When we consider pedagogy as the change in consciousness between three agencies: the teacher, the learner and the knowledge they produce together, it becomes a formative site for uniting research, methodology and practice. Feminist perspectives offer us ways to resist patriarchal traditions that can empower, embody and em-brain,[2] re-positioning the actor as cultural worker.[3] Working alongside Chapter 1, this chapter constructs a methodology to evaluate the feminist potential of the acting pedagogies examined in Part Two.

How might the esoteric knowledges of the hidden curriculum in acting, with its pedagogy of disappearance, be observed, theorised and analysed?[4] The hidden curriculum, which I overview in Chapter 1, refers to the personal, social and political knowledges of acting, which operate under, beside and through technique.[5] This has variously been described as 'dispositional attitudes',[6] 'transitional skills'[7] and the 'invisible dimension'.[8] If somatic knowledge is positioned as female and the female condition necessitates a 'separate vigilance',[9] then qualities such as relationality, instinct, empathy, generosity, collaboration, vulnerability and reflexivity might be attributed to a female domain. From this position, the hidden curriculum has the potential to enable a feminist way of being in the world, built on the positivity of difference and an affirmative politics. Giving focused attention to the teaching and learning of these skills/qualities re-orientates thinking about acting knowledges beyond technique.

In this chapter, I consider feminist interventions in actor pedagogy in three parts: the first seeks a pedagogical framework to analyse the specific interactions between actor and teacher/director in practice; the second re-calibrates acting pedagogy in terms of power and gender relations to reveal an alternative affirmative politics and a different teaching authority, which I term the '*via positiva*'; the third suggests a shift towards a relational ideology, underpinned by new feminist materialisms, to reconfigure acting as a critical pedagogy, which *re-makes* mimesis.

## Acting and pedagogical frameworks

Several scholars have drawn upon developments in neuroscience and cognitive situated scientific models to map acting as a human science.[10] However, the particular and specific intersections with educational frameworks are rarely considered.[11] Theories of social constructivist education (Dewey, Kolb, Vygotsky and Lave & Wenger)[12] and critical, feminist and performative pedagogies (Freire, Giroux, hooks, Weiler, Pineau)[13] can help us understand how the hidden curriculum is produced.

As the process of knowledge construction is dependent, in part, on the interaction between actor and teacher/director, my primary concern is to interrogate these points of exchange to consider what teachers do in practice to develop an actor's knowledge. Lev Vygotsky's educational construct 'The Zone of Proximal Development' (ZPD) provides a useful starting point. ZPD describes the gap between what an actor brings with her at the start of her training or rehearsal process and the progress she might achieve independently with the value added to her knowledge or skills by her teacher or peers.[14] Lave and Wenger identify different interactive strategies, which support this in practice, such as scaffolding (structuring) the learning at the start and throughout the process.[15] Mary Thorpe defines 'scaffolding support' in teaching to identify seven ways that learning is facilitated. These prove useful when thinking about the interactions between teacher/director and actor in practice:

1. Modelling (comparing to an image)
2. Feedback (comparing to a standard)
3. Contingency management (discipline and re-enforcement)
4. Instructing (requesting specific action)
5. Questioning
6. Explanations
7. Task structuring (chunking and sequencing).[16]

In a workshop, class or rehearsal all seven of these interactions will be observed. The teacher/director might show or demonstrate *how* to perform a technique or play a moment (1); feedback and give notes on a performance (2); organise the logistic, practical and operative structures necessary for working (3); instruct, question and explain (4,5,6); organise the time into specific tasks to enable development of the process/rehearsal (7). Of course, these interactions do not only exist between actor and teacher, but in a relational and constructed exchange with fellow actors in the rehearsal room. Lave and Wenger's research shows how communities of practice, with a sense of membership, characteristic biographies and professional legitimacy, construct learning socially. This is seen in the shared knowledge of theatre companies who have relationally shaped their training approaches over years through a familial apostology. This enables an inherited 'knowledge with' and any explicit consideration of pedagogy is deemed to be unnecessary.[17"]

Donald Schön's research into professional learning practices draws a distinction between professional knowledge as facts, rules and techniques and professional knowing, explained in terms of 'thinking like an actor'.[18] For Schön, the generation of this knowledge depends on the reciprocally reflective dialogue between teacher and student. In his study of professional coaching in music, two dominant approaches are explained: mimicry of modeled examples, which, once mastered, enable improvisation; and joint experimentation. Here the relationship constructed is not so much teacher and student, but rather partners in an enquiry, where the learner is asked to consider their choices and preferences and in this way learning is mutually structured. Schön identifies the actions of immediate reciprocity in performance coaching practice as:

- Setting and solving the substantive problems in performance
- Tailoring demonstration or performance to a student's particular needs
- Joint experimentation
- Follow me (where the coach models for the student who copies them).[19]

This reciprocal construction of knowledge between 'partners in enquiry' is at the centre of notions of collaboration. These two approaches 'follow me' and 'joint experimentation' tend to dominate acting pedagogies with learning scaffolded through a process of repetition, trial and error, in order to achieve mastery.

Arts linguist, Andrea Milde, has developed what she claims is the only method for analysing the ways that language operates in rehearsal between actors and director, which she terms 'spoken artistic discourse' or 'rehearsal analysis'.[20] Milde breaks down modes of exchange as: providing feedback; providing explanations; using improvisations; providing instructions and using keys (meaning spontaneous coaching or 'side coaching') as a way of providing instructions; framing one's own activity; sharing ideas, thoughts, stories, anecdotes; providing/making suggestions; providing/asking questions.[21] Milde's work offers a useful analytical framework, focusing on recorded and empirical speech interactions. However, this approach doesn't analyse the more intangible conditions of learning such as: the atmosphere or mood in the room, the behavioural and expressive communication, the way that authority is physically communicated and how the dynamic of space, time and objects impact learning. When we think about pedagogies through the lens of new feminist materialisms, we can look beyond language to understand the subtle and complex ways that agency is relationally produced in the learning exchange and to include the non-human.

This current thinking, prompted by the work of feminist scientists and social philosophers (Barad, Harraway, Braidotti, Bennet, Grosz),[22] and increasingly explored in the scholarship and practice of educationalists (Taylor and Ivinson, Jackson, Juelskjaer),[23] offers new paradigms for pedagogical enquiry. New feminist materialisms seek alternative ways to understand being in the world that are not only bound to patriarchy – laws of causation, the supremacy of the word and the inscribing apparatus of culture. They also pay attention to nature and the body, to the multiple ways that the body as matter can affect and transform itself, things around it, and the meanings produced through its exchanges. In this way, we can expand our thinking about agency to include transformations *within* the body *in relation with* non-human agents. Furthermore, we can re-think how actors and teacher/directors are constituted to question why certain categories, persons and things come to matter differently.

Whilst Camilleri doesn't position his thinking as new materialist, his scholarship similarly responds to the deep materiality of actor training to propose an ecology of practice. He constructs a seven-point methodology for thinking about training that acknowledges: the materiality and physicality of bodies (age, gender, ethnicity, class, ableism); the materiality of the workplace; the objects, tools and artefacts employed; the language and discursive practices; the groupings and communities; the background and context of the community; the rules, both tacit and explicit, that impact the community. Camilleri does not explicitly direct his model towards pedagogic practice; however, it usefully highlights the specific materials of the training exchange, pointing towards post-psychophysical approaches where the bodymind becomes a *bodyworld*.[24]

Observing the way that the hidden curriculum is produced in actor training pedagogies, we should be alert to the numerous agents affecting ways in which power is experienced. When, as argued in the Introduction, the pedagogical exchange in acting can teeter precariously on the edge of abuse, then sharpening our understanding of how power is produced and passed between, who is included and excluded and what are the stakes, becomes vital. Only then can we dismantle patriarchal systems of oppression, equipping ourselves with more nuanced understanding about the choices we make in practice and nourish ourselves with alternative approaches. Of course, power comes into being not only through the learning exchange between teacher/director, but also other agents that might include: the demographic of participants; the time of day; the way that space, objects, or technology are being used; the proximity or distance between people; the ways that touch, breath, listening or laughter transforms the learning exchange. Using the models of Thorpe, Milde and Camilleri as a launch pad, I propose a fluid analytical methodology for analysing the critical potential of pedagogy in practice, which considers:

- How the hidden curriculum of personal and social knowledge is delivered
- How an atmosphere of trust and relationality is built
- How vulnerability is supported
- How authority operates in the room
- How choice and action are scaffolded for the actor
- How instruction, explanation and feedback are given
- How non-human agents operate within the teaching/learning
- How individual and group progress is managed within time constraints
- How gender, sexuality, ability, class and ethnicity operate within the learning[25]

These nine factors recognise that verbal and non-verbal communication work simultaneously in the learning exchange.

Returning to Schön's overarching model, whether working with 'follow me' or 'joint experimentation', the process of learning in acting is structured around solving substantive problems. *How* the actor is brought to solve these problems defines the pedagogical approach. Different methodologies and aesthetics lend themselves more to particular practices and this, in part, affects the ways that power structures operate and are produced. In some acting processes, particularly in Eastern traditions, the actor is taught specific somatic forms from a master teacher, the mastery of which enables improvisation within that structure. This 'follow me' methodology can also be seen in Western practices where physical training dominates. In these approaches, which are mostly developed by male pedagogues, the learning process is navigated through the experience of repetition and failing. Feminist interventions refigure this formative way of learning to mediate potentially oppressive pedagogies in acting.

## *Foundational pedagogies: Play and the 'via negativa'*

Mark Evans, in his examination of teaching notions of the self and identity in actor training, presents 'foundational practices' as 'practices that underpin the system and the techniques they use'.[26] In acting, two foundational practices can be seen to underpin a variety of training approaches: constructs of 'play', and learning through the experience of 'failure', which I consider in relation to the term '*via negativa*'.[27]

Play as a medium of learning was recognised by Jean-Jacques Rousseau and Friedrich Froebel in the early nineteenth century and developed in the thinking of Jean Piaget and Lev Vygotsky, who saw symbolic play as a way to construct meaning as opposed to being purely for pleasure.[28] Playing within strict rules increases the intensity of choice and the sense of challenge. The seminal work of female drama educationalist Finlay Johnson at the turn of the last century privileged play to reposition the authority of the teacher as equal to the learner and their peers in constructing meaning.[29] In theatre, the construct of play has emerged as formative in many theatre practices: Barker (1977), Johnstone (1979), Lecoq (2000), Gaulier (2006) and Wright (2006).[30] Whilst the scope of this book precludes a detailed study of play it is important to acknowledge its foundational practice and potential to open up ideas of mimesis beyond feigning and imitation. This is necessary in order to re-position mimesis in feminist acting practices.

A distinction should be made between play and games, where play is the action and the game is the structure. Johan Huizinger (1949) and Roger Caillois (1958) theorise the game structure as part of social and cultural activity.[31] In acting, games might form the warm-up practice, structure training exercises or inform rehearsal techniques. This type of play can lead to the discovery of characters' motives, reveal staging choices or generate a particular openness or quality of alertness between actors. Then there is the play-acting of situation, which can be framed as a mimetic play, with characters and narratives exploring social settings and dilemmas, or abstract and surreal realities, enabling movement between realism, the symbolic and the semiotic. This dual existence, where one is both subjectively experiencing being *inside* the drama, whilst objectively conscious of the role one is playing, is a fundamental condition of being in acting. This type of play enables the development of spontaneity and openness within a structure where *mimesis-as-play* is a way of coming to learn.[32] In this process reality is not so much a reflection but a constant, relational state of flux, a diffraction, revealing new possibilities in action, moment to moment.

Lynne Kendrick's scholarship interrogates play through the complex pedagogies of Jacques Lecoq and Philippe Gaulier, to construct a *'ludic* performance theory', which enables analysis of the pedagogical approaches that produce a particular *'paidic aesthetic'*.[33] Here, *ludic* means playing and engaging in games as the act of learning. *Paidic* describes the particular type of performance, which is 'playful, exuberant and imbued with pleasure'.[34] Drawing on the play theory of Callois,[35] which focuses on a ludic dialectic between *paida* (the play instinct) and *ludus* (the structure of the game), Kendrick looks at how acting professionalises play.[36] The pleasure of game play is, in part, dependent on the experience of avoiding failure and the games are constructed around winners and losers. There is a difference between playing a game in the spirit of competition and the notion of 'playing well', which generates a playful and responsive connection between actors. Inherent in play is the architecture of failure that structures the learning for the actor, whether this is through repetition in rehearsal or in training exercises. Through learning by failing, either literally through losing the game or by making mistakes through rehearsal, the actor and teacher/director add value to the ZPD. This necessary negative economy in the learning of acting, which is both intrinsically and extrinsically motivational, is managed and structured by the teacher/director. Their position of authority can sit on a spectrum from despot controlling the game, to partner in the game. One question that arises is how does gender function in this type of strategic power play?

The term *via negativa* is mainly associated with Grotowski, who used the term to explain the way that the actor learns through an encounter with failure. In the Catholic tradition the *via negativa* is the negative pathway to God and it points to a dialectical way of learning. The transcendence of God can only be approached in terms of what God is not; negativity references positivity and failure references success. This draws attention to the space between one state and the next and so neither become fixed but are states of becoming, with a liquid architecture. One person's 'failure' or 'block' is uniquely experienced and the subjective nature of the teacher/director's decree of failure on another in the realms of performance constructs a heightened authority. How this authority manifests depends on *how* the teacher/director facilitates failure in their context and approach. Evans, reflecting on his own training, explains that when a teacher does not make their approach to failure explicit, the experience of learning to act becomes 'inward' and self-referencing, which he experienced in terms of 'not being man enough', and the power of the teacher becomes even more pronounced.[37] Stephen Wangh presents this process of 'unlearning' as empowering for the student, as long as they have been given the reflective and reflexive skills.[38] To be clear, my suggestion here is not that learning through failure is necessarily a bad thing but that this type of meta-learning needs to be scaffolded for the actor.

For Grotowski, *via negativa* references the psychophysical 'blocks' that the actor must confront, which stop her from being able to achieve her potential. He explains,

> The education of an actor in our theatre is not a matter of teaching him something; we attempt to eliminate his organism's resistance to this psychic process ... Ours then is the *via negativa* – not a collection of skills but an eradication of blocks.[39]

This 'unlearning' demands a condition of internal passivity, which in Eastern training practices is seen to be a strength.[40] The extreme physical nature of Grotowski's training in the 1960s and 1970s with its sustained, durational challenge (particularly as experienced in his para-theatre experiments), confronted the participants with the same types of psychophysical exertion as might be faced in extreme sport or in Eastern performance and martial art traditions, which still tend to be perceived as male able-bodied domains. In this context, the participants do not *want* to do the work because it is so physically challenging, but they do it anyway. Grotowski's approach was to side coach the actor to help her identify her blocks and to find her own solutions, an approach that reflects the authority of a guru. Whilst the term 'guru acting traditions' implies a despotic or even abusive tyrant, in Eastern religions, such as Hinduism, the guru does not *instruct* but *coaches* to help one independently discover one's own answers – to become an autodidact.[41] A similar pedagogy works in somatic practices such as Feldenkrais and Alexander Technique where the coach might direct attention to a particular point of focus, withholding full explanation, diagnosis or treatment, thus enabling heutagogy for the participant. I'm interested in the different ways that this sensitive process is brokered and how gender operates within this exchange.

Through the 1960s, 1970s and 1980s, in the rehearsal rooms and laboratories of 'the founding fathers' of acting curriculums, accounts from actors repeatedly suggest that the *via negativa* was achieved through fear and anxiety. This, one could argue, was indicative of the time, which pursued exclusive, stereotypical ideas about the technologies of the body. Many pedagogues, including Grotowski, worked from the negative imperative in their language with actors. Duncan Jamieson's research draws attention to the many kinds of negative verbal interventions that Grotowski used for specific purposes. He would be highly economical with words, often giving the feedback 'I don't believe' or 'I don't understand'. He felt that negative phrases, pointing to what *not* to do, enabled the self-reflexive active/passive state required and guided the actor away from actions that were habitual, clichéd or disconnected.[42] Whilst the use of non-predetermined language intended to shift behaviour from routine patterns towards the desired passive state of readiness, it could be experienced as diminishing. Actor Antoni Jaholkowski commented, 'And sometimes we'd have dreams about our scary Boss shrieking alternatively: 'I don't believe it! "Not true!" "I don't believe it!"'[43] This tendency to work from negation as a way to coach actors is replicated in different ways in other approaches.

Jacques Lecoq has been seen to work with *via negativa* in the explorations of play and failure inherent in clown training. Simon Murray explains this as, 'an approach which rejects prescription and illustration by example, in favour of a search for the truth through negation'.[44] Like Grotowski, Lecoq would alert the actor to her failure, but would not offer a solution or a model. For some, this process of learning is empowering and liberatory, but for the less resilient it can be intimidating and damaging. This more despotic position of authority is also seen in American Method training and it ensures the heightened state of habitual vulnerability of acting students. The structure of 'a master' watching and failing you without explaining why can feel ruthless, and the predication of male pedagogues to operate with this form of oppressive authority dominates traditions of acting pedagogy and presents ethical problems.

Maggie Irving considers how gender features in the power dynamic of the *via negativa*, reflecting on her negative experience in workshops with Philippe Gaulier, who also works with this pedagogy.[45] She questions the position of her gender, her frustration with being denied explicit or useful feedback and how 'the positioning of pupil/teacher, high status/low status, youth/maturity, male/female might impact upon students'.[46] Gaulier explains his authority in combative terms: 'When I teach clown, I box'.[47] Kendrick notes the ways that this metaphorical violence is made manifest through the 'unexplained cruelty' of physical punishments; for example, 'Guantanamo' (he presses the player's fingers into the palm of the hand) and to finish off, he administers a Chinese burn on the arm'.[48] This physical abuse is an 'intrinsic pedagogical act' in an advanced form of ludic training, to place the actor in a state of genuinely awful feelings where acts of idiocy may occur.[49] Although this form of actor training is particular to clowning, as argued in the Introduction, notions of punishment and shaming result in habitual servitude becoming a professional trait of acting.[50] Although Irving questions the ethics of the approach, one can also recognise in Kendrick's analysis how the sophisticated manipulation of failure is a way of initiating creative tension in the performer. This kind of oppressive power play, which ignores the particularity of bodies, teeters on the edge of abuse and relies on producing fear. In what ways might the *via negativa* be scaffolded to ensure a more positive and ethical learning experience for the current time? Foucault drew attention to the positive potential of power play when experienced as 'a sort of open-ended strategic game where the situation may be reversed'.[51] In acting, within a process of joint experimentation, learning through failure can liberate when it is explicitly understood as a productive, creative exchange. Building on Irving's enquiry, in the next section I consider the extent to which the gender of the teacher/director might impact and potentially re-frame *via negativa* in the pedagogy of acting.

## *Feminist interventions: Power, affirmativity and the 'via positiva'*

The male-dominated tradition in the history of actor training, with its masters' laboratories, can be seen to replicate the notion of apprenticeships and the master/student power dynamic of Oriental training practices. The guru tradition of passing on knowledge and spiritual guidance is predominantly a male domain, which is modeled on a father–son relationship, 'intimate yet hierarchical rather than a meeting of friends or equals'.[52] It involves absolute discipline, faithfulness and obedience. Many Western twentieth-century teacher/directors have been and continue to be influenced by Eastern performance traditions, the apprenticeship model and the distinct power hierarchy in the rehearsal room or acting class.[53] The kind of master/mentor/sage/guru/father/son dynamic that Stanislavski constructs through the pedagogic relationship between Kostya and Tortsov in *An Actor Prepares* has influenced perceptions of male authority in actor training and directing. This authority is problematised when viewed through a gendered lens. Malague in *An Actress Prepares* attends to the misogyny of American Method training systems and how teachers, even unconsciously, can misuse their authority.[54] Looking at the work of Stella Adler and Uta Hagen as alternative approaches to Lee Strasberg and Sanford Meisner, she identifies a positively different approach to the power dynamic in teaching, which tries to re-think hierarchies, mindful of the ethical responsibility that such a marked power dynamic necessitates.

Working collaboratively within re-imagined power structures has been identified as a feature of female directing/teaching practices.[55] Phelan explains power in the collaborative act of performance-making as a fluid architecture, constantly shifting, appearing and disappearing as the nature of sociality in performance means that there is always someone being looked at and someone doing the looking.[56] This way of thinking about power illuminates the pedagogy of the UK female collectives in the 1970s who initiated collaborative devising practices as a radical shift in the traditional hierarchies of theatre-making.[57] Female collaborative practices are presented as an alternative to phallocentric structures and egoistic traditions. But how can such collaboration operate within the marked status positions of teacher/director and actor?

Rather than interrogate the pedagogy of women's collaborative practice, which others have considered, my concern is to better understand the multitudinous nature of the female teacher/director's leadership. Joan Schenkar suggests that the feminist director resists ideas of control as her own authority necessarily means robbing someone else of theirs. She suggests that, for a feminist director, the model of production 'should look less like a pyramid and more like a series of odd sized interceptive spheres with each person who contributes to the production responsible for her or his special circularity'.[58] This cartography differs from Phelan's organic power play in the way that it is a stable and concrete architecture, built on mutual dependency and interconnection. In this way, learning is facilitated within a supportive structure to enable empowerment, which is the operative mode of production in feminist pedagogy.

From this perspective, the female educator is a joint learner with her students, holding authority by virtue of a greater knowledge and experience. She presents herself not as the guru, but as the expert whose expertise is a condition of a lack of ego, a respect for the unknown, a willingness to get things wrong and a recognition that all knowledge is socially constructed and relational. This openness to diffusing knowledge and power enables others to take more ownership of their learning, trusting that they will be safe in conditions that allow them to fail, but crucially that they will be supported to find solutions. Gore states that the 'differentiation of power as domination, to power as creative energy, is central to the reclaiming of authority for feminist pedagogy'.[59] This offers an alternative affirmative position from which to learn through failing in acting.

The *via negativa* process of learning requires the actor to exist in a state of habitual vulnerability. In interviews for this book, actors, irrespective of gender, repeatedly expressed the opinion that they feel more able to be vulnerable with a female director. Actor Fiona Shaw explains: 'You need your bad ideas to be celebrated and not to be made to feel that you've failed. You need to be willing to be stupid and sometimes it's easier to do that with a nurse than with a doctor'.[60] Looking beyond Shaw's gendered stereotypes, she recognises that sexed bodies have different power and that she can be more vulnerable with another woman. Actor Tristan Sturrock, who, during the last two decades has mostly worked with female directors agrees, 'Female directors probe much more in different ways, using their own approaches they push harder but softer, in a way that you feel that you can develop or be riskier'.[61] Female authority can be more enabling for the actor in a training process where learning happens through failing. While enabling vulnerability might be considered a more female domain, such essentialist claims, the female disposition for nursing/caring and the notion of 'mothering' for example, are of course limiting. Vanessa Ewan, Co-Course Leader in MA/MFA Movement: Directing and Teaching at RCSSD, asks: 'How do you get the positives, or the really rich, deep understanding that the female has, without developing this archetype mother thing?'[62] I suggest that we turn from notions of servitude and flattening power towards the positive authority of the mother as problem solver, fixer or diagnostician. The ability to respond diagnostically, in the moment to what one is seeing, without preconceptions, was described as a 'female space' by Shona Morris, Course Lead in Movement at RADA,

> Facilitating sounds like you know what you want. You don't know what you want, you're going on that discovery with them, but when you get there you have to hold it for them, so that it is safe. Or you have to have enough judgment to know when it is going too deep. That feels very female to me.[63]"

Morris' female space points to the relational and mutually receptive exchange of joint experimentation. The teacher/director closely observes and adjusts to the signs of the actor, not working with some master code or holding preconceived ideas about fixing a product. This shift in authority is a feature of the positive economy of feminist pedagogies.

Similarly, the positioning of *via negativa* in acting pedagogy can be reconsidered from a feminist perspective. Negativity, through the construct of melancholia, has been presented as the most viable form of political action but an affirmative politics, rooted in relations and looking to the future offers a productive alternative. This affirmative position is not naïve optimism, but endurance, transformation and ethical principle, where the body can sustain its pain threshold without being annihilated by it.[64] This paradigm reflects Sedgwick's move away from the negative affect of 'paranoid reading' towards a 'reparative reading'. Like Sedgwick, I problematise the prescribed paranoia necessary for a critical stance, where any other position is seen to be 'naïve, pious or complacent'.[65] For Melanie Klein, a change of direction from the paranoid to the reparative is fueled by love and this imagines a more hopeful and sustainable critique for minoritarian societies.[66]

Looking to black feminist thinking opens perspectives when considering the politics of love and constructs of difference. Jennifer Nash proposes that black feminist love politics, particularly associated with second-wave feminism, offers an alternative to the institutionalisation of intersectional identity politics, which she suggests re-inscribes identitarian models of relationality, fixed in the present rather than looking to the future.[67] Nash maps the development of this politics, starting with Alice Walker's (1983) *In Search of Our Mother's Gardens* which places love at the centre of relations – with other women, with humanity, with the spiritual world and with herself. Walker's political project of womanism is 'a radical investment in difference' where love is 'a practice of self-work'.[68] Black feminist love politics is utopian, invested in a radical ethic of care. However, Sarah Ahmed cautions that this has the potential to inscribe new claims for power as 'those who don't love, who don't get closer, become the source of injury and disturbance'.[69] What is vital in working from a politics of love is that we recognise that 'how we love matters'.[70] Although, within the parameters of this book, I can only point towards this important strand of feminism, I hope that this might be a focus for future research as I see many connections here with Critical Acting Pedagogy. Relating this thinking to acting, working with a politics of love offers an alternative position. When viewed in the context of the *via negativa*, where learning operates through the negative affect of paranoia, a reparative position, working with a politics of love, can produce a feminist alternative – a *via positiva*.

In Catholic doctrine the *via positiva* assumes the presence of God in nature with the idea that God is knowable. In the context of acting, the *via positiva* ensures that the nature of the learning is made explicit and facilitates the actor as auto-didact in a productive creative exchange. Rather than being left to manage negative feelings of fear, anxiety, blocks or failure, s/he is supported to endure and sustain the habitual vulnerability necessary as part of her/his practice. By making the practice of coming to learn explicit, the transferable skills and dispositional attitudes of the hidden curriculum are facilitated. A feminist pedagogy works in joint experimentation to diagnose problems and facilitate solutions. The *via positiva* recognises that one might equally be motivated by what feels good and gives pleasure. The idea of 'no pain, no gain' and 'suffering for the art' fuels the melancholic assumption that depression is somehow noble and that happiness is vulgar, which is challenged through an affirmative politics. I have repeatedly observed female practitioners' teaching and directing from a position which shifts the focus to a positive economy of learning, where the actor, whilst identifying their failure, is supported to view this in positive terms. Talking of her approach Morris reflects:

> The *via negativa* is a Lecoq thing that comes from my training but I never, never use it. I've never felt interested in running a class where people stand up and then you go 'no'. I've never been able to do it. … What pleasure would I take from that? What I took from that is to be playful … if people are playing then there is pleasure.[71]

By repositioning power as creative energy and pleasure as equal to suffering in learning, a female reorientation emerges. Evans has recently asked:

> What value does pleasure in actor training and acting have? Can pleasure and discipline go hand in hand? Or is part of actor training learning to deal with discipline, setback and even failure?[72]

The *via positiva* allows pleasure and discipline to operate *beside* each other and opens up the possibility of endurance and sustainability as affirmative experience. In Part Two of this book, we will look at the specific and varied ways that women, working in voice, movement, acting with text and devising apply *via positiva* in their practice with actors. In Chapter 4, the idea of pleasure is considered as a feminist material through the construct of *jouissance*; this can be seen in the movement practices of Vanessa Ewan and Niamh Dowling. In Chapter 6, pleasure is seen to be central in Emma Rice's rehearsal process. Turning now from the foundational pedagogies of acting, I propose a Critical Acting Pedagogy, responsive to new feminist materialisms, that foregrounds the politics of the body.

## Towards a Critical Acting Pedagogy: Difference, the critical position and feminist acting approaches

### Difference

> What is hidden by the neuter?
>
> *Luce Irigaray*[73]

In the field of acting, which struggles to address inequalities (gender, class, race, ableism) in training and employment opportunities and which absents women from training lineages, the neutered body in pedagogies becomes an urgent concern. When acting, an embodied practice, ignores the gendered and sexed body as constituent of embodiment, a formative experience of being in the body is shut off. However, there seems to be an apparent disconnect between the act of teaching an acting class, the effect of the gender dynamic, and the specific acknowledgement of the particular body in the scholarship and practice of acting.[74] This is odd given the ways in which gender influences many aspects of decision-making: What scripts might be best suited to the group? How to group successfully? How to work with the individual and collective bodies in the room? The impact of gender in UK acting and drama at Higher Education cannot be ignored. Over the last five years drama schools have moved towards gender equality in recruitment, in spite of double the ratio of female to male applicants. In the university sector, applications for drama degrees also reflect significant biases in gender.[75] It is evident that females seem to be more attracted to the enabling 'knowledges' of the subject. Without detailed qualitative data we can only speculate on why this might be so. One conjecture is that the hidden curriculum, which develops knowledges perceived to be more female, such as empathy and vulnerability, affects this preference. Another possibility is that, rather than it being the *types* of knowledge or *ways* of thinking, it is the minoritarian doubling of the female state as both subject and object, simultaneously 'being' and 'being seen', which attracts females to acting.[76] The gender of the subject teacher might also be an influencing factor as the majority of drama teachers working in the UK secondary school system are female.[77]

In 1980, Audre Lorde cautioned 'we have no patterns for relating across our human difference as equals ... we do not develop tools for using human difference as a springboard for creative change within our lives'.[78] In 2020, at this cultural moment, questions of difference remain an urgent concern. The gender of the teacher has an impact on the experience of students. The scholarship of feminist educationalists notes the ways that women tend to foreground difference in their pedagogies, as their marginal position alerts them to this.[79] Aston and Harris remind us that any negotiation of difference is demanding and certainly should not be viewed naively. Differences cannot be dealt with 'by listing them, embracing them, celebrating them or remarking their proliferation'.[80] Navigating difference is risky, often teetering on the edge of confrontation and collapse and yet it is vital for a sustainable future. Constructs of difference, equated with 'diversity', 'inclusion' and 'equality' can become catch-all terms that disguise all sorts of problems, operating as a form of institutional damage control. It is vital that we recognise a practice of difference to be a slow and ongoing process of repair as opposed to a quick-fix solution.[81] Working from a positivity of difference we must remember there are differences *within* a particular body as well as *between* bodies. In her consideration of a post-intersectional position Nash cites Jasbir Puar to suggest that the term 'difference', which seems to organise identity into some sort of neat categories, might be better thought of as 'assemblage', always in motion and looking to the future and affect.[82] We are all relational in our understanding of ourselves, so I compare and construct my difference to your situatedness and through this I question my own assumptions. From this position, any notion of difference moves from a fact to an effect, to enable an enactive way of seeing and being, which is always moving and never complete.[83] Working from the positivity of difference the politics of the actor's body becomes a potential site of resistance. I situate this within the paradigm of critical pedagogy.

## *The critical position*

Pioneering work in Drama in Education (DIE) at the end of the last century enabled students to explore themselves and society through play, producing a critical pedagogy.[84] Performance Studies also positions itself in this way. However, whilst the hidden curriculum of acting develops 'personal and social knowledge',[85] the political exigent of actor training is rarely given space.[86]

As Broderick Chow notes, the fact that the embodied technique of acting exists in relation to lived material reality, including social, political, cultural and historical contexts means that 'embodied knowledge is always in some ways embodied political knowledge'.[87] At a time when the cultural agency of the performer is seen to be an imperative, re-conceptualising acting in this way can provide an alternative to limiting ideas of acting as mimesis and to notions of professional servitude.[88] Looking to educational models of critical pedagogy offers a context for this shift.

The idea that the learner might be empowered through the process of learning to act is drawn from modes of critical pedagogy, which place the notion of the self and the other, or in other words relationships between identity and society, as its central concern. Although I would argue that constructs of critical pedagogy are inherent in DIE, its origin is attributed to the pioneering work of Brazilian educationalist Paulo Freire. In his concern for the oppression of illiterate groups, Freire theorised how education should escape 'fill em up' structures, where students passively receive knowledge, and move towards a more critical and personalised approach to learning with the student as an active participant.[89] A critical pedagogy allows us to critique oppressive power structures in order to activate alternative ways of being.[90] Students critique the mechanisms of power at work in language and behaviour to understand how oppressive marginal positions are constructed and to re-imagine the status quo. The negative view of 'the other' is challenged to enable empowerment where there is difference. Critical pedagogy's features can be summarised as: recognising that *how* you teach something is as important as *what* you teach; flattening power structures; individualising learning with a commitment to develop the individual's political, personal and social awareness; recognising the complexities of problems as opposed to seeking conclusions; taking notions of difference and particularity as productive sites for resistance.

Feminist educational theorists have criticised a number of aspects of critical pedagogy. They have commented on the neutering of gender, the heroic claims that fail to root theory in practice and the extent to which a recognition of difference paradoxically strengthens the most privileged voices.[91] Feminist pedagogy is a strand of critical pedagogy that confronts concerns of difference to foreground the position of women as both subjects and objects. It developed in the UK in the late 1960s and 1970s in response to the consciousness raising of the Women's Movement. As with feminist theory there are many different positions: radical, socialist, black, postmodernist, liberal and intersectional, but all use gender as a central tool for analysis. Women challenge the de-valuing of personal experience in learning and look at power not only as a constraint but also as a possibility, not dichotomous but as mutually informing relations of contradiction. They try to make all students feel valued as individuals and use their experience as a learning resource. The reciprocity between teacher and student is inherent in the pedagogy of bell hooks, which she describes as an 'engaged pedagogy' that 'moves beyond critical or feminist pedagogy, in the way that it empowers wellbeing'.[92] For hooks, wellbeing and a shared enjoyment of the act of learning is crucial, so that teachers grow alongside their students. In order for this to happen there needs to be a step away from set and routine practice towards a more changeable and spontaneous response to the needs of the individuals in the moment. This requires both students and teachers to listen to each other and share in risk taking and vulnerability. In this way, notions of power shift from domination to a creative and affirmative exchange based on pleasure as opposed to pain. These features of shared vulnerability, reciprocity and relationality are central to the processes of joint experimentation in the pedagogy of acting.

However, the discourses of critical pedagogies tend to be driven by dialogic structures rather than through bodies. Performative pedagogy, which foregrounds materiality where thinking happens through the body, has developed as a field of scholarship and practice over the last decade alongside the establishment and growth of Performance Studies as a discipline. Elise Pineau recognises the intersections between these two fields as a fruitful site for liberatory practice and has coined the term Critical Performative Pedagogy (CPP).[93] The social constructivist nature of learning is made explicit through close attention to the sociological and anthropological conditions for action, which determine the way that people behave. Attention is given to the space between the dialectic, the moment of choice and, by making this space explicit, the learner comes to develop personal and social understanding. Identity and exploration of the self and other is explored through structures of role play and improvisation, which become both the content and the form for investigation. The body is a site for historical, political and ideological inscription and seen as a canvas for creating alternative possibilities through bodily play. Like forms of DIE and the liberatory practice of Augusto Boal,[94] performative pedagogy enables unique insights through the body that often elude disembodied, intellectual reflection.[95] In many ways this is the knowledge of acting, but Pineau maintains a distinction between performative pedagogy and 'simply acting out' to argue that performance 'probes beyond the surface of observable behaviours' and that 'It is a shift from mimesis to kinesis'.[96] This reminds us of Kirby's positioning of acting as 'feigning' outlined in the Introduction.[97] It reduces 'mimesis' to reflection, ignoring the wider possibilities of *mimesis-as-play* which underpins the improvisation used within Performance Studies. Acting is thus reduced to a style – naturalism – foreclosing its political potential as a critical pedagogy. Performative pedagogy directly positions itself as such. It is concerned with issues of power: politics, history, conflict, appropriation and resistance and openly calls for more interdisciplinary research with education to develop this pedagogy.[98] Although scholars and practitioners confidently assert the critical and political possibilities of performative pedagogy and the necessity for interdisciplinary scholarship, it is only recently that acting pedagogy has been mined for its political potential.[99]

Acting pedagogies, re-considered through the lens of feminist new materialisms, develop and extend CPP to work with an added layer of knowledge – notions of embodiment. This allows for a double thinking, where analysis of the 'social body' is entangled with the phenomenological exploration of the 'lived body' as necessarily interactive.[100] This *beside thinking* places notions of embodiment alongside performative pedagogy where the lived body can be seen as 'the tool' and the social body 'the text', thus recognising the beside nature of bodily learning.[101] This pedagogical approach responds to Spatz's call to reconceptualise the techniques of acting alongside techniques of identity in order to interrogate their transformatory potential.[102] It pursues what Chow calls 'the thinking body', reframing training as a form of critically creative thought.[103] A new materialist acting approach considers how the social body intersects with the lived body in its specific context, to produce a Critical Acting Pedagogy (CAP). Here the actor develops her/his relational awareness, the reflective beside the reflexive, exploring how meaning is produced in the spaces *within* the body and *between* people or things. One area where acting has been granted this type of critical agency is in feminist acting pedagogies.

## Feminist acting approaches

Different types of feminisms are evident in women's approaches to theatre. Aston overviews the three dominant feminist positions as liberal, radical and materialist. Broadly speaking, the liberal minimises difference between men and women and works for reform as opposed to revolt. The radical maintains the superiority of female attributes and favours a separate female system. The materialist stresses the conditions of production that shape race and class, whilst minimising biological differences between men and women.[104] To this we can add two more positions: the intersectional feminist, who highlights the complex stratifications of power that work to oppress marginalised groups and the differences *between* women; the new feminist materialist, who recognises the entangled doubleness of the body as both inscribed and inscribing and recognises the differences *within* a women.[105] A feminist acting pedagogy facilitates a feminist acting approach and will be contingent on the type(s) of feminism and the form/aesthetic/cultural context of the practice, be that devising, text based or purely training focused. To suggest that this falls neatly into particular camps denies the messiness of this practice as pedagogies inevitably cross over and collide ideologically and in practice.

At the risk of stating the obvious, it is important to reiterate that feminist acting pedagogies seek out alternative approaches to traditional patriarchal practices. In the 1970s and 1980s radical female countercultures, which drew on the international languages of myths, symbols and archetypes, where approaches to knowing the body were central, sought ways to reject traditional ideas of character. Women's acting methods were often based on autobiographical material, including areas of experience recognised as common to women and this gave permission for the performer to be 'herself'.[106] Through the 1990s, when the first wave of feminist theatre scholarship emerged in force, there was increasing resistance to actor training programmes that assumed a masculine norm.[107] Aston, Harris and Stroppel problematise extreme physical regimes and exercises that draw attention to bodily strength. Female students can be 'abused' by training practices that foreground strength and weight to create body anxiety.[108] Malague, in her feminist reframing of the American Method, advises that any feminist acting technique should stress the importance of developing emotional strength alongside physical strength.[109]

In its essence, a feminist acting pedagogy –whatever its parameters and context – seeks out the spaces that allow for choice and authorship. Whenever women make theatre it is immediately politicised because of their marginal position. Harris notes that any performance is 'already double, marked in quotation marks' but that the artist authors *how* these quotation marks are viewed – as citation, iteration, mimesis, mimicry, representation or appropriation.[110] A feminist acting pedagogy looks for choice in the slippage between competing discourses: nature/culture, performance/performativity, the social body/the lived body, the inscribed body/the inscribing body, human/non-human. Stroppel, noting feminist responses to the Method in the U.S., recognises a more explicit or implicit approach in the way that citation is revealed as a double marking. 'Explicit' exposes the constructed-ness of characters and can be seen to reflect a Brechtian strategy. 'Implicit' relates to realistic performance, which has been created with an individual psychology and a social critique. She explains that a feminist acting technique '[V]isibly highlights differences of gender, race, sexual preferences and class as cultural representations rather than subsumes them as natural reflections of society'.[111] Moving on from Diamond's seminal text *Unmaking Mimesis,* and following Stroppel's search for post-Brechtian strategies, what feminist critical theories best illuminate these spaces?

Feminist materialisms highlight the critical potential in these slippages. In *Bodies That Matter,* Butler addresses the space between the construct of performance and the performative. Feminist scholars had questioned the way that the explanation of performative action in *Gender Trouble* suggested the unalterability of gender. Butler seemed to be suggesting that through iteration, gender became embedded and unalterable. In this light, possible actions of resistance were closed down.[112] Butler clarifies that performance is 'a bounded act',[113] operating within its particular constructions and the performative is repeated actions, which, through repetition, establish gender as technique. However, the action of repetition inevitably opens up the possibility for change. No embodied repetition will be exactly the same and this enables a 'hiatus in iterability',[114] reminding us of Irigaray's impossible original, or 'non-truth' of truth. The blurred space between performance and performativity can therefore be seen as intra-active, relational and potentially transformative as both constructs operate *in relation with* each other. Butler posits 'it is necessary to learn a double movement: to invoke the category and, hence, provisionally to institute an identity and at the same time to open up the category as a site of permanent political contest'.[115] I see Butler's double movement as operating in different ways from Brecht's not/but, either/or, dialectical double gesture. In her thinking there is the sense of 'and/with', an awareness of beside-ness, mobility and the potential in polyvalence.

Irigaray also offers a useful strategy for feminist pedagogies to explore the space between performance and performativity when she calls for a female mimicry, which draws attention to the masquerade through its exaggeration. In this case, performing female is offered as 'an actively offensive rather than defensive strategy, so as to make visible, by means of a playful repetition, that which was supposed to remain invisible'.[116] Through examining the possibilities of repetition a feminist acting pedagogy enables the actor to foreground the processes of representational production, as a space of future re-articulations. In Part Two, Chapter 5 looks at the ways that Alison Hodge and Kristine Landon-Smith work with 'the hiatus of iteration'. Chapter 6 recognises the same quality in the work of Katie Mitchell and considers how Emma Rice explores female mimicry.

Stropple's scholarship points to the subtle, implicit ways that the 'natural' might be critiqued in acting. How can feminist acting pedagogies work within the context of realism? As we noted in Chapter 1, new feminist materialisms, in refusing to privilege culture/society above nature/the body/matter, revisit 'the natural' and offer a powerful ideology for a post-psychophysical acting pedagogy. Vital materialism is a different way of thinking about the agency of the body, with phenomenological theory of embodiment working *beside* Marxist and post-structuralist ideas about the intersections between bodies and power. From this perspective, bodies are simultaneously embedded and embodied, inscribed and inscribing. Understanding the body as matter has evolved since 1990s materialism as ideas intersect with developments in science. Matter is seen as active and self-organising, not simply something done to. Bio-literate feminists such as Donna Haraway,[117] Fausto Sterling,[118] Karen Barad,[119] Elizabeth Grosz[120] and Jane Bennet[121] fight matter with matter to re-think the unity of the human being and to foreground the positivity of difference. When we recognise the specificity and plasticity of each body in its constant state of becoming we are reminded that, in neutering the body, we foreclose the rich resource of difference in actor training. Placing movement and mobility at the heart of thinking in pedagogies allows us to give value to what is normally sidelined. Rather than matter being produced by some master code, *in relation to,* each encounter is an ethical opportunity for empowering through connection *in relation with* others, including the non-human. This expands feminist acting pedagogies beyond ideas of the bodymind into the bodyworld, an ecological body, ethically accountable.[122]

In the U.S., Rhonda Blair's feminist acting pedagogy develops an implicit/post-Brechtian feminist pedagogy within the realm of realism in ways that draw on new materialisms. She draws attention to how feminist scientists have advanced knowledge about cognition, behaviour and sexuality and how these might be embodied in the brain. Blair works at the intersections of theory, practice and science and she challenges 'feminist actors and acting teachers to be more rigorous in their understanding of bodies, consciousness, and feelings … with the awareness that these processes are reflective of brain structure and function'.[123] Like Katie Mitchell, Blair guides the actor to interrogate intention so that, through detailed analysis, she might author her action as a possible site of resistance within the constructs of realism. The actor is brought to critically understand the historical, political and social assumptions underlying the representations they are playing and the methodologies they are working with. Simultaneously, they develop a heightened awareness of their 'body-in-movement-within-a-changing environment'.[124] In this way, new approaches are possible, working with choice from an affirmative position. Blair explains that the actor is 'acting for herself' with the simple knowledge of being 'in oneself', as opposed to *for* 'some other', which is based on anger and fear, 'for to react to something is to acknowledge its power by trying to control or destroy it'.[125] This position moves away from a practice of reflecting, in *relation to* society, towards a diffraction, in *relation with*; the intra-action of society *with* the body. As I explained in Chapter 1, this becomes an important feminist strategy to *re-make mimesis*.

A succinct example of this is Carrie Noland's exploration of agency and embodiment, through the gesture of the curtsey. In considering this gendered gesture as technique, Noland recognises that through the hiatus of iteration, one can work from a double awareness of social role beside a bodily, felt sense. She asks, 'what if in performing the curtsy the subject felt not only "feminine" but also sore? What if the socially established meaning of the act were overwhelmed, at least momentarily, by the somatic experiences of pressure, friction and pain? What if, in other words, the body spoke back?'[126] Blair's feminist acting pedagogy gives space to how bodies speak back, developing the hidden curriculum of acting through building self-acceptance, critique and compassion. As I turn to practice in Part Two, I build on Blair's insights to examine women's pedagogic practices through the lens of new feminist materialisms.

Thinking about acting pedagogies intersecting with feminisms opens up its epistemic scope. When we adopt a gendered position to consider the ideology, the foundational pedagogic practices and the politics of the body, acting operates as a critical pedagogy, concerned with notions of identity and power. The feminist interventions I have examined here re-direct attention to the hidden curriculum to explore the value of learning to act from a minoritarian position. They propose alternatives to patriarchal pedagogies to point to alternative power structures, working from an affirmative position, where the experience of failing is positively supported – a *via positiva*. This enables a CAP, where *mimesis-as-play* is a kinetic praxis. These feminist interventions in acting offer valuable insights for pedagogy in its broadest context.

# Notes

1. Ross Prior, *Teaching Actors: Knowledge Transfer in Actor Training* (Bristol UK/Chicago USA: Intellect, 2012) 55–56.
2. In the Introduction to this book I problematise the lack of pedagogical enquiry to suggest that this disempowers disembodies and 'dis-embrains' the actor.
3. Maria Kapsali, 'Training for a Cold Climate', *Theatre, Dance and Performance Training*, 2, (2014): 103–106.
4. This was considered in Chapter 1 through the work of Peggy Phelan.
5. These include, but are not limited to: imagination, emotional intelligence, being in the moment, focus, impulse, intuition, instinct, flow, emotional availability, trust, respect, generosity, inner listening, curiosity, self-care, polyphonic awareness, empathy, altruism, collaboration, reflection, reflexivity, learning through failure, playfulness, knowing the value of fear, self-discipline, resilience and relational awareness.
6. Simon Murray cited by Maria Kapsali, 'Training for a Cold Climate: Edited Transcript of Roundtable Discussion', *Theatre, Dance and Performance Training*, 5(2), (2014): 2019–2231.
7. Stephen Wangh, *The Heart of Teaching: Empowering Students in the Performing Arts* (London & New York: Routledge, 2013) 139.
8. Frank Camilleri, *Performer Training Reconfigured: Post-Psychophysical Perspectives for the Twenty-First Century* (London & New York: Methuen Drama, 2019).
9. Noelle McAfee, *Julia Kristeva: Routledge Critical Thinkers* (London & New York: Routledge, 2003) 98.
10. Phillip Zarrilli, Jerri Dabbo and Rebecca Loukes, *Acting: Psychophysical Phenomenon and Process* (Basingstoke: Palgrave Macmillan, 2013).
11. Ibid. 233–238.
12. In the context of this study I draw on John Dewey, *Experience and Education* (West Lafayette, Indiana: Kappa Delta Pi, 1998), David Kolb, *Experiential learning: Experience as the Source of Learning and Development* (Vol. 1) (Englewood Cliffs, NJ: Prentice-Hall, 1984), Lev Vygotsky, *Thought and Language* (London: MIT press, 1988), Jean Lave and Etienne Wenger, *Situated Learning: Legitimate Peripheral Participation* (Cambridge: Cambridge University Press, 1991).
13. Paulo Freire, *Pedagogy of the Oppressed* (New York & Great Britain: Continuum, 2000), Henry Giroux, *Schooling for a Democracy: Critical Pedagogy in the Modern Age* (London: Routledge, 1989) 189, hooks, op.cit., Katherine Weiler, 'Freire and a Feminist Pedagogy of Difference', *Harvard Educational Review*, 61 (1991): 449–474, Elyse Pineau, 'Pedagogy: Fleshing Out the Politics of Liberatory Education', in Nathan Stucky and Cynthia Wimmer (eds), *Teaching Performance Studies* (Carbondale, Illinois: Southern Illinois University Press, 2002) 41–54.
14. Vygotsky defines this as, '[T]he distance between the actual developmental level as determined by independent problem solving and the level of potential development as determined through problem solving under adult guidance or in collaboration with more capable peers'. Lev Vygotsky, *Mind in Society: Development of Higher Psychological Processes* (Cambridge, Massachusetts: Harvard University Press, 1978) 86.
15. Lave and Wenger, op.cit.
16. Mary Thorpe, 'Re-Thinking Learner Support: The Challenge of Collaborative Online Learning', *Open Learning*, 17(2), (2002): 111.
17. Ross Prior, *Teaching Actors: Knowledge Transfer in Actor Training* (Bristol, UK, Chicago, USA: Intellect, 2012) 188.
18. Donald Schön, *Educating the Reflective Practitioner: Toward a New Design for Teaching and Learning in the Professions* (San Francisco: Jossey Bass, 1987) 37.
19. Ibid. Chapter 8.

20 This was explained in Chapter 2. Andrea Milde, 'Linguistics in Drama Processes', *Working Papers in Urban Language & Literacies,* Paper 251 (2019) https://www.academia.edu/39625216/WP251_Milde_2019._Linguistics_in_drama_processes [accessed 25.07.19].
21 Ibid.
22 Karen Barad, 'Posthumanist Performativity: Toward an Understanding of How Matter Comes to Matter', *Signs,* 28(3), (Spring, 2003), 801–831, Donna Haraway, *Simians, Cyborgs and Women: The Reinvention of Nature* (London & New York: Routledge, 1991) 127–149, Rosi Braidotti, *Nomadic Theory: The Portable Rosi Braidotti* (New York: Columbia University Press, 2011), Jane Bennet, *Vibrant Matter: A Political Ecology of Things* (Duke University Press, 2010), Elizabeth Grosz, *Volatile Bodies: Towards a Corporeal Feminism* (Indiana University Press, 1994).
23 Gabrielle Ivinson and Carol Taylor, 'Material Feminisms: New Directions for Education', *Gender and Education,* 25(6), (2013): 665–670, Alecia Youngblood Jackson, 'Making Matter Making Us: Thinking with Grosz to Find Freedom in New Feminist Materialisms', *Gender and Education,* 25(6), (2013): 768–775, Malou Juelskjaer, 'Gendered Subjectivities of Spacetimematter', *Gender and Education,* 25(6), (2013): 754–768.
24 Camilleri, 124.
25 As explained in the Introduction, when I observe pedagogy my primary focus is gender but I am alert to these other factors.
26 Mark Evans, 'Playing with History: Personal Accounts of the Political and Cultural Self in Actor Training Through Movement', *Theatre, Dance and Performance Training,* 5(2), (2014): 149.
27 Richard Schechner and Lisa Wolford, *The Grotowski Sourcebook* (London & New York: Routledge, 1997) 31.
28 Nicolas McGuinn, *The English Teacher's Drama Handbook* (London & New York: Routledge, 2014).
29 Harriet Finlay-Johnson, *The Dramatic Method of Teaching* (Boston & New York: Ginn and Company, 1912).
30 Mark Evans, *Performance, Movement and the Body* (London and U.S.: Macmillan International, Red Globe Press, 2019) 50–52.In this section Evans points to the following: Clive Barker, *Theatre Games: A New Approach to Drama Training* (London: Methuen, 1977), Keith Johnstone, *Impro: Improvisation and The Theatre* (London: Methuen, 1979), Jacques Lecoq, *The Moving Body: Teaching Creative Theatre* (London: Methuen, 2000), Philippe Gaulier, *The Tormentor: Le jeu- light-theatre* (Paris: Filmiko, 2006), John Wright, *Why Is That So Funny: A Practical Exploration of Physical Comedy* (London: Nick Hern Books, 2006).
31 Johan Huizinga, *Homo Ludens: A Study of the Play Element in Culture* (London: Routledge and Kegan Paul Ltd, 1949), Roger Callous, *Man, Play and Games* (Paris: Librarie Gallimard, 1958).
32 In *Performance Movement and the Body,* Mark Evans explains play as 'a form of human behaviour whose rational justification is not necessarily required; in which pleasure, unpredictability and excitement in physical engagement is at least as important as any outcomes; in which physical imagination is at least as important as rational intention; and in which meaning is present but always fluid and embodied. It is in this sense not only an activity but also an attitude towards an activity'. 50.
33 Lynne Kendrick, 'A Paidic Aesthetic: An Analysis of Games in the Ludic Pedagogy of Philippe Gaulier', *Theatre, Dance and Performance Training,* 2(1), (2011): 72–85.
34 Ibid. 74.
35 Ibid. 76–77.
36 Ibid. 77.
37 Evans, 145.

38 Wangh, 13.
In reflective practice the learner personally reflects on what they have learned (inner awareness); in reflexive practice the learner considers the implications of what they have learned within a wider social context (outer awareness).
39 Richard Schechner and Lisa Wolford, *The Grotowski Sourcebook* (London & New York: Routledge, 1997) 31.
40 Grotowski explains, 'But if one learns *how to do*, one doesn't reveal oneself; one only reveals the skill for doing. And if someone looks for means … In the end one has to reject it all and not learn, but unlearn, not to know how to do but how not to do and always face doing'. Ibid. 230.
41 When Grotowski's approach is understood through his writings or through observation, the ethics and the aesthetics that underpin the practice and scaffold the learning for the actor are obscured. See Eugenio Barba and Nicola Savarese, *The Secret Art of the Performer* (London & New York: Routledge,1993) 26–33.
42 Duncan Jamieson, 'Between Craft and Metaphysics: Voicing Acting Process at the Laboratory Theatre', paper presented at International Platform for Performer Training, Kent University, 9th January, 2020.
43 See 'Curiosity and a Readiness to Search for the New', Antoni Jahołkowski talks to Tadeusz Burzyński, trans. by Duncan Jamieson and Adela Karsznia, in *Voices from Within: Grotowski's Polish Collaborators*, ed. Paul Allain and Grzegorz Ziółkowski (London and Wrocław: Polish Theatre Perspectives, 2015) 95–99, 97.
44 Simon Murray, *Jacques Le Coq* (London & New York: Routledge, 2003) 49.
45 Maggie Irving, 'Clown Training, Preparing for Failure' unpublished paper presented at TAPRA in 2010.
46 Ibid.
47 Gaulier (2007) 290 cited by Kendrick, 73.
48 Kendrick, 80.
49 Ibid.
50 Roanna Mitchell, 'The Actor's Body: Identity and Image', talk given at Royal Central School of Speech and Drama (15.10.13).
51 Michel Foucault, *Power: Essential Works of Foucault 1954–1984. Volume 3* (London: Penguin, 1984) 298.
52 Rosemary Jeanes Antze, 'Oriental Examples' in Eugenio Barba and Nicola Savarese, *A Dictionary of Theatre Anthropology: The Secret Art of the Performer* (London & New York, 1991) 31–34.
53 Brecht, Grotowski, Artaud, Brook, Bogart, Mnouchkine have all declared the influence of Eastern theatre on their practice.
54 Rosemary Malague, *An Actress Prepares: Women and "The Method"* (London & New York: Routledge, 2011) 16.
55 Rachel Daniels, *Women Stage Directors Speak: Exploring the Influence of Gender in Their Work* (North Carolina: MacFarlan and Company, 1996).
56 Peggy Phelan, *Unmarked: The Politics of Performance* (London & New York: Routledge, 1993) 173.
57 Duska Radoslavljevic, *The Contemporary Ensemble: Interviews with Theatre Makers* (London and New York: Routledge, 2013) 10.
58 Ibid. 256.
59 Louise Alcroff and Elizabeth Potter, *Feminist Epistemologies* (London & New York: Routledge, 1993) 72.
60 Interview with Fiona Shaw, Glyndebourne (30.09.13).
61 Interview with Tristan Sturrock, Bristol (30.01.15).
62 Interview with Vanessa Ewan, RCSSD (15.11.13).
63 Interview with Shona Morris, Drama Centre, London (01.11.13).
64 Ibid. 21.

65 Eve Sedgwick, *Touching Feeling. Affect, Pedagogy, Performativity* (Durham and London: Duke University Press, 2003) 126.
66 Ibid. 128.
67 Jennifer C. Nash, 'Practicing Love: Black Feminism, Love-Politics, and Post-Intersectionality', *Meridians,* 11(2), (2011): 1–24.
68 Ibid. 12.
69 Sarah Ahmed, 'In the Name of Love', *Borderlands E-Journal,* 2(3), (2003) http://www.borderlands.net.au/vol2no3_2003/ahmed_love.htm [accessed 20.06.20].
70 Ibid.
71 Morris (14.02.20).
72 Mark Evans, *The Actor Training Reader* (London & New York: Routledge, 2015) xxx.
73 Luce Irigaray, *Sexes and Genealogies* (New York: Columbia University Press 1993) 171.
74 For an extended discussion on this see Ben Spatz, *What a Body Can Do: Technique as Knowledge. Practice as Research* (London & New York: Routledge, 2015) 113–217.
75 Referring to the UCAS conference presentation in 2014, Stephen Lacey asked that universities question the difference in participation between males and females. From 2009 to 2013 there were twice as many females to males applying, with between 7,800 and 8,500 women compared to well under 4,000 male applicants. These statistics were posted by Mark Taylor-Batty on SCUDD http://www.scudd.org.uk/2014/04/24/ucas-application-stats-04–14/ [accessed 24.04.14].
76 This idea has been mapped by feminist scholars through readings of Lacan, in particular through the work of Judith Butler, Peggy Phelan, Jacqueline Rose and Rosi Braidotti.
77 Applications and offers were notably gendered during the eight years I led the Post-Graduate Certificate in Education (PGCE) in Drama at the University of Sussex (2007–2014).
78 Audre Lorde 'Age, Race, Class and Sex: Women Redefining Difference' in Audre Lorde, *Your Silence Will Not Protect You* (UK: Silver Press, 2017) 95–96.
79 Esther Beth Sulliven cited by Ellen Donkin, *Upstaging Big Daddy: Directing Theatre as if Gender and Race Matter* (Ann Arbor: The University of Michigan Press,1993) 28.
80 Elaine Aston and Geraldine Harris, *Feminist Futures?:Theatre, Performance, Theory* (Palgrave Macmillan, 2007) 12.
81 This idea of 'repair', first suggested by Broderick Chow and Royona Mitra, was offered as a provocation by Arabella Stanger in conversation 25.06.20.
82 Ibid. 13.
83 Phillip Zarrilii, *Psychophysical Acting: An Intercultural Approach after Stanislavski* (London & New York: Routledge, 2009) 46–63.
84 Harriet Finlay-Johnson, *The Dramatic Method of Teaching* (Boston & New York: Ginn and Company, 1912).
85 Prior, 91–92.
86 Unlike the U.S., as seen in Ellen Margolis and Lisa Tyler Renaud (eds), *The Politics of American Actor Training* (New York & London: Routledge, 2009).
87 Broderick D.V. Chow, 'How Does The Trained Body Think?' in *Thinking Through Theatre and Performance,* ed. Maaike Bleeker, Aidrian Kear, Joe Kelleher, Heike Roms (New York & London: Methuen Drama, 2017) 148.
88 Kapsali, op.cit. 104.
89 Freire, op.cit.
   Also note Jacques Rancière explores this position in *The Ignorant Schoolmaster,* where he describes a move away from 'the circle of powerlessness' to 'the circle of power', which emancipates students to teach themselves. Jacques Rancière, *The Ignorant Schoolmaster: Five Lessons in Intellectual Emancipation* (Stanford, Carolina: University Press Stanford,1991) 15.

90 Educationalist Henry Giroux describes this process of learning as 'the process of appreciating and loving oneself', reflecting an affirmative politics. Henry Giroux, *Schooling for a Democracy: Critical Pedagogy in the Modern Age* (London: Routledge, 1989) 189.
91 Katherine Weiler, *Feminist Engagements: Reading, Resisting and Revisioning Male Theorists in Education and Cultural Studies* (New York & London: Routledge, 2001).
92 hooks, op.cit. 13.
93 Elyse Pineau, 'Pedagogy: Fleshing Out the Politics of Liberatory Education', in Nathan Stucky and Cynthia Wimmer (eds), *Teaching Performance Studies* (Carbondale, Illinois: Southern Illinois University Press, 2002) 41–54.
94 Augusto Boal, *Theatre of the Oppressed* (London: Pluto Press, 1979).
95 Elyse Pineau, 'Teaching Is Performance: Reconceptualising a Problematic Metaphor', *American Educational Research Association,*. 31(1), (1994): 16.
96 Ibid. 16.
97 Michael Kirby, 'On Acting and Not-Acting', *The Drama Review: TDR*, 16(1), (1972): 3–15, 3.
98 John Warren, 'The Body Politic, Performance and the Power of Enfleshment', *Text and Performance Quarterly,* 19 (1999): 266.
99 I indicate this scholarship in the Introduction.
100 Elizabeth Grosz, *Volatile Bodies: Towards a Corporeal Feminism* (Indiana University Press, 1994).
101 Mia Perry and Carmen Medina, 'Embodiment and Performance in Pedagogy Research: Investigating the Possibility of the Body in Curriculum Experience', *Journal of Curriculum Theorizing,* 27(3), (2011): 63.
102 Spatz, 163.
103 Chow, op.cit. 147.
104 Elaine Aston, *An Introduction to Feminism and Theatre* (London & New York: Routledge, 1995) 8.
105 Braidotti, op.cit.
106 Ibid. 67.
107 This came to the fore in the landmark year 1988–1989, and the work of:Sue Ellen Case, *Feminism and Theatre* (London: Routledge, 1988); Jill Dolan, *The Feminist Spectator as Critic* (Anne Arbor: University of Michigan Press, 1988); Lynda Hart, ed., *Making a Spectacle: Feminist Essays on Contemporary Women's Theatre* (Ann Arbor: University of Michigan Press, 1989).
108 Aston (1995), 101.
109 Malague, 11.
110 Geraldine Harris, *Staging Femininities. Performance and Performativity* (Manchester & New York: Manchester University Press, 1999) 77.
111 Malague, 106.
112 Ibid. xi.
113 Judith Butler, *Bodies that Matter: On the Discursive Limits of Sex* (London & New York: Routledge, 1993) 234.
114 Harris, 72.
115 Butler, 222.
116 Irigaray, (1985) 46.
117 Donna Haraway, *Simians, Cyborgs and Women: The Reinvention of Nature* (London & New York: Routledge, 1991) 127–149.
118 Anne Fausto-Sterling, *Sexing the Body: Gender Politics and the Construction of Sexuality* (New York: Basic Books, 2000).
119 Karen Barad, 'Posthumanist Performativity: Toward an Understanding of How Matter Comes to Matter', *Signs*, 28(3), (Spring, 2003): 801–831.

120 Elizabeth Grosz, *Volatile Bodies: Towards a Corporeal Feminism* (Indiana University Press, 1994).
121 Jane Bennet, *Vibrant Matter: A Political Ecology of Things* (Duke University Press, 2010).
122 Sandra Reeve, *New Ways of Seeing a Body* (Devon: Triarchy Press, 2011) 48.
123 Malague, 189.
124 Reeve, 48.
125 Rhonda Blair, 1995. 'Liberating the Young Actor: Feminist Pedagogy and Performance', *Theatre Topics,* 2(1): 23.
126 Carrie Noland, *Agency and Embodiment* (Cambridge: Harvard University Press, 2009) 194, cited by Chow, 153.

# PART II
# Considering Practice

# 3
# WOMEN AND THE MATTER OF VOICE

Di Trevis, the first woman to direct and lead a company at the National Theatre in the 1980s, believes it is 'the combination of the physical and vocal life of the actor' that sets UK acting apart.[1] If voice and movement work define actor training then it is important to note that women dominate these fields. In this chapter I focus on voice, mapping the women who have made significant contributions and thinking through how a gendered (re)consideration of voice pedagogies can open up the specific knowledges of the hidden curriculum.[2] I look at the pedagogic practices of Jane Boston and Nadine George, practitioners who, to some extent, position themselves on the edge of voice practice. Their work, which operates at the intersection between gender and voice as technique, develops personal and social knowledges in acting, advancing critical pedagogies from a feminist perspective.

The poetic tradition of the literary canon has established the UK as a centre for excellence in voice training. The dominance of the classical text requires actors to be cogent in textual analysis and vocally capable. Generations of UK female practitioners have shaped the field, many inspired by Cicely Berry (1926–2018), world-renowned teacher and Voice Director at the Royal Shakespeare Company between 1969 and 2014. Other notable practitioners are Patsy Rodenburg, Head of Voice at Guildhall School of Music and Director of Voice at Michael Howard Studios New York and Kristin Linklater, Head of Acting at Columbia University. These women have authored a significant body of work – Berry (1991, 2000, 2001);[3] Rodenburg (2009, 2015, 2019);[4] Linklater (2006, 2010)[5] – to establish voice work as a female domain. Many practitioners taught by these women or at The Royal Central School of Speech and Drama, which is the longest-running centre for UK voice training,[6] have authored their methodologies and branded their work, for example *The Fitzmaurice Voicework,* widely taught in the U.S., developed by RCSSD alum Catherine Fitzmaurice.[7] These practitioners, along with Kate Fleming at The Old Vic, form a body of internationally renowned UK voice specialists. Indeed, in *The Actor Training Reader* the only female to be represented amongst thirteen international practitioners is Kristin Linklater.[8]

Although these particular women dominate the field, a network of practitioners have been formative in developing voice training, and looking to a small selection of these more hidden histories, recognising them as part of a much wider landscape, helps to broaden the focus:[9] Elizabeth Pursey (1923–2012), course leader for Voice at RADA between 1962 and 1976 and Betty Mulcahy (1920–2012), who made an important contribution to verse speaking and broadcasting; Iris Warren (1900–1963), voice tutor at London Academy of Music and Dramatic Art; Frankie Armstrong, singer and writer who was an initiating member of the Natural Voice Practitioners' Network (NVPN) and who co-founded the Feminists Improvising Group (FIG) in 1977; Barbara Houseman worked alongside Cicely Berry at the RSC and became Associate Director for The Young Vic. Houseman continues to work as a voice coach in the West End, teaches in the U.S. and set up the company 'Dangerous Spaces' in 2017, with the remit to develop a wider range of roles for women, especially women of colour and older female actors; Rebecca Clark-Carey, previously senior voice tutor at RADA who, along with her husband David Carey, former course leader of MA voice at RCSSD, now writes about voice and works in the U.S.; Mel Churcher, writer and voice practitioner, prolific in her coaching for film; Catherine Weate, course lead for voice at Rose Bruford College who now coaches internationally; Jeannette Nelson, Head of Voice at the National Theatre since 2007; and Nadine George whose *Nadine George Technique* (NGT) is taught at the Royal Scottish Conservatoire and across Europe. It is worth noting that this snapshot reveals a predominantly white middle-class demographic reflecting the lack of diversity in the field. Most of these women have published texts/workbooks that map their methodologies, in stark contrast to the relative absence of women authoring approaches in acting. Many of them trained at RSCCD on the Diploma in Voice Studies or on the subsequent MA, MFA Voice Studies in Teaching and Coaching, currently led by Jane Boston. The synergy between gender and voice as techniques, inherent in Boston's pedagogy, forms one of the two case studies in this chapter.

Why is it that women, marginal in actor training lineages, dominate the field and brand their practices in voice? Treading the line between complicity and critique, adopting a strategic essentialist position points to some possibilities: perhaps it is because the process-based exploration of voice, which investigates the particular individual, the self in relation to the other, is rooted in the corporeal geography of female knowledge; or that women's labour is more readily associated with nurturing jobs such as teacher or care-giver and thus more attuned to the emotional intimacy associated with voice, which, in turn, grants entry into the field.[10] On a more pragmatic note, it may be that female actors, struggling to find work, are more likely to refocus their careers as voice practitioners and so the dominance of women in the field becomes a self-fulfilling prophesy. Perhaps male directors, who continue to dominate the UK industry, are more comfortable in negotiating the relationship between director and voice director within a male/female dynamic? Whilst such essentialist suggestions might be quickly dismissed as inherently reductive, one must acknowledge that intrinsically, voice practice enables a level of success within the industry, which women struggle to achieve in actor training and directing. It seems important to ask why this might be so?[11]

Inevitably voice pedagogies tend to evidence female orientations towards teaching and learning, directly confronting ideas of identity and developing the hidden curriculum of acting. They operate through a holistic relationship between method (*what* to do), and pedagogy (*how* to do it) and are often presented in a kind of self-help format, which might be practised independently of a teacher.[12] Because of the intensely personal nature of voice work, the practitioner's power is magnified in the mostly one-on-one pedagogical exchange, where 'knowledge giving' and 'facilitation' work *beside* each other. This situates voice teaching as a liberatory pedagogy, empowering the student through an intimate encounter with the whole person, the social body and the life body, within a diagnostic exchange.[13] The voice, in its connection to breath, communication and emotion, reveals and withholds information about our being-ness in the world. As such, the politics of the voice is intrinsic to the learning and this is evident in the titles that pedagogues choose for their books. For example, Rodenberg's *The Right to Speak,* Berry's *Your Voice and How to Use It,* and Linklater's *Freeing the Natural Voice* all convey a liberatory commitment, the necessity to speak out and to explore the full potential of our voices.[14]

In its organising structures, however, the field of voice replicates certain aspects of hegemonic actor training. In their written form at least, some of these texts might be seen to offer linear methodologies, which seem at odds with a diagnostic practice, appearing systematising and universalising. Whilst being inclusive and facilitative, some texts capitalise on the promise that the author's 'insider' industry knowledge will deliver vocal agency, thus producing a commodified and commercialised product.[15] The branding of practice offers methodology as the commodity for sale. Indeed, the branding of voice, particularly in the U.S., mirrors the familial apsotologies in acting, which can result in conservatoires employing practitioners who will perpetuate certain lineages of training, as opposed to seeking out new approaches. Some question the extent to which voice teaching liberates within institutions when issues of identity are side-lined.[16]

Historically, the discourse around voice has struggled to reconcile theory and practice. In response to an article critiquing the perceived 'neutrality' inherent in voice training, Boston, calling for new frameworks, suggested that materialist paradigms might offer productive ways to re-consider voice practices.[17] Voice scholarship inherently questions the matter of voice, to question *who* is given voice with a natural concern for marginal voices.[18] As such, it operates in very different ways to acting pedagogies which tend to work from the position of a 'masculine I' and invisiblise gender. Inevitably, within a gendered field of knowledge, practitioners interrogate the subject of the female voice. A survey of vocal preferences at The National Theatre showed that theatre audiences preferred male voices, perhaps revealing an unconscious resistance to *hear* female voices.[19] Voice practitioners identify the 'cultural sound house' as patriarchal, whilst women's domain is situated in 'the domestic – singing, storytelling, laughing, weeping and calling'[20] and they propose an ideal chorus, equally represented by male/female voices.[21] Patsy Rodenburg, in an essay entitled 'Powerspeak: Women and Their Voices,' reflects on four decades of working as a voice coach, responding to changing perceptions in gender and voice techniques. She points to dominant male and female behavioural and vocal habits and how, in searching for the optimum voice, she works from the positivity of difference which she describes as, 'The middle way. A balance between male and female energy. A place of absolute strength and absolute vulnerability.'[22] This hybridity chimes with the search for 'female knowledge' pursued by male acting practitioners mentioned in Chapter 1. In this chapter, I consider how 'the middle way' is re-understood and produced through the pedagogies of women. Part of this involves teaching people how to listen without prejudice and I situate techniques for achieving this within the hidden curriculum of acting which operates within a critical acting pedagogy. In his incisive study on technique as knowledge, Ben Spatz asks:

> Can we envision projects that use embodied methodologies to develop substantive new techniques for dealing with race and gender and acting/performance as overlapping areas of practice?'[23]

The two case studies which follow (Jane Boston and Nadine George) respond to Spatz's provocation.

## Jane Boston: Thinking through voice

> I knew from quite early on that I didn't have a 'method' for voice. It's a bunch of exercises, but *what* you do with those exercises, *how* you put them in a room with everybody and what you hope to get, these are things that interest me more.[24]

Jane Boston is course leader of the MA, MFA in Voice Studies: Teaching and Coaching and leads the International Network for Voice Studies (INV) at The Royal Central School of Speech and Drama (RCSSD), where she has worked since 2010. She was part of the original team to develop the BA in Acting in 1990 when UK Drama School training was first affiliated by universities. Previously, Boston worked as a voice tutor at Royal Academy of Dramatic Arts (RADA) for eight years. Her first degree was English at the University of Sussex and she was one of the first cohorts to complete an MA in Women's Studies at Kent University. When considering her pedagogical practice, her own formative education seems significant: her early education in the UK was the progressive, child centered A.S Neil approach; her secondary education was in Madison Wisconsin in the U.S. at the height of the Civil Rights Movement where she was immersed in radical politics and protest; she completed her further education at Dartington Hall School in Devon, an alternative experimental free school; at university, Boston was a founding member of the lesbian feminist theatre collective Siren, with whom she continues to perform as lead singer/songwriter. Her ideology in working with voice reflects the various formative influences of liberatory pedagogies, feminist and lesbian politics, women's writings, protest theatre, music and poetry.

Boston's pedagogical practice can be viewed through the lens of new feminist materialisms, in the ways that it fights and/or positions matter with matter. Through Women's Studies she came to recognise how the presence of the body itself was a necessary antidote to the linguistic turn. She realised that:

> We need the body here. We need to put the body in the room. We need to find other ways to approach the problems that Women's Studies raises – the problems of identity, the problems of dislocation, the problems of disempowerment, and it's not all talking.[25]

Unlike her colleagues, Boston hasn't chosen to map a methodology or to brand her practice. In fact, she is uncomfortable about any formulaic system that limits freedom and offers a method, more inclined to open up thinking through voice, using it as the material through which to resist and transform ideas around representation. In her monograph, *Voice*, she interrogates the multi-faceted field of voice studies, its stylistics, tensions and spaces to foreground issues of power in relation to and in relation with voice.[26] In her teaching and through the MA curriculum she explores ways to dismantle the systems and structures, which constrain aspects of voice work – the canon, the text, the word, the speech – to embrace the chaotic, messy and gendered space of voice as a material.[27] Her feminist pedagogy is built upon a relational ontology, which makes issues around gender and inclusivity explicit. Since 2015, she has researched intersections between gender and voice technique in various ways, leading yearly 'Voice and Gender' symposiums at RCSSD in partnership with the Voice Care Network and The International Network of Voice. Her research considers the relationship between pitch, politics and performance.[28] Boston hosted an INV Study Day in 2016, at which Dr David Reby, from the University of Sussex, presented findings about the pitch of a baby's cry as en-gendered. She used the research to support ideas about the ways in which the construct of pitch itself might be sharpened as a performative tool to challenge representation. In 2018, Boston led a series of workshops with speech therapist Matthew Mills, researching the transgendered voice. In her creative work as poet and singer she explores her feminism through forms of language, resisting hegemonic structures to seek, an 'écriture féminine'.[29] Her own sexuality mobilises her to promote a 'positivity of difference' at the heart of her pedagogy.

Boston rejects oppressive systems which insidiously filter into any field of 'expertise' to offer a critical acting pedagogy, a type of un-learning and un-teaching, where learners can become autodidacts. Since 2010, Boston has been able to rigorously investigate pedagogical practices within the world leading MA/MFA Voice Studies Teaching and Coaching.[30] At the time of writing, the curriculum is constructed with a central spine – the Linklater approach – intersected with alternative interventions. However, an inherent tension in Boston's pedagogy is an antipathy towards the idea that voice can be commodified or 'bestowed' as part of a linear method.[31] Reflecting on her ambivalence towards documented, method driven voice practices, she explains:

> It's not my thing to lay out the actual steps because it [printed voice methodology] is actually very didactic. The paradox of this whole thing is that it actually just says 'do this' or 'do that'. Didactically linear, it wants you to obey, although there are many other permissions in it.[32]

As noted in Chapter 2, feminist pedagogies frequently reject systems of learning that operate within set or linear structures to recognise the cyclical, unpredictable and diagnostic practice of coming to learn. Boston is acutely conscious of the potency of the voice teacher's power 'to get into the body of the other'[33] and how this dynamic needs to be constantly checked and the processes of exchange made explicit.[34] Certain foundational techniques emerge as traits of her pedagogical practice and recall the *via positiva* approach examined in Chapter 2: Boston is quick to correct or challenge students when they are moving off track, not taking up opportunities or making mistakes; she scaffolds failing as a positive, supported and mobilising experience as opposed to a negative, isolated and paralysing one;[35] a dominant feature of the teaching and learning exchange is her use of questioning;[36] she consciously avoids giving students answers and instead encourages them to take responsibility for their own learning, searching for the most pertinent questions to activate self-discovery. This approach reflects a coaching model, where the more expert teacher joins the learner in a process of joint experimentation, where they are, in an individualised and embodied way, coached to find their own solutions to problems. The teacher must be particularly receptive and responsive to the needs of the student, and rather than 'pronouncing' on them, a dominant mode of conservatoire training, Boston's questions allow her 'to open up a space of internal monitoring'.[37] This 'unlearning', which recognises existence as a state of becoming, facilitates a processual learning exchange where power is shared.

In 2018–2019 Boston's interventions included workshops exploring voice, gender and identity, focusing on the transgendered voice and feminist approaches to working with text. In this work, gender in relation *with* voice is explicitly critiqued and explored as embedded and embodied technique. Through a close analysis of four sessions, working with the nine-point methodology explained in Chapter 2, Boston's pedagogy and its intersections with critical feminist theories can be used to tease out its foundational practices.[38] In responding to the teaching and learning exchange I am mindful to resist imposing theory onto practice but to remain open to emerging synergies. My goal is three-fold: to document these nuggets of practice as examples of critical pedagogy; to draw attention to the ways in which the personal and social knowledge of acting is produced and to focus on the ways that gender operates in the training ground. Through Boston's pedagogy the matter of voice becomes an ethical accounting, a way to resist and reshape phallogocentric systems of control.

## *Becoming voice*

> There is a thing I can impart and what is that thing? Maybe forever the thing is the unfolding of the thing. The becoming. And maybe that's enough.[39]

In February 2018, Boston led two sessions at the RCSSD with seventeen MA voice practitioners (thirteen cis-females and four cis-males) in collaboration with Matthew Mills, speech and language therapist and voice coach working with gender dysphoria from the Gender Identity Clinic in Charing Cross, London.[40] Gender dysphoria includes birth assigned females (cis females) who are transitioning to become trans males and vice versa, as well as gender-neutral or non-binary people. These sessions explored the intersections between voice in theatre (voice technique) and the therapeutic clinic (gender technique). Speech and language therapists are specialists *with* the voice, but not necessarily specialists in their *own* voice, maybe working in ear, nose and throat (ENT), in psychologically orientated fields or therapeutic environments. For Boston, all voice work (in this case the theatrical voice and the therapeutic voice) is concerned with promoting individual choice, awareness and perception to enable self-determination.[41] In these sessions, issues of pitch, tone, vulnerability and how to hear voice, were explored through embodied exercises. A new matter of voice emerged, simultaneously embedded and embodied – a *becoming* voice.

Mills and Boston framed this work as experimental research that placed gender technique and voice technique beside each other to examine their convergences and conflations. From the start Mills drew attention to the unconscious bias that underpins gender and how, as a set of behaved socially inscribed actions, the perception of gender and the experience of gender might be very different: 'We affirm and confirm each other's gender identity by how we behave'.[42] From this position, the body is both inscribed and inscribing with the agency to affect and change cultural perceptions. The first workshop focused on pitch and vulnerability and an atmosphere of trust and relationality was built through the opening exercises. Boston led the students in a vocal warm-up that opened up different types of spatial awareness through the voice, following and extending from Rodenburg's circles of presence.[43] The group first connected to their physical space and then to each other through breath and sound, working with throwing and catching an imaginary ball of sound at a distance from each other. Mills then led the group into a more therapeutic, reflective space, inviting individuals to privately remember a time of vulnerability and then to think forward to a space of possible resolution.

The embodied exploration of gender was introduced through a deceptively simple but revealing task. The group explored what it was like to speak in a different pitch in improvised pair exchanges: the cis-males exploring a higher register and the cis-females a lower register. Some of the men immediately revealed their discomfort by performing a stereotype, which was explained later in discussion as, 'I felt like I was putting on an act'.[44] The marked disconnection between the perceived 'natural voice', natural in the sense that they were speaking in their habitual pitch, and an 'other', 'performed' voice opened up the assumptions and un-conscious bias prompted by these easy gendered definitions. Through voice work, people with gender dysphoria are invited to 're-naturalise' the voice, particularly in terms of pitch, through exploring their multiple, plastic, material voice in a state of becoming.[45] For trans men this may involve taking hormones to lower pitch, which is not the case for trans women, and so each uniquely becoming voice is discovered through work with the voice therapist.

This practice speaks to the biopolitics of new feminist materialisms, which foregrounds how bodily power can affect culture. The deep materiality of the embodied, becoming voice is reminiscent of Braidotti's nomadic theory, which cautions how notions of fixed identities are produced within the oppressive mechanisms of advanced capitalism.[46] However, working with the possibilities of the multiple voice and being open to difference is hard to achieve in practice and a number of tensions emerged.[47] For example, it was acknowledged that the goal for some trans people is to 're-naturalise' the voice to conform to the gendered voice they are happy with, recognising that this involves balancing listener expectations. There was general consensus that the unconscious bias in listening is very hard to shift. Even so, Boston and Mills' intervention brings to the fore notions of difference to question ideas of 'the neutral', or 'the natural' in voice and gender techniques as fixed states. This reconsiders Rodenburg's 'middle way' to foreground the liberatory potentiality of the voice in its constant states of becoming.

In the second workshop, responding to the challenge of the unconscious bias in confirming gender, Boston led the group to explore non-judgemental listening. Mills played samples of his clients reading the same text: Fairbank's

*Rainbow Reading Practice*.[48] The group listened and noted their responses, and in the following discussion, where each person's gender was revealed, they were brought to re-evaluate *how* they heard voices to examine the extent to which hetero-cis-normativity was their unconscious bias. Through a process of questioning, Boston opened up the ways that power constructs operate through voice, language and sense-making where 'Voice text as language is a great site of investigation if you want to challenge power, because the grammar of power is constructed into the English language'.[49] Learning how to hear, through the patterns and divisions in voice, the ways that power is operating on and through the voice feeds into the hidden curriculum of personal and social knowledge. Adopting the nomadic paradigm, where we inhabit a state of relational becoming, the voice can be seen to be mobile and free. The 'client', seeking voice support in whatever form, theatrical or therapeutic, might be wanting to explore the full potential of their multiple voice, as opposed to fixing it and limiting its possibilities.

In seeking to open up this space of choice Boston introduced what she referred to as 'the pre-linguistic voice', asking the group to imagine themselves in a pre-historic cave before language (the word), when sound itself was imagined as the principal communicative medium before print. In this cave the echo of the voice returns to us, so that we are not listening with social judgement, but are able to hear our sounding in its pure, unadulterated form. As such, we receive the return of sound with less judgement than when it is imbricated within language structures. The opening of Boston's poem, *The Arrival of Sound,* offers a compelling provocation,

> When I entered the cave, my eyes saw nothing
>
> Seeing nothing, I listened with my eyes open.
>
> I waited in the static of silence
>
> And in the press of sediment static
>
> I heard the resound of water somewhere falling
>
> Singly into water. Its origins preceded me
>
> A message with no receiver, until now, in my presence
>
> It became a gift. A stone pressed gift of sound.
>
> And in sounding to me I became a subject

> A subject of the cave's life sounding me out.[50]

The materiality of Boston's cave, its chambers, fissures and sediment produce sound in relation *with* the material body. This questions *who/what* is subject and *who/what* is object? In other words, when sound is relationally constructed through vibration and echo, who is the originator and who is the receiver – 'I' or the cave? This materialist position recognises that all existence is relational, mobile and transforming. It speaks to Irigaray's feminist re-working of Plato's Cave in Book 4 of *The Republic*, where she re-positions the duplicity of mimesis through the metonymy of a womb-theatre.[51] If Irigaray's womb-theatre dismantles notions of male original truth and in doing so shatters the idea that mimesis has a true referent, Boston's pre-historic cave similarly looks behind 'the word of the Father'[52] and phallocentric language constructions to return us to the relational origin of sound. Sound which, drawing on Karen Barad's agential realism, is constructed through a reverberating diffractive affect, where both cave and the human body are transformed as the apparatus of sounding.[53] In this way, students experience the body's power to shift and transform cultural re-presentation, as equally inscribing as inscribed. This feminist re-orientation of voice was explored through an embodied learning, which was scaffolded in highly creative ways.

Boston invited the group to imagine the world of the cave, transforming the spaces in the room into echo chambers; the crevices, cocoons, wombs and places of resonance within the body and within the spaces of the cave. Both body and cave became sounding landscapes within the natural world. The students drew around their hands as a 'body script' and pinned these to the walls, recalling the early hand-prints of pre-historic communities. Boston asked them to embellish their body script with pencil marks responding to the sounds they made through the reverberations of their bodies. Then, moving round the room, the group encountered a series of images of pre-historic abstract paintings and masks, which Boston had placed around the space. They responded to these, again through sounds, and made additional marks on their body text. Throughout this task Boston coached, 'What do they give you? Do they repel you? Magnetise you? Find yourselves to them. Has everyone found another voice to voice with a non-human presence'?[54] Finally, each individual created a sound score in response to their body text and shared this in performance with the rest of the group. The resulting individual vocal propositions had a spectral quality, resonant and textural with a sense of connection to the essential materiality of the body. The group reflected on the moving quality of these performances, where the body appeared porous and vulnerable but at the same time strong in its emotional connection. In attempting to articulate the emotional quality in the work Boston suggested:

> Because we have these spaces, the more we can perceive these spaces in our own terms, without other people telling you *what* you're perceiving. That activates something. Maybe that is part of the 'moving' quality?[55]

The activating and moving potential of this work seemed to point to the liberatory possibilities of the body. In its deep materiality, it provides space to transform and in doing so potentially moves cultural parameters to resist reductive representations.

These mobile chambers or spaces of becoming voice recall Kristeva's semiotic chora. Taking Plato's idea of the chora as a liminal space, which receives the seed of the father and gives shape to beget his offspring, like Irigaray's womb-cave, Kristeva's chora is a womb type space of becoming, located within the female domain. Adriana Caverero describes it:

> [T]he [chora], in addition of being a site of indistinct, is a place of continuous movement, a constant motility that knows no quiet. The [chora] has its rhythms, which cannot be comprehended or catalogued by a symbolic system. In the [chora], a vertiginous motility and movement prevent anything from being separate from anything else.[56]

I find synergies in Boston's pedagogy, its ideological positioning and methodologies with Irigaray's cave and Kisteva's chora as she explores the fundamental motility of the material voice. Her cave is an anthropomorphic moving, sounding chamber that foregrounds sound before language, voice before speech. In its motility and diffractions it offers a relational paradigm and new ways of listening, all of which activate a multiple voice.

Boston scaffolds this radical proposition through provocations, in the form of questions, images and use of objects (the paper and pencils to create the body script and the images of masks and paintings around the room). Her interactions are open and encouraging, soliciting responses and making connections between ideas to initiate further questions. In this way, Boston extends the exploration of gender and technique to investigate what Camilleri terms a post-psychophysical *bodyworld* in its essential material state, alert to social judgement.[57] In experiencing this freedom the group was reminded of the extent to which the social body limits and inscribes, producing unconscious biases. They were introduced to the idea that, by turning to the natural world and knowledge of the body, we might find ways to resist this oppression.

## *The second text*

> It seems to me, as a feminist, that there is a lot of philosophical thought that says that language itself is part of the problem.[58]

In 2016, Boston presented a paper at Training and Performance Research Association (TAPRA) entitled *The Second Text,* a play on Simone de Beauvoir's feminist tome *The Second Sex*.[59] She argued that the male dominated canon used for actor training practices should include female writers and feminist approaches to textual analysis. A male dominated canon, apart from perpetuating inequality, requires the female actor to speak words, which originate from a male perspective, and this can present significant challenges. Boston's session on voice, gender and the dramatic text confronted some central questions in voice practice: how can we enable inclusivity for actors when working with texts? How do we move from the voice warm-up into embodying the text ensuring that the body is part of the discovery? How can we make room for the multiple voice when working with text?

Boston problematised the ways in which printed text operates as a material in voice pedagogies, questioning domains of authorship, to ask who is included and excluded in the curriculum and to raise the stakes concerning choice of texts. When we work with a wide range of texts we can destabilise patterns and habits to open up the possibilities for new discoveries in the voice. One immediate challenge for the voice practitioner is to shift people from the inclusivity and freedom of a vocal warm-up, into the cerebral or interpretive space of textual analysis, which has the potential to alienate and exclude. Boston modeled an inclusive approach to voice and text, working with Caryl Churchill's *Escaped Alone*, which premiered at the Royal Court in London in 2016. This all-female play, with five actors all over sixty, offers an immediate challenge to the hegemony. Churchill's writing enables a critical pedagogy, as it produces a theatre for the oppressed, where gender, sexism, colonialism, capitalism, class and race are placed under interrogation. Gendered orthodoxies are challenged within the text itself through character representation, content/themes and an evocation of imagery that critiques dominant hierarchies. In looking at the Preface, Boston excavated the myriad of ways that a first encounter with text can include or exclude. She asked the men in the room how they felt about the prospect of engaging with a text that featured no male characters. This highlighted the ways in which we inevitably bring our gendered unconscious bias into reading and alerted participants to the relative ease with which we invest and connect to text when we feel represented. Although gender and ageism were the focus for the discussion, on that occasion, race, sexuality, class or able-ism were not mentioned and I was reminded how, in focusing on one exclusion, we can inadvertently sideline another.

Boston led the group in a playful exploration into how to embody text using sets of words, related to the play, as provocations: nouns – pigeon, rat, cat, poison; prepositions – over, under, behind, in, on; senses – smell, touch, taste; and emotions – fear, anxiety. The students first explored breath patterns and sound possibilities associated with these words and then worked in pairs to create a playful response to their patterning, a sonic landscape, which might or might not work with a sense of narrative. In sharing these responses there were multiple perspectives of the possible tone, atmosphere and currents in the text, which had come from the impulses of the body as opposed to emerging through cerebral interpretation. The group was able to somatically explore the text's sensorial and thematic possibilities within an inclusive, multi-perspective framework.

A close analysis of one section of the text, Sally's monologue,[60] pointed to the ways that feminist writing ruptures linguistic structures in a number of ways: through the absence of punctuation, through rhyme, repetition, alliteration, assonance, dialect, images, metaphors, colloquialisms, aphorisms and onomatopoeia. It works with elisions, fragments and non-sequiturs to draw attention to the space between ideas. These in-between spaces resist traditional language structures, where the rational or logical forms of language are replaced with a more sensual and emotional logic, working in patterns and cycles, as opposed to linear movements. When we only work within the canon we shut down women's voices and instigate a prescribed metric, accepted as the authorial voice, which Irigaray refers to as 'the law of the Father'.[61] Exploring the text in pairs, the group examined what the absence of punctuation had made present in terms of sense, rhythm and emotion and how, in managing the torrent of this text, the breath sought to connect to the sense. They spoke the text together, their plural voices falling into an agreed rhythm, producing a feeling of unity and shared responsibility.

Boston used Churchill's writing as a provocation to destabilise the expected laws of language and in so doing she showed how text might operate in different ways: ways that enable an inclusive practice where there is no right or wrong way to interpret text. In starting with the embodied response she modeled ways of ensuring that the liberatory possibility of the language was mined for its potential. In doing so, the oppressive structures of language were made explicit and questioned. From a feminist materialist position Boston showed how the embodiment of the text, and the ways that language affected the body, was as important, if not more so, than the cerebral textual analysis of socio-cultural meanings. Moving beyond a hierarchy in which the actor's body serves the text, Boston's pedagogy enables a diffractive, thinking-beside position, where the text and the body claim equal power.

Boston stands apart from the lineages of UK voice training in a number of ways. Although she recognises that, in her position, there is pressure to produce some sort of 'method', she resists what she describes as the 'pleasing the mother' approach, referencing Cicely Berry, to reflect, 'I would like to be the figurehead for multiple possibilities'.[62] She straddles two camps, with one foot in conservatoire training practice and another in feminist studies, and she intellectualises the voice while developing a rigorous industry-responsive practice. As such, her approach is activist and interventionist, placing the mattering discourse of voice at the center of her work and testing its limits. Boston makes the hidden curriculum explicit through the relational possibilities of voice: the political voice that challenges hegemony; the philosophical voice that attunes and sharpens ways of listening, ways of questioning, ways of thinking; and the ethical voice, which strives for equality. Her thinking through voice makes a vital contribution to the development of UK voice pedagogy.

## Nadine George: The healing voice

> This work is philosophical and professional. We must touch our labels and our limits. For me it's very important to say that it's spiritual.[63]

*The Nadine George Technique* (NGT) is taught at the Royal Scottish Conservatoire and in Sweden, Denmark, Norway, Finland, Iceland, France and the Faroe Islands. George, encouraged by her voice teacher Miss Mitchell whilst at boarding school in Lincolnshire, and inspired by the pre-war actors she had seen performing with the Royal Shakespeare Company at Stratford, trained as an actor at the Royal Central School of Speech and Drama in 1960. Her teachers included Gwynneth Thurburn, Cicely Berry (voice) and Liz Pisk (movement). In 1964, a year after graduating, George met the South African actor Roy Hart (1926–1975) and her life took a different direction. Hart had previously completed a degree in English and psychology before securing a scholarship to RADA and working with the singing teacher Alfred Wolfsohn.[64] Wolfsohn's later practice was rooted in the Jungian collective unconscious, archetypes (anima and animus) and individuation, ideas that underpin Hart's approach.[65] When George first heard Hart sing she was struck by the extraordinary quality of his voice, which spanned eight octaves. She followed him to the South of France where, along with forty English artists, they established a commune in the crumbling chateaux Melérargues and established the Roy Hart Theatre which, until Hart's death in a car crash in 1975, gained a reputation across Europe for experimental theatre practices, particularly their work with voice.[66]

After Hart's death George returned to the UK where, working with BA Drama students at Birmingham University, she honed her practice. In this way she discovered how to make the demanding experimental approach of Melérargues accessible for a student group. This progressive pedagogical process responded to consistent student feedback, which allowed George to finetune and adapt the work, shifting from Hart's 'four qualities of voice' (baritone, tenor, alto and soprano) to terms the students could relate to (high male, low male, high female, low female).[67] At this time she approached Ros Steen, who taught voice at the Royal Scottish Academy of Music and Drama, now the Royal Conservatoire of Scotland, to suggest a potential collaboration. Subsequently, their shared exploration allowed the practice to be adapted across an institution where, with commitment from the principal John Wallace, NGT became core practice on all programmes, replacing the methods of Berry, Rodenburg and Linklater.[68] To transform an entire school curriculum is a significant undertaking, and George worked with every member of staff at all levels to 'break down the fear' for non-performers working with voice.[69] In *Growing Voices: Nadine George*

*Technique: The Evolution of Its Influence in Training and Performance*, students, teachers, actors and directors consider how the work is more than a technique. John Wallace explains it as 'the journey to the centre of the self', crucial for all human beings as it instills 'a core methodology of self- determination'.[70] This approach, innately personal and exploring ideas of identity and relationality, contributes to the hidden curriculum of acting.

Through the ongoing work of teachers trained by George her practice has moved beyond the training ground into professional theatre and further too. Ros Steen has brought the technique into the National Theatre of Scotland with her work on acclaimed productions, including *Black Watch*.[71] Since 2006, the voice department at RSC has evolved into the 'Centre for Voice in Performance' and George's practice is disseminated to voice practitioners across the world as part of ongoing research. Beyond theatre practice, NGT practitioners in Scotland have worked within the arts and health sector and across different sectors of the community including teachers, police, young offenders and business leaders. George, having worked in Glasgow with older adults in and out of hospital, with female recovering addicts and young offenders, is now hoping to work with school-refusers in the UK, looking towards her ultimate goal, to combat knife crime through the healing voice.

In London during July 2018, I undertook an intensive two-week workshop with George as participant researcher. The workshop was designed for professional actors and there were twelve actors from across Europe, eleven females and one male, many returning to George's practice. The training moved between three strands: work on breathing, opening and centering; work on the four qualities of voice and work on the text. Each day followed the same structure, breath work, exploration of the four qualities and then text in the afternoon. This pedagogical scaffolding allowed for development to be checked and monitored as, through the repetition, we were able to embed ourselves more into the practice and work at a deeper level.

George can be seen to work with a feminist pedagogy in a number of ways. Bodily knowledge eclipses rational knowledge so that we think *from* and *through* the body, recognising its power to heal itself. Hierarchical structures are flattened through discourse and in practice George rejects the controlling methodologies of a training regime, insisting that technique 'fixes you in something' and that 'No one can teach anybody acting. All you can do is get them to stand in who they are'.[72] Rather than 'direct', she 'intuits' the actor's needs.[73] Like Boston, George is alert to the potential misuse of power as a voice pedagogue reflecting, 'I loath the guru, ego role. I hate the idea of controlling people'.[74] She is at pains to make her practice explicit, and in this way she brings the teaching and learning exchange to account, reflecting, 'You are receiving yourself through yourself. I am receiving myself through you'. Marie-Anne Gorbatchevsky, a workshop participant, offered an alternative way of thinking about George as a teacher, describing her as ' le réveiller', meaning 'the one who wakes us up'.[75] Another participant, David Walshe, affectionately referred to her as 'The Dr'[76] alluding to the ways that George foregrounds fear, pain and the possibility of the body to heal itself, thus enabling theatrical voice technique to intersect with therapeutic technique.

The affirmative politics that underpins George's work operates from 'the positivity of difference',[77] where the uniqueness of the individual is celebrated within the plurality of the group. There are constant reminders that pain can be productively managed in positive terms and that there is 'force in fragility'.[78] As George explains, 'None of us want to experience pain. The question is how do you relate to that pain? Do I identify with it or do I distance myself? I have to be able to move forward'.[79] George makes this humanistic bodily knowledge explicit through her teaching as an antidote for the negative reparative, in a way that I term *via positiva*. She recognises all blocks, restrictions and impediments as a positive opportunity for change where 'The moment of obstruction is, for me, an opening'.[80] Her teaching persona is central to the way that power operates in the room. She projects a maternal quality, which is caring and nurturing, built upon her ideology of kindness, love and spirituality but which, at the same time, is exacting and direct. Her positive energy and generosity is generated through her language, which is consistently encouraging: 'Enjoy the release'! 'Don't withdraw'! 'Open, open'![81]

This liberatory practice invites us to examine our uniqueness and to tap into what George calls, 'the real root of the self'.[82] Awareness of cultural identity and the specific vocal traits that emerge in different nationalities is part of her professional knowledge born out of her work in Scandinavia, France, Scotland as well as the UK. Indeed, the particular notion of identity that exists in Scotland, a nation that has staunchly defended its independence, has no doubt been a determining factor in the way it has embraced George's work, as actors tap into Scots *beside* English. For George, in the roots of language resides creative and artistic power. Power is produced and passed between teacher and learner through two key forms of dialogic exchange: personalised feedback, where George gives specific coaching to each individual, ensuring time and space for individuals to respond; and sharing feedback, which establishes a collective responsibility. This pedagogic practice bonds the group and encourages autonomous learning, equipping actors with tools to apply to their own practice. Ysmahane Yaqini reflects, 'I will never be the same on the stage because it has helped me to know how to work alone … to connect to my own humanity. I've been given the tools to be autonomous in a project and to be *in* a research'.[83] As life-long learning, this practice opens up the epistemic scope of acting technique to examine the self as technique. Reflecting on my own experience as participant researcher, two aspects of George's work emerge as foundational practices: how breath and voice become materials for accessing or touching feeling and how, through the queering of voice, George re-defines Rodenburg's 'middle way'.

## Touching feeling in voice

> The more you know who you are, the more you can open and connect to your own humanity.[84]

The first two hours of every day in George's workshop were given to deep breathing through primary massage techniques, originally developed by dance practitioner Dominique Dupuy, taught and supervised by George. Working in pairs, the massage allowed us to connect with our partner through breath, shifting into a heightened awareness of the body. The prescribed breathing took breath from the stomach and out through a wide, open mouth with lips taught and energized to form an 'AW' sound. Standing, we breathed towards a far horizon and then connected into energetic walking, led by the breath, opening up our awareness beyond the confines of the room. At points, George directed us to come together in pairs, to maintain eye contact, hold wrists and breathe together, raising and lowering our arms and then feeling the breath through an embrace. In a circle, connecting with breath and eye contact, we occupied the space of shared dynamic breathing, our attention outwards, passing the energy between us.

The breathing underpins a practice built on relationality and interconnectedness, where the space between is brought into focus. The key terms that pervade the discourse are 'spirituality', 'space' and 'love'. For George, spirituality is recognising ourselves in relation with natural forces, as a necessary antidote to advanced capitalism. Viewed from a new feminist materialist perspective George privileges the bio-politics of the body and its ability to heal itself. Throughout the work, spaces materialise in a myriad of forms as 'voids', 'cracks', 'channels', 'openings', 'gates'.[85] In the spaces within the body, between inbreath and outbreath, between sound and silence, between different human beings, meaning and potential is produced. Through its relational focus George's practice attends to the complexity of these spaces and foregrounds how we can tend to shut down our potential through fear. She makes awareness of fear explicit, 'Fear is a part of life. It's how we work with this and relate to this that matters so that fear can be released into the space'.[86] Through this release, perceptions of human fragility can be reframed within a positive economy, where vulnerability becomes a strength. Fear closes down freedom of emotion and accessibility to others and to ourselves, stopping us from being able to live in the present moment. Finding a way to break through this negative position is not easy and requires substantial commitment but, recalling Eve Sedgwick's reparative position, it can be actioned through love. George doesn't shy away from using this term, working from an affirmative position to allow space for a compassionate and caring relationality, which offers us, as individuals and as a group, a potentially developmental experience. George scaffolds her pedagogy through breath and touch and this resonates with Irigaray's claim, 'Breathing and loving need one another'.[87]

In the essay 'To Begin with Breathing Anew' Irigaray takes up the argument, explored through earlier works, for the need to cultivate an 'autonomous breath'.[88] In George's practice the autonomous breath produces a state of self-determination, which enabled participants to explore a reciprocal breath. During her workshop, we worked from the inside out to 'cultivate a silent availability'[89] and to access our individual power before connecting with each other to generate a shared power. For Irigaray, 'Giving more breath to meaning and more meaning to breath' is necessary for us to achieve a spiritual, relational life built on love. Through breath we can unite the social body with the natural (lived) body to produce a culture of love and compassion for each other and for ourselves with respect for our differences, which for Irigaray, begins with 'sexuate' difference.[90] According to Irigaray, breath and touch enable a relational culture, which can re-shape hegemony. She posits:

> Joined to a culture of love for the other, as well as for ourselves, in respect for our difference(s), a culture of breathing establishes in us a place where the perception and the development of consciousness are henceforth founded on touch as much and even more than on seeing and listening. It is an intimate touch that can inform us about the sound decision to be made in accordance with life and its sharing.[91]

Moving away from an aspectual consciousness, intrinsically patriarchal and based on commodities of exchange, enables a feminist re-framing of being-in-the-world and an ethical and ecological accounting. During the breath work I felt a psychophysical shift in myself; an opening of the spaces within me, between myself and others, within the space of the room, the building, the wider geography and beyond, reaching out towards an elemental or spiritual space.

Touch was intrinsic in the exploration of breath, working beside it and through it. At the start of the day George welcomed each individual with touch, a holding of the hand, a touch on the shoulder, or a rub of the back, which established her relational authority. In pair massage we learned how to touch each other with care and purpose. In dynamic breathing exercises, where we opened up our awareness to each other, we touched each other through direct eye contact. In reciprocal breath work, we touched each other through holding wrists, raising them on the inbreath, dropping them with the outbreath. In embrace, we felt the movement of our shared breath through held bodies. Touch became the primary mattering apparatus, to scaffold this learning exchange and, as we will see, this extended into listening to the individual voices and exploring the four qualities (low male, high male, low female, high female). Here there is a concrete sense that the voice touches, both the individual experiencing its powerful possibilities and for the rest of us receiving the sound, through vibrations and through emotional connection. Breath and voice allow us to touch ourselves, a sort of enveloping hug, which feels like self-healing. George makes the touching voice concrete. She says,

> The voice touches different levels of feeling. It touches different parts of the body when you vibrate the voice. And I would like to question, what's happened in the world that's made people so afraid of the voice, so afraid of touch, so afraid of not even physical touch, but touch through the voice. Touch through the sound into the feeling?[92]

Taking Irigaray's theory into practice, George enables voice technique to work beside self-as-technique (developed personal and social awareness), through activating the matter of the body and its inscribing possibilities to re-shape culture.

## *Queering voice*

The second stage of George's workshop practice involved exploring the four qualities of voice. Breath worked as a prelude to song, with George playing scales on the piano, shifting between low male, high male, low female, high female. The deep male is sounded in the stomach on the vowel AW, starting on the middle C for women and an octave lower for men, going up and down four notes on the scale. Once the voice has opened to the sound through song, text is spoken on the sound. George experimented with Shakespeare's texts during her time at Birmingham to discover the right line for the sound. On the deep male sound we speak, 'Is this a dagger, which I see before me,/The handle toward my hand.'[93] The high male sound is in the chest on the vowel AH, starting on middle C, an octave lower for men and runs up and down the scale by four notes with the line, 'The raven himself is hoarse, that croaks the fatal entrance of Duncan/Under my battlements'.[94] The deep female is sounded in the chest on the sound OO, four notes up and down the scale from middle C, with the text, 'But soft, what light through yonder window breaks'.[95] High female is in the head, connected to the stomach, on the vowel AH; four notes running up the scale and back from middle C, with the text, 'Gallop apace you fiery footed steeds'.[96] Following the piano, we sounded each quality and then applied it to the line of text. In this way we opened up to our vocal possibilities in preparation for 'self-research' with the four qualities.

During the first four days of the workshop, the afternoon text work was preceded by individual focus into each quality. Facing George behind the piano, sitting in a line, we took turns to stand and follow the octaves, sounding each note until we reached our optimum range. George coached each individual to examine their own rhythm, limits and blocks. There was a powerful unspoken contract in the giving and receiving of sound between the pedagogue, the actor and the audience of peers, a carefully held intimacy that the deep breath work had enabled. This was not a case of singing the notes accurately but of opening and connecting, to give space for the breath and sound to explore the possibilities of pitch. Sounding the four qualities was intense, exhilarating and challenging, psychologically and physically.[97] I found that my body produced new, previously unheard and unbounded sounds, both liberating and alarming. I was aware of previously unexplored potential through my body and in myself. Boston, referring to George's extended pitch work posits,

> It gives rise to a range of feelings and sensations associated with third-party exhortations, self-beliefs and opinions, only parts of which are linked to a unified sense of self.[98]

I would agree that sounding in this way is a profound experience through a seemingly simple act. It opens the channels to the deep recesses of consciousness, where impulse, memory, association, feeling and sense, both innately psychological (inner) and socially imposed (outer) are not so much unified as operate *beside* each other. What emerges is a palpable bodily awareness of the multiple self, in a state of becoming, equally felt in the act of hearing this mobility in others, as in hearing one's own voice. This heightens an awareness of oneself in relation with others, ethical and ecological, both human and non-human, and gives space to engage with this responsibility.

Although the gendered architecture of George's practice might appear problematic in the way it is structured through a seemingly essentialist binary, these categories are simply used as jumping off points, forms through which to explore the possibilities of the voice. George reflects,

> Instead of fixing them [*the four qualities of sound*], one is singing them in order to move them, so the vibration of the sound is moving. So there isn't this definition, as there was so much with Roy, so much of male and female energy, it's more something to do with humanity itself.[99]

Starting from the different octaves recognises the physical, sexuate difference between male and female pitch. However, when moving through the four qualities the focus is not on hitting and holding the 'right' note or making a beautiful sound. The point of the practice is to work with the breath to *sound* the sound, whether that is fully audible and external, or internal as a strange rasping echo, almost imperceptible. What is perceptible are the different energies these qualities have and how they seem to tap into different emotional centres. Consequently, one becomes aware of the variety and potential we hold *within* ourselves, through the possibility of our voice locating us to our roots, our sex, our emotion, our self. Revealing the possibilities of our 'multiple voice' we can expand our agency and potentially transform reductive cultural codes.[100] George recognises the way that her approach enables this multi-dimensionality. She says,

Because the balances of everybody are so different and this work is allowing the whole thing to move without really fixing on gender itself as an issue, but more on the human being and what lies in the human being itself. So that allows something to be much more fluid.[101]

In practice, the qualities of the voice are tangled together playing with and through each other, where male and female co-exist – a type of queering the voice. This was made manifest in what George referred to as 'the crack'.[102] There were moments when, climbing or dropping through the scale, the voice would shift between two pitches, cracking and breaking to create a third sound. In the crack new vocal possibilities are made material; a beyond-human sound is released, other-worldly, echoing an ancient pre-human world whilst pointing forward to post-human possibilities. This brings Rodenburg's 'middle way' into sharper focus, as it produces a third space, where potential energy is waiting to be tapped.[103] George explains, 'It's an emotional thing affecting the break … this double sound is about the development of the individual. You are seeing yourself as multi-dimensional'.[104] From this perspective, the material voice holds the potential to change the ways that we hear and to shift cultural consciousness.

Although George's approach seeks to undo gendered categories, a number of aspects feel rooted in qualities of 'female-ness'. George acknowledges that as a woman, her approach differs from that of Wolfsohn's and Hart's, principally in her commitment to make the work accessible and inclusive. She offers a process which might be personalised and adapted to suit the individual's needs, as opposed to producing a methodology. At the time of writing George has not set out her practice in written form. During the two weeks' training, the female body was particularly present, in part due to only having one male in the group, but also through the forms and content of the work itself: the complex female characters of the chosen text;[105] the opening of the body in the breathing; the repeated images of opening channels connecting to the physiological opening in birth. The open force of the lips and the mouth and the connection to breathing from the stomach is reminiscent of the breathing encouraged through birth in opening the pelvis and the birth canal.

An extraordinary event happened to David Walshe as he was sounding the high female voice on the fourth day. As his voice steadily climbed the octaves the sound vibrated through his trembling body and he appeared almost illuminated. The energy transmitted through the voice was intensely connected to a female quality, both vulnerable and powerful, in pain and ecstasy. Reflecting on the experience immediately after the exercise David spoke of feeling strangely connected to being born, the pain for both mother and child. George suggested that he 'was giving birth to himself … Your energy vibration is central to the body. The spiritual connection. This work with the voice is taking us back to the first scream'.[106] This idea of primal energy, a life force deeply connected to the power of nature, is inherent in this practice and potent in its potentiality.

To my mind, George's work responds to Barad's feminist new materialism which, in part, draws on Bohrs' work on atomic physics, re-thinking ideas around agency and power to recognise that everything, including the human body, exists in a constant state of becoming and transformation.[107] Harnessing and focusing the energies of the body through the voice we can tap into vibration, vibrations of the breath, through the vocal chords, through the resonant chambers of the body and, in this vibration, there is a sense of molecular or cellular power. George refers to the vibrations, 'vibrating at 5000 miles an hour' and how we 'move the cellular structure of the body' to transform ourselves.[108] Indeed, in a state of full vibration the actor appears transformed, larger than themselves, sometimes luminous with life force. One should note that vibration doesn't only occur through sound. There is also vibration in silence when the actors are fully attuned to each other. This physical, cellular action is palpable for the actor within their own body, but George ensures that this is made external, so that one is aware of the doubling in the transmission of this energy. This doubling is the space between receiving and perceiving. Yaqini describes this experience:

> For me there is one eye inside myself connected completely to me and one is outside and this work helps me to be aware of that. It's like this with the voice also, with the sound and with the breath. It's how we bring this outside because it's cool to know how deep you are, but how you put it into the world in a way to change it, to make it more delicate, more soft.[109]

This state of being doubled, central to the knowledge of the actor, shifts the actor from a body/mind paradigm to a post-psychophysical body-world.[110] It is as though the vibrations directly alter the materiality of the other's body in what Cavarero refers to as 'musicality in relation' where the reverberations of vocal exchange expose 'uniqueness as understanding [un'intesa] and a reciprocal dependence'.[111] This work produces an ethical and ecological voice pedagogy, which offers transformative possibilities for the self through technique.

Both Boston and George, in making offers that extend beyond methodologies of practice, stand on the edge of UK voice training: Boston, with her position of 'multiple possibilities' and George with her 'healing voice'. Their work expands the epistemic of theatrical voice technique to develop the personal and social knowledge of the hidden curriculum through critical pedagogies. Both practitioners, in specific and particular ways, use constructs of gender to push back against socio-cultural inscriptions and to harness the body's inscribing potentiality with voice as a mattering discourse. Boston's chora-like space of becoming voice and George's 'third space' look beyond Rodenburg's 'middle way' to offer new ways of thinking through gender in voice studies.

## Notes

1. Di Trevis was the first female to direct at The National Theatre in 1986. Interview with Di Trevis, London (09.09.13).
2. In Chapter 2 I consider the hidden curriculum of acting. These are the personal, social and political knowledges of acting. These include, but are not limited to: imagination, emotional intelligence, being in the moment, focus, impulse, intuition, instinct, flow, emotional availability, trust, respect, generosity, inner listening, curiosity, self-care, polyphonic awareness, empathy, altruism, collaboration, reflection, reflexivity, learning through failure, playfulness, knowing the value of fear, self-discipline, resilience and relational awareness.
3. Cicely Berry, *Voice and the Actor* (New York: Wiley Publishing, 1991), Cicely Berry *The Actor and Text* (London: Virgin Books, 2000), Cicley Berry, *Text in Action: A Definitive Guide to Exploring Text in Rehearsal for Actors and Directors* (London: Virgin Books, 2001).
4. Patsy Rodenburg, *Presence: How to Use Positive Energy for Success in Every Situation* (London: Penguin Books, 2009), Patsy Rodenburg, *The Right to Speak: Working with the Voice, 2nd Edition* (London & New York: Bloomsbury Methuen Drama, 2015), Patsy Rodenburg, *The Actor Speaks: Voice and the Performer* (London & New York: Bloomsbury Methuen Drama, 2019).
5. Kristine Linklater, *Freeing the Natural Voice, 2nd Revised Edition,* (London: Nick Hern Books, 2006), Kristine Linklater, *Freeing Shakespeare's Voice* (New York: Theatre Communications Group, 2010).
6. Other UK drama schools and universities have developed Centres for voice study including: Rose Bruford (Centre for Voice), Essex University and The University of Portsmouth (Interdisciplinary Centre for Voice Studies).
7. For an overview of contemporary voice teaching see Paul Meier, 'Training the Trainers: A Review of Some of the Leading Programs for Training Voice Trainers,' in Voice and Gender' ed. by Mandy Reese Cincinatti, *Voice and Speech Review*, vol 5 (2007) 53–67.
8. Mark Evans, *The Actor Training Reader* (London & New York: Routledge, 2015).
9. It is useful to question what the term 'hidden' forecloses and the ways that it exposes characteristic gender/race/class biases.
10. Indeed, voice work is not limited to actor training and practitioners may also work in therapeutic fields.
11. These speculative suggestions first emerged from a discussion concerning the gendered domain of voice with a focus group from the 2017/2018 cohort of MA Voice at RCSSD. These views have been echoed in interviews with practitioners for this study.
12. The movement towards a self-help format can be seen in most voice texts from the 1950s onwards. A good example is Kirstin Linklater, *Freeing the Natural Voice* (New York: Drama Group Publishers, 1976). Here, Linklater acknowledges that she is looking beyond technique to recognise that the voice work can be beneficial to everyone. The self-help format recognises that individuals will adapt these methods to their own unique positions.
13. This recalls the work of Paulo Friere, Henry Giroux and bel hooks.
Paulo Freire,1974. *Education for Critical Consciousness* (London & New York: Continuum, 1974); Henry Giroux, *Schooling for a Democracy: Critical Pedagogy in the Modern Age* (London & New York: Routledge, 1989); bel hooks, *Teaching to Transgress* (London & New York: Routledge, 1994).
14. Cicely Berry, *Your Voice and How to Use It: The Classic Guide to Speaking with Confidence* (London: Virgin Books, 2000); Kristine Linklater, *Freeing the Natural Voice*

(London: Nick Hern Books, 2006); Patsy Rodenburg, *The Right to Speak*, 2nd Edition (London & New York: Bloomsbury Methuen Drama, 2015).

15 For example, Patsy Rodenburg, *Presence: How to Use Positive Energy for Success in Every Situation* (London: Penguin, 2009). Rodenburg uses her experience training actors to give non-actors all the presence and charisma that the 'stars' have.

16 Micha Espinosa and Antonio Ocampo- Guzman, 'Identity Politics and the Training of Latino Actors,' in Elin Margolis and Lissa Tyler Renaud, *The Politics of Actor Training* (London & New York: Routledge, 2010) 150–161.

17 In 1996, Sarah Werner suggested that the conservatoire voice training of Berry, Rodenburg and Linklater de-politicised the voice giving actors a *neutral* set of tools when reaffirmed, rather than challenged the underpinning cultural biases of the field (Sarah Werner, 'Performing Shakespeare: Voice Training and the Feminist Actor', *NTQ*, 12(47), (1996): 249–258). Although the practitioners defended the inherent politics of their practices (Cicely Berry, Patsy Rodenburg and Kristine Linklater, 'Shakespeare, Feminism and Voice: Responses to Sarah Werner', *NTQ* 13(50), (1997): 48–52), there was a sense that the voice work in conservatoire training served an industry as opposed to working to change it. In 2014, Jane Boston, commenting on the exchange in *The Voice and Speech Review*, suggested that a close-up examination of the faultlines between conservatoire and academy might benefit voice studies. Noticing what is absent in the discourse enables the production of new knowledge, and she urged that we think about each practitioner's practice, both in the studio and in written form, as contextually specific and ideologically distinct. Boston points to the ways in which, intricately embedded within these practitioners' ideologies, were the traces of the radical political movements of the 1960s and 1970s. In particular, the feminist and Civil Rights movements transformed understandings of *who* was given voice. She suggests that voice studies use different critical theoretical tools to consider practice, citing feminist historical materialism as a way to re-think the power play operating on and through the voice to question what is heard and unheard in the discourse.

18 Frankie Armstrong and Jenny Pearson, eds, *Well Tuned Women: Growing Strong Through Voicework* (London: The Women's Press, 2000).

19 *The Female Voice* was hosted at The National Theatre on 20 November 2014. Jeanette Nelson, Head of Voice, joined by actors and directors, considered attitudes towards voice and women in theatre. This was in collaboration with Central's project 'Voicing Gender: Vocal Authority for the Public Platform'.

20 Ibid. 28.

21 Ibid. 29.

22 Armstrong and Person (2000) 109.

23 Ben Spatz, *What a Body Can Do: Technique as Knowledge. Practice as Research.* (London & New York: Routledge, 2015) 163.

24 Interview with Jane Boston, Hove, 16/03/18.

25 Boston, ibid.

26 Jane Boston, *Voice* (London: Macmillan Publishers, 2018).

27 Jane Boston, 'Voice and the Practitioners, Their Practices and Their Critics: Reassessing the Controversy in Its Historical Context', *NTQ*, 13(51), (1997): 248–254.

28 In 2016, at the second Voice and Gender Symposium at RCSSD, Boston's keynote was entitled *Pitch Politics and Performance*.

29 Hélène Cixous, 'The Laugh of the Medusa', *Signs,*1(4), (1976): 875–893.

30 The course is designed to train practitioners of voice, post-graduates, who might have trained as actors, or practitioners with voice experience, such as directors, teachers or coaches.

31 Ibid.

32 Interview with Jane Boston, Hove, 16/03/18.
33 Ibid.
34 This position is a common trait in women's pedagogy where there is a conscious flattening, or re-shaping, of hierarchical structures, and power is passed *between* teacher and learner as opposed to operating from a top-down approach.
35 Discussing Boston's pedagogy a student noted how she scaffolds failure, 'she doesn't mind letting you fail'. Interview with RCSSD MA Voice students, The Hampstead, 05/03/2018.
36 Her students note that, 'She takes your question and she suggests possibilities and it's your job to find the answer for yourself ... that is integral to her form of teaching and what she wants from her students'. Interview with RCSSD MA Voice students, The Hampstead, 05/03/2018.
37 Interview with Jane Boston, Hove, 16/03/18.
38 The nine-point methodology is: how the hidden curriculum of persona and social knowledge is delivered; how an atmosphere of trust and relationality is built; how vulnerability is supported; how authority operates in the room; how choice and action are scaffolded for the actor; how instruction, explanation and feedback are given; how non-human agents operate within the teaching/learning; how individual and group progress is managed within time constraints; how gender operates within the learning.
39 Ibid.
40 After completing the MA Voice Studies Teaching and Coaching at RCSSD, Mills worked in voice therapy and continued his collaboration with Boston through their shared interest in gender and voice.
41 First Workshop, Clean Rehearsal, Royal Central School of Speech and Drama, 05/02/2018.
42 Ibid.
43 Patsy Rodenburg, *Presence: How to Use Positive Energy for Success in Every Situation* (UK: Penguin, 2009).
44 First Workshop, Clean Rehearsal, Royal Central School of Speech and Drama, 05/02/2018.
45 When I use the term natural I am not referencing Linklater's 'natural voice' but referring specifically to habitual pitch.
46 Rosi Braidotti, *Nomadic Theory: The Portable Rosi Braidotti* (New York: Columbia University Press, 2011).
47 Adrianna Caverero, feminist philosopher, whose work responds in part to Hannah Arendt's, sees what she terms 'the multiple voice' as being vital for a democratic and inclusive society. For Caverero, vocal uniqueness is dependent on enabling a voice where many 'I's can emerge in the register of the unconscious. She asks that we look to the female voice to access our multiple voice, because the female is associated with voice as opposed to speech. Adriana Caverero, *For More Than One Voice: Towards a Philosophy of Vocal Expression* (Stanford University Press, 2005).
48 Second Workshop 1, Clean Rehearsal, Royal Central School of Speech and Drama, 12/02/18.
49 Ibid.
50 Ibid.
51 Luce Irigaray, *Speculum of the Other Woman* (New York: Cornell University Press, 1985) 243–364.
52 Ibid.
53 Karen Barad, 'Posthumanist Performativity: Toward an Understanding of How Matter Comes to Matter,' *Signs*, 28(3), (Spring, 2003): 801–831.
54 Second Workshop 1, Clean Rehearsal, Royal Central School of Speech and Drama, 12/02/18.

55 Ibid.
56 Adriana Cavarero, *For More Than One Voice: Towards a Philosophy of Vocal Expression* (Stanford University Press, 2005) 134.
57 Frank Camilleri, *Performer Training Reconfigured: Post-Psychophysical Perspectives for the Twenty-First Century* (London & New York: Methuen, 2019) 57.
58 Third Workshop, Clean Rehearsal, Royal Central School of Speech and Drama, 19/06/18.
59 Simone de Beauvoir, *The Second Text* (London: Penguin Books, Vintage Classics, 1997).
60 Caryl Churchill, *Escaped Alone* (NHB Modern Plays, Ebook, 2016) 41.
61 Irigaray, op.cit.
62 Ibid.
63 Cecile Fontaine, Toynbee Studios, 11/07/18.
64 Wolfsohn's fascination with the voice was prompted by hearing the dying cries of soldiers on the front line during the Second World War.
65 Nadine George, 'My Life with Voice', *Voice and Speech Review*, 4(1), (2005): 33–42.
66 Jane Boston, *Voice* (London: Palgrave Macmillan, 2018) 157–160.
67 George (2005), ibid.
68 Acting, Contemporary Performance Practices, Musical Theatre (BA and MA) and Masters in Classical and Contemporary Text.
69 Interview with Nadine George, 9/07/18.
70 Ros Steen, ed., 'Growing Voices: Nadine George Technique: The evolution of its influence in training and performance,' Royal Conservatoire of Scotland (2013).
71 Steen, ibid.
72 George, ibid.
73 Ysmahene Yaqini, a workshop participant explained this as 'impulsing us'. Notes from Nadine George Workshop, Toynbee Studios, 2/07/18–13/07/18.
74 George, ibid.
75 Notes from Nadine George Workshop, Toynbee Studios, 2/07/18–13/07/18.
76 Walshe, ibid.
77 Braidotti, op.cit.
78 Cixous, op.cit.
79 George, ibid.
80 George, 2/07/18–13/07/18.
81 Ibid.
82 Ibid.
83 Interview with Ysmahane Yaqini, 12/07/18.
84 George, ibid.
85 Ibid.
86 Ibid.
87 Luce Irigaray, 'To Begin with Breathing Anew' in Lenart Skof and Emily A. Holmes, *Breathing with Luce Irigaray* (London & New York: Bloomsbury, 2013) 224.
88 Irigaray, ibid. 217–226.
89 Irigaray, ibid. 220.
90 Irigaray, ibid. 225.
91 Irigaray, ibid. 226.
92 George, 9/07/18.
93 William Shakespeare, *Macbeth,* Act 2:1.
94 Ibid., Act 1:5.
95 William Shakespeare, *Romeo and Juliet,* Act 2:2.
96 Ibid., Act 3:2.
97 One impediment to making the sounds is the fear of damaging the voice. In this respect, George's work is controversial and she believes that traditional voice

pedagogies and contemporary practices for voice health have placed reductive technical limitations on the actor. In the voice training of the 1960s little consideration was given to voice care, and in George's view contemporary voice work is resistant to opening sound and accessing emotion when 'You should go through the pain. When we try to control it is much more painful'. (George, 9/07/18). This attitude may be seen to reflect a post-war robustness. Indeed, George's practice can seem old-fashioned in its return to the actor's art of voicing emotion, and working with 'the full voice'. However, in its seeming simplicity it is intricate and rigorous, offering the actor a comprehensive set of tools to apply to every type of work, from the challenges of playing large outdoor arenas, to the nuances of film.

98 Boston, op.cit., 158.
99 George, ibid.
100 George, 2/07/18–13/07/18.
101 George, ibid.
102 Ibid.
103 Ibid.
104 Ibid.
105 We worked with scenes from Ibsen's *John Gabriel Borkman* with the same scene partner for the two weeks. For the first week, the readings were in chairs as we sat facing each other whilst the others watched. We moved through the script in its entirety, then in three sections in full voice. Full voice is speaking in a very loud, full-energy voice. The point isn't to try to bring expression into the text or interpretation but to feel the vibrations and potential energies connecting with your partner. In the second week we worked off-book, in a slightly reduced voice, sometimes with George's direction, for example, 'speak with a smile'. We moved on to stage the scene working with George's movement instructions working with two chairs and a central sofa. By this point we were off-book and still working in full voice. The final stage was to reduce full voice, and work through the staging score, to embody the text in relation to our partner. The practice was repetitive and ritualised so that everyone quickly knew what to expect. There was a clear sense that this work was building systematically and in a highly measured and controlled way. As a result, we were able to feel in ourselves, and observe in others, the ways in which the text was becoming fully embodied through the voice. This happened without any analysis of the text, discussion about psychology or character intentions. The process felt organic and embodied, where the body was leading the decision-making and the vibration created through breath and sound gave permission for emotional connection.
106 George, ibid.
107 Barad, ibid.
108 George, 2/07/18–13/07/18.
109 Interview with Ysmahane Yaqini, 12/07/18.
110 Frank Camilleri, *Performer Training Reconfigured: Post-Psychophysical Perspectives for the Twenty-First Century* (London & New York: Methuen, 2019) 57.
111 Caverero, op.cit., 182.

# 4
# WOMEN AND THE MATTER OF MOVEMENT

Feminist critical theories, interrogating the construction/deconstruction of female and feminine materiality, have actuated the bodily turn of the twenty-first century. However, intersections between this thinking and the specifics of movement training are rarely considered. When the field of UK movement for actors is recognised as a female domain, it is strange that seminal contributions are not more visible and that gendered implications are not interrogated. Mark Evans, in his detailed contextual survey, has gone furthest in mapping women's practice in this field.[1] In this chapter, I consider the specific ways that women produce liberatory pedagogies that establish movement as a technology of the self, with social/cultural critique operating *beside* anatomical/biological awareness. In opening up its epistemic scope, we can recognise movement as a critically embodied way of knowing, where constructs of difference are re-considered. A feminist lens sees movement as a critical pedagogy, fueled by *via positiva*, harnessing the vital materialism of the body.[2]

Women dominate this field, with practitioners from a variety of backgrounds, including acting and dance, moving into movement direction and teaching. Like voice, vocational movement for acting is taught as discrete classes in conservatoire curriculums. MA Movement Teaching courses perpetuate recruitment alongside apprenticeships and mentoring systems.[3] Whilst acknowledging this list as partial, a female genealogy of UK practitioners includes: Trish Arnold (London Academy of Music and Dramatic Art, Guildhall), Wendy Allnutt (Guildhall), Jean Newlove (Theatre Workshop, East 15), Jane Gibson (The National Theatre), Litz Pisk (the Old Vic and RCSSD), Lorna Marshall (RSC, RADA), Shona Morris (RADA, Drama Centre, Rose Bruford College, Stratford Festival Theatre, Canada), Sue Lefton (the National Theatre), Jackie Snow (Guildhall, RADA, the Globe), Glynne MacDonald (the Globe), Vanessa Ewan (Film Coach, RCSSD) and

Niamh Dowling (West Yorkshire Playhouse, Library Theatre/Maly Theatre, Manchester Met, Rose Bruford College). These women have careers that move between teaching in institutions and collaborating with actors and directors in rehearsal.[4] Many have worked with, or been trained by, each other. For example, those trained by Trish Arnold (1918–2017) recognise her Pure Movement and work with the spine as a formative influence.[5]

The majority have developed cross-fertilized practices underpinned by the branded somatic methods of F.M. Alexander, Moshe Feldenkrais, Rudolph Laban, and/or the work of Jacques Lecoq which, according to Evans, produces 'the neutral body' and/or 'the natural body', primed for efficient labour in the industry.[6] Each of these distinct approaches enable particular interpretations of the 'efficient' body. These practices continue to dominate movement curriculums, supplemented with the work of Jerzy Grotowski, Eugenio Barba, Wlodzimierz Staniewski, Tadashi Suzuki, Gabrielle Roth, Mary Overlie and Anne Bogart, according to the movement practitioner's interest and expertise.[7] As with acting, female movement teachers have tended to 'author' their practice, as opposed to branding it, as is the case with Litz Pisk, Annie Louie, Dymphna Callery, Lorna Marshall, Jackie Snow, Vanessa Ewan and Niamh Dowling.[8] Whilst I recognise that developing and transmitting a practice is, in itself, a type of authoring, here I mean documenting a methodology in written or digital form. It may be that, because women continue to teach practices that are seen to stem from male lineages, their contribution to the field is somehow diminished.[9] It seems clear that when one thinks about pedagogy as praxis, that *how* you teach something is as important as *what* you teach, a thorough consideration of the pedagogies of women dominating this field is most necessary. In movement, as with voice, there appears to be a holistic relationship between pedagogy and method, with the focus on individual experience/exploration, books written in a self-help format and digital materials demonstrating practice. As such, movement training can be considered as a critical pedagogy, guiding actors to discover what makes them unique and empowering them as autodidacts.[10]

I start from the premise that movement, as 'the basic experience of existence', is cultural and political.[11] Shona Morris, Movement Director and actor, currently Lead Movement Tutor at RADA, reflects: 'Politics and economics is everything. I teach this in my movement classes – so there is an intersectionality for me between class and gender and race'.[12] In turning our focus to the political imperative of movement for actors, we should be reminded that teachers in conservatoires do not create practices in a vacuum. Throughout the 1970s, 1980s and 1990s developments in theatre, contemporary dance and somatics variously influenced practitioners. Many of these developments stemmed from the progressive and sometimes radical work of women.

In theatre training, the innovations of improvisation techniques taken from Lecoq and aspects of Michel St Denis' work (animal study), alongside scenario work from Stanislavski and Laban, as adapted by Jean Newlove, shifted movement approaches in theatres. This responded to a wave of writing, influenced by Epic theatre, which required large casts and actors to multi-role.[13] The development of movement directing came from an understanding of acting. For example, movement directors Jane Gibson and Sue Lefton trained at RCSSD, then went to Lecoq. Lefton trained with Litz Pisk who was influenced by developments in modern dance/free dance – an exploration of the body in space. Geraldine Stevenson, movement director at the National Theatre, was influenced by Jean Newlove and Claude Chagrin (Lecoq trained). Trish Arnold led two acting departments, LAMDA and Guildhall, and worked at Stratford Festival Theatre. These movement practitioners worked with movement systems adapted for acting and theatre, made them their own, and passed them on. However, their seminal contributions to theatre practice have been, until recently, largely overlooked.[14] It may be that, because this work is 'discrete' in a production, it has been easily sidelined. Or perhaps, as they were mostly assisting male directors, an underlying sexism contributed to this silencing. Anecdotally, voice practitioner Patsy Rodenberg ironically described voice and movement directors as 'handmaidens' to the director.[15] That said, these fields afforded women greater agency than acting and/or directing.

Throughout the 1970s and 1980s some movement pedagogies for acting were shaped in the context of the political turn of contemporary dance. Following in the path of new developments in experimental dance in the U.S., in particular the seminal Judson Dance Theatre, new forms of dance emerged in the UK that challenged the hierarchical structures of traditional/classical dance pedagogies. Ludus Dance, whose work continues today, was founded as a touring company in 1975 by teachers, creatives, dancers and political activists with the remit to inspire and empower new audiences.[16] Extemporary Dance Theatre, established by students from The London School of Contemporary Dance, ran between 1976 and 1991 making work that pushed at the boundaries of dance, theatre and film.[17] Between 1976 and 1980, the X6 Dance Collective, running from the X6 Dance space, a warehouse in Butler's Wharf, established a countercultural movement, seeking new pedagogical practices and aesthetics. This group, founded by dance artists Emily Claid, Maedée Duprès, Fergus Early, Jackie Lansley and Mary Prestidge, was informed by emerging feminist and queer theoretical frameworks, critical of the highly gendered structures of ballet and much contemporary dance. The collective produced a radical programme of performances, a magazine, *New Dance* (1977–1988) and ran classes and workshops. They were pioneers in the development of the British New Dance movement, and through their work with a variety of international collaborators, such as Mary Fulkerson (Release Technique) and Nancy Stark Smith and Steve Paxton (Contact Improvisation), they introduced new approaches to performance training.[18] Also significant, but with less media coverage, was Natural Dance Workshop based at The Diorama, at Peto Place, London.[19] Although revolutionary dance isn't part of the curriculum content of movement at drama school, it's likely that its affects were felt.

Movement teachers in conservatoires were developing practices at a time fueled with questions around power and the materiality of bodies. From their marginal position, female practitioners, caught between the paradox of serving an aspectual industry, where the body of the actor is commodified (outer), with developing 'the hidden curriculum', the personal and social knowledges of the actor (inner), produced pedagogies inextricably rooted in the politics of the body.[20] However, such approaches remained implicit, as movement practitioners rarely had the agency to significantly shape conservatoire curriculums.

A third influence was the development and experimentation in 'somatics'.[21] This term encompasses a wide range of movement practices fostering close internal and external awareness: the holistic experience of movement as expression, exercise and/or therapy.[22] Early somatic innovation, borne from the health and strength training movements in Germany, UK and the U.S., gained momentum in the nineteenth century and was dominated by female practitioners. Following the seminal practice of German bodywork pioneer Elsa Gindler (1885–1961), women created innovative systems of physiological practice that integrated the body, mind and the imagination. Mabel Ellsworth Todd's (1880–1956) 'ideokenisis', Gerda Alexander's (1908–1994) 'Eutony' and Irmgard Bartenieff's (1900–1981) 'Bartenieff Fundamentals' developed alongside Feldenkrais and Alexander Technique, in response to movement related injuries in order to enable holistic body–mind health and expressivity.[23] Throughout the twenty-first century these approaches have been passed on to practitioners who brought them into their own practices, developing influential schools particularly in the U.S.: post-modern dance pioneer Anna Halprin integrated Feldenkrais into her work and co-created the system 'RSVP Cycles'; Elaine Summers, founding member of Judson Dance theatre developed 'Kinetic Awareness'; Trisha Brown (1936–2017) developed 'Pure Movement'.[24] Throughout the twenty-first century cross fertilization characterises the field of somatics, used in occupational therapy, clinical psychology and in the arts. Directors create training systems that foreground somatic experiences, such as Ruth Zaporah's 'Action Theatre', Marie Overlie and Anne Bogart's 'Viewpoints'.[25] In 2020, movement practitioners work with a wide range of practices that seek holistic integration of body/mind/imagination.

At this cultural moment, movement training continues to navigate the inner/outer paradox, developing personal and social knowledges alongside the need to serve the industry and it responds to some key pressures: the influence of Hollywood, where most actors aspire for film careers and movement training is perhaps seen (wrongly) to be less necessary; the shifting face of theatre, where intra-medial performance refigures ideas of embodiment; the growing expectation that training must be personalised, enabling the development of the particular self/identity of each actor although taught in a group; the production of 'branded' movement in the industry, where the work of high-profile movement directors is commodified; the need for movement training to be more diverse, with some institutions actively seeking more male tutors to redress the perceived gendered knowledge in the field.[26] For Morris, it seems that now women pedagogues have established a field that is starting to gain traction in the industry, men are being encouraged to participate. From this perspective, the move towards diversity could be seen to mask an inverted prejudice against the gendered knowledge developed by women in somatic practices.[27] Evans' recognition that more men in movement signifies its shifting cultural status, also indicates the lack of value given to knowledges seen to be female, perceived to be less worthy of study.[28] Certainly, theorising the intersections between post-modern articulations of the body and movement training has, until recently, received limited academic attention.

What happens when we start from the premise that a field is gendered and so give space to examine the positivity of difference? Re-examining actors' movement training from a feminist position seems more important than ever during this #MeToo and Black Lives Matter era.[29] The shifting consciousness in the industry around the ways that certain bodies can be exploited and abused, alongside increasing concern about the relative absence of women and BAME performers/creatives in training canons, and systemic racism in drama schools has sharpened attention around mechanisms of power and bodies.[30] The ripples of this are felt strongly in movement teaching where the potential for the misuse of power is marked. The movement space can easily mirror the master/student dynamic of martial arts, sports coaching or ballet, where the suppliant body receives instruction through close observation, usually in silence, often through pedagogic touch and where the authority of the teacher is magnified. As previously noted, the welcome introduction of a code of conduct around consent in UK drama schools foregrounds issues of power and the pedagogic exchange.[31] This has drawn attention to the ways that practitioners across all fields (acting, directing, voice and movement) work with touch, and the gendered effects of this are complex. However, it seems vital to recognise that, in spite of the perceived power dynamic of the movement space, actors tend to reflect on their experience as empowering and liberating. I would suggest that this is, in no small part, contingent on the way that power is passed between teacher and actor.[32] When the majority of movement practitioners are female, it is not unreasonable to suggest that the gender of the teacher has something to do with the success of this reconstituted power exchange. When we re-consider movement pedagogies through a feminist lens, celebrating what Braidotti calls 'the positivity of difference', we can attend to the valuable knowledges that are produced beyond skills acquisition.[33]

## Feminist ways and movement teaching

What is revealed when we think about developments in UK movement training intersecting with feminist articulations of the body? When we start from the premise that critical theory situates the body as female knowledge, then movement practitioners, albeit unconsciously, can be seen to work in the feminist tradition.[34] Let us revisit Evans' central tenets of the natural/neutral body and *jouissance* through the lens of feminist materialisms.

Evans identifies two 'types' of body that movement training aspires to make available to the actor – the 'natural' and the 'neutral' body, both of which are understood within the context of 'the efficient body', a specifically twentieth-century trope. This double imperative is inherent in somatic practices where, through a process of becoming alert to 'inhibitions', one finds one's own solutions.[35] The term 'neutral body' becomes formative in the discourse when used by Lecoq, specifically in his neutral mask training which, confusingly, required different sexes to wear either a female or male 'neutral' mask. It is only recently that this practice has changed and students are now allowed to pick the mask they are most comfortable working with.[36] As with ideas around gender, the cultural psyche has shifted and there is an inherent problem with the idea of neutrality in the twenty-first century. Indeed, Morris, whose work had been previously framed as neutral body work, no longer recognises her practice in this way:

> I was using that term then to talk about a kind of placement of poise and openness and readiness but I don't think I'm training people to find a neutral body. I think I'm training people to find a state of physical readiness, elasticity and ease but also the potential for making meaning through their bodies through text, with breath and obviously with space. A kind of elasticity of expression rather than a sort of neutrality.[37]

Similarly, in Jackie Snow's application of Pure Movement she conflates the 'neutral state' with the 'universal state', meaning a 'state of readiness'.[38] In Vanessa Ewan's practice, rather than the search for a neutral body, she guides actors towards the essence of an action – neutral action – free from adverb or adjective.[39] Morris also describes this state as a kind of 'middle ground', de-cluttering gender stereotypes. This recalls Rodenburg's 'middle way', 'a balance between male and female energy' examined in Chapter 3.[40] Morris's rejection of the term reflects a sea change, propelled in part by feminist scholarship, where ideas of neutrality are exposed as hegemonic, i.e. the white, non-disabled, male body is the norm. Women, from their marginal position, are immediately alert to these discourses of the centre. In actor training, which continues to struggle to address the question of equality,[41] and is tasked to serve an industry increasingly lambasted for its lack of diversity,[42] questions of neutrality are loaded. As previously mooted, there is an increasing expectation that movement training be personalised and specific, recognising the differences *between* and *within* individuals. It therefore seems vital to wrangle with the word neutral. How might terms such as 'the neutral body' and 'the neutral state' perpetuate the neuter in acting? Is this yet another way to invisibilise the female body, the disabled body, the aging body, the body of colour? Rather than being viewed as a state of being, 'the neutral body', we might better appreciate the construct of 'the neutral state' as a pedagogic process, a product of *via positiva*, helping the actor to reconfigure habitual inhibitions and find a state of readiness. However, even when recognising this process as a critical pedagogy, potentially empowering and resistant, the term seems outdated. Morris's 'elastic body', or 'middle ground' or Elizabeth Grosz's 'plastic body' are more pertinent for today's pedagogic discourse: a polymorphous body in a state of becoming.[43]

In 1994, Elizabeth Grosz's *Volatile Bodies* made a seminal contribution to reframe the matter of the body, foregrounding feminist re-configurations of knowledge and subjectivity, to call for a theory of the body.[44] Her work offers a foundational underpinning for thinking about feminist ways in movement teaching. Grosz critiqued the three Cartesian perspectives that situate the body as passive: as a natural object belonging to natural science; a metaphor for social construction; or as a conduit for expression. These male-constructed philosophical positions maintain the body as something to be acted upon and this is compounded for female bodies, seen to be '*more* biological, *more* corporeal and *more* natural than men'.[45] Grosz, harnessing Spinoza's monism, points to an integrated bodymind, constantly in process, producing fragmentations, fracturings and dislocations that orient bodies and body parts to other bodies.[46] As such, the body is relationally constructed and offers the possibility for change and transformation. Grosz urges feminists to look to a range of thinking in order to move a conception of the body from the natural/social, mind/body dualisms, to consider embodied subjectivity or psychophysical knowledge. She posits that corporality can no longer be associated with one sex, but must recognise the plural, multiple body as the cultural product. New models must demonstrate some sort of internal or constitutive articulation, or even disarticulation, between the biological and the psychological, between the inside and the outside, representing the subject's lived body *beside* the physical, social body. Both psychic and social dimensions must find their place in reconceptualising the body, not in opposition to each other but as necessarily interactive.[47] This double awareness of feminist materialism underpins the 'inside/outside' approaches of movement teaching.

Two decades on, how have feminists responded to Grosz's call? Harnessing Eve Sedgwick's 'thinking beside' we can re-consider approaches to the inside/outside, which maintain the social/cultural as operative, moving beyond binaries to recognise the power of the natural to *re-shape* culture.[48] New feminist materialisms resist ideas of the body *in reaction to*, to position the body *in relation with* where, like a mobius strip, the biological and the social affect each other.[49] In applying this thinking to efficient 'natural' and 'neutral' bodies we can see how the 'natural' actor's body might be many things: the expressive or 'life' body, the 'inner', the emotional or spiritual life, the biology, the anatomy, the erotic effects of movement, the personal knowledges. Likewise, the 'neutral' might be understood in a number of ways: the social or physical body, the 'outer', the gendered, classed or racialised expressions of codified movement. In the process of exploring both *beside* each other we can realise what we are and what we are not in relation to others and, in this way, we are drawn irrevocably to a critical pedagogy of difference, which opens up a space of possibility.

Actors experience this difference through their lived sexed and gendered states and, as I considered in Part One, the marginal position of being female, with its inherent objectification and unequal visuality, is central to the way that space and movement are experienced and understood. This manifests in gendered movement habits that include females taking less space, displaying what Iris Young, in her seminal text *Throwing Like a Girl,* calls 'inhibited intentionality', shown as a lack of confidence in physical tasks.[50] Of course, sexed and gendered behaviour is contextually specific and constantly changing but the disconnect between our self-perception and how we are seen remains a constant. I maintain that the very condition of 'being' female initiates the double consciousness of being and being seen, which becomes a positive advantage when learning to act.[51] It is in the space between that one can explore what Butler calls the 'hiatus of iterability', to question expected behaviour and to potentially re-shape cultural norms.[52] For the female actor, a critical movement pedagogy enables her to use her body in ways that allow her to take up *more* space and to work from a point of pleasure.

Evans uses Grosz's discussion of 'the unruly body' to open up a consideration of pleasure and *jouissance* in movement through the thinking of Barthes.[53] In considering a feminist pedagogy of acting I am drawn to the ways that women tend to work with pleasure, as opposed to patriarchal acting traditions, associated with pain, and this principle is central to my concept of *via positiva*, examined in Chapter 2. Pleasure is closely associated with play, enabling the neurological, hormonal and physical changes that happen to the body when working with a state of release. This state also initiates an openness that allows for positive, empathetic connections with others. However, unlike Evans, I have come to constructs of *jouissance* through French feminisms, which situate this experience 'beyond pleasure' as belonging to a female domain. Cixous, Irigaray and Kristeva seek to liberate or move the construct beyond Lacanian psychoanalysis, where it refers to the loss of the child's extreme bliss in relation to the mother as it moves into the symbolic order. Like this state of mutability, the word itself resists being pinned down, and as such has come to mean different things. Jane Gallop, in her essay on the untranslatability of *jouissance,* concludes that it is 'beyond principle'.[54] For me, the term resonates with a number of feminist constructs: Kristeva's semiotic chora,[55] Cixous' *écriture feminine*,[56] Irigaray's feminine enjoyment[57] and Braidotti's nomadic theory.[58] Whilst each is distinct and uses the word discretely, like Kirstu Lempiäinen, I see an overlap in feminist readings of *jouissance* and a relational space of becoming, where it transforms into 'a between area ... the moment of knowing oneself in a multiple or social manner ... becoming an "I" especially because of the presence of others who share the same pleasurous space'.[59] To my mind, *jouissance*, which enables the actor to experience 'excitement, risk, danger, thrill, and sublimated erotic pleasure',[60] is essentially relational, coming into being through the body in relation to space, time, others, objects. When viewed as a feminist material, *jouissance* opens up a space where, through a process of simultaneous construction through pleasure (play) and deconstruction through *jouissance*, the actor reconfigures, however subtly, bodily matter.

Evans cautions that, in order to empower students, movement training must move beyond skills and techniques or it may 'run the risk of simply confirming that movement is "about the body", is (within patriarchal ideologies) predominantly a feminine activity; and is extrinsic to human experience'.[61] I suggest that, adopting a strategic essentialism and interrogating the ways in which these knowledges *are* gendered, ideologically and in practice, maps a female genealogy of movement as a critical pedagogy. In the two case studies that follow I consider the specific ways that women work relationally, through *jouissance*, to explore the plastic, polymorphous body. As I explained in the Introduction, the position I take, the lens I apply and analysis I work through is my own and I hope that this offers interesting perspectives on pedagogies. In the movement practice of Vanessa Ewan we can see gender as technique, exploring what Sandra Reeve calls 'the cultural body', and in the work of Niamh Dowling a nomadic pedagogy emerges, where 'the ecological body' comes into being.[62]

## Vanessa Ewan: The cultural body

Vanessa Ewan is Senior Tutor in Movement for Actors at the Royal Central School of Speech and Drama (RCSSD) where she has developed her pedagogy since 1990. Ewan was trained in the Laban ideology of the 'thinking dancer' and cites Marion North and Bonnie Bird, from her time at the Laban Centre in the 1970s, and Jean Newlove and Maggie Bury, who started East 15, as key influences.[63] She teaches actors how to 'see', or to perceive, qualities of movement and performative action. Her ideology is rooted in her Laban training, where 'difference' was celebrated and any notion of a 'neutral' body or 'normative' dancer's body was challenged. She supports actors to find a 'unique way of seeing and being in the world'[64] through the politics of the body, developing the Laban efforts into 'codes and keys', a form of somatic critique.[65] Alongside technique, she develops the actor's personal and social knowledge, 'teaching things that an actor needs to know about human beings; about people and the games they all play, including themselves'.[66] For Ewan 'teaching actors to be physical ambassadors of the human condition is inherently feminist' as it strives for equality and compassion.[67]

Her commitment to making pedagogy explicit can be seen in her book, *Actor Movement: Expression of the Physical Being*.[68] Written with long-time colleague Debbie Green, it is designed for actors, movement tutors, choreographers, movement directors and directors.[69] Here, Ewan foregrounds the teaching/

learning experience with notes for tutors, such as the need for specific and accurate dialogic practice in feedback where,

> [R]eference may be made to cultural difference, skin colour and sexuality ... The tutor's choice of language can also keep an actor 'on track' as [they] find a more sophisticated way of seeing (for example, the tutor might drop in masculine and feminine as clearer descriptors than 'male' and 'female').[70]

Looking at how Ewan teaches actors to 'do' gender and intimacy, with a heightened sense of double consciousness, we can reconsider movement as a Critical Acting Pedagogy (CAP). The double vision required of acting, which Elin Diamond terms 'looking at being-looked-at-ness', underpins Ewan's practice which, through simultaneous construction and deconstruction, opens up space for a heightened reflexive awareness.[71]

## *Foundational practices: Learning 'to see' through keys and codes*

Ewan teaches through *via positiva*, scaffolding a learning process that enables the actor to discover the agency of her body through pleasure as opposed to pain. In Chapter 2 I've suggested that this positive alternative to the male constructed *via negativa*, is a formative feature of a feminist pedagogy, where, as Landon-Smith explains in Chapter 5, actors learn 'from the crest of a wave', rather than being negated and left to find their own solutions.[72] Ewan expresses this difference when she reflects:

> For me, the *via negativa* is a journey of discovery where travelling is the adventure. The search is endless and the Student Actor does not aim for or retain any sense of the negative. It is a case of transfer and shift of mindset. It could easily promote a powerplay between tutor and student but my focus is on the shared event, to enable the actor to be positively excited by their own volition.[73]

This orientation towards pleasure can be experienced through relaxation and release, not pushing to achieve results but trusting in the process, another feature of feminist pedagogy. Imogen Hale, who studied for three years with Ewan, reflects that she moves beyond technique acquisition to help actors to see the value of 'not working', of 'day-dreaming', to 'drop the work and to trust that if I understood the pattern or the being that I was in, then it would be there effortlessly'.[74] A foundational feature of this approach is to *re-learn* how to see, working from outside-in.[75]

Like Brecht, Ewan believes that 'Observation is a major part of acting'[76] as the actor observes the social, cultural and political gestus, in order to demonstrate the character with a critical attitude. She notes, 'So many exercises that the actor encounters develop [their] eye and ability to read the body'.[77] I recognise this ability as a 'transferable skill',[78] or 'dispositional quality'[79] in the hidden curriculum of acting. For Ewan, observation is 'more than seeing', a bodily memory that can be usefully stored, and she breaks this down into three parts: 'The actor starts by looking outwards: [they] look at the world, then at the influence of the world on the person and finally at the person [them-self]'.[80] In this way, they learn to read socially inscribed, performative movement. Ewan reflects on observation from a gendered perspective:

> I looked after the watches at the football matches when I was a child. I was so happy to have this part to play in the boy's world. But whilst later I bemoaned my lack of all that boys gain from engaging and playing and preparing for life, I simultaneously realised that my observing from the sidelines had actually been a place of learning. Actors who enter the world of rehearsals with the skill of seeing can hugely develop their understanding. After all, the opportunity of observation is at the edge of the rehearsal room. You know, most of an actor's life is spent sitting on the sidelines.[81]

The quality of close observation that she noticed in her female teachers at Laban made her aware of certain gendered characteristics. The women seemed less concerned with 'performing themselves' and therefore more able to watch the class and 'Bonnie Bird's acute understanding of watchfulness' was a key influence.[82] This 'watchfulness' reminds us of the 'separate vigilance' seen by Kristeva to be essential to the female condition.[83] Actors are taught to exist simultaneously in the two states of being and being seen, honing a double vision, which, in part, comes from learning how to observe the other.

Dialogic scaffolding is established through the vocabulary of Laban's Motion Factors (Weight, Time and Space)[84] and to enable the discovery of the eight Efforts of Action Drive (dabbing, gliding, floating, thrusting, flicking, wringing, pressing, slashing).[85] Key to Ewan's critical pedagogy is this discovery process, where she guides the actor to 'celebrate their journey, to discover their personal understanding of Efforts'.[86] This, along with the language of metaphor, enables them to put the somatic translations they are observing and experiencing into words. Ewan's students undertake 'live' research through the observation of place, people or animals, noting observations and recognising patterns in movement and the way in which everything is interconnected, socially enactive and relational.[87] This activates what Reeve calls 'The Cultural Body', where 'observing different emergent movement approaches may offer different, unexpected but distinct cultural, generational or gendered resonances'.[88] Moving beyond Laban, Ewan's 'codes and keys' are a way of exploring *how* to play types of behaviour that reflexively interrogate performative action. 'Codes' refers to states of being 'instantly recognised through physical expression', for instance 'old age' and 'drunk'. 'Keys' access 'codes', for example the key to playing old age might be 'bound energy' or 'doing one thing at a time'.[89] There are social codes, which belong to the world of the play and will reflect the historical, political and social landscape and physical codes, which belong to the character's movement and are more universal but still specific and relational.

Hale, who in her first year after leaving drama school was cast in the lead role in Kneehigh's production of *Rebecca*, an adaptation of the novel by Daphne du Maurier, illustrates Ewan's pedagogical discourse through her explanation of working with keys and codes to author her performance of Mrs de. Winter:

> I'm working with her being not balanced physically as a kind of metaphor ... she's wringing inside and she's heavy, but it's like a full woman and she's not yet in her power and she's lighter than that, so quite flicky and light and she's kind of not able to fully sink into her power until half-way through the show.[90]

From this we can see how Ewan's outside-in approach offers Hale a way of critically applying movement choices to interrogate the cultural body, providing her with a vocabulary to articulate these decisions. She guides actors to 'train their instinct by developing curiosity, observing the world and 'questioning "why"? and "how"? about everything'.[91] This critical pedagogy becomes particularly necessary in arming actors with ways to maintain agency in the complex territory of gender and intimacy in performance.

## *'Doing' gender: Gender as technique*

In a workshop at RCSSD with sixteen second-year BA actors, Ewan worked with keys and codes to explore gender. She located her investigation in the UK during the 1950s to access 'a very performative extreme of stereotypically "idealised" men/women'.[92] As Diamond identifies in her overview of a gestic feminist criticism, historicisation allows actors to examine situational gendered positions obliquely, making comparisons with their contemporary experience.[93] The three-hour workshop examined how certain actions construct perceptions of gender. The first exercise compared males and females play-fighting in a playground; through this Ewan encouraged the actors to explore the idea that 1950s males are not encouraged to touch each other and so, in fight, they use contact as an opportunity for a 'gathering' drive or effort, which engages the whole body. In comparison, 1950s females touch each other as part of their socialised behaviour, so are less habituative to physically connect in fight; the code they are given to lead their efforts is 'scattering' and they connect more in the upper body. The actors observed each other's playing within gendered roles, then swapped male and female roles to try out the observed behaviour, then reflected on the shift in experience.

The feminist thinking of Joan Riviere, Judith Butler and Jacqueline Rose, considered in Chapter 1, can helpfully sharpen pedagogical perspectives on this thick description of the class.[94] Ewan introduced the first exercise to the female actors in distanced, historicised terms: 'So, actors playing females – in this exercise you are a "thing". We're going to take this a step further. Your relationship with your "object"'.[95] She moved around the room, pointing to an object and then back to herself, 'This is me – this is a chair – this is me – this is a door – this is me – I've got an outline – this is a chair – it has an outline'.[96] The actors tentatively moved around the room with a sense of doubt and some resistance to naming themselves as an object. The actors playing males were asked to build an improvisation: 'Your key is "the guardian". So, one person is going to leave the room and basically one of you is going to be the potential threat'.[97] A bar environment was set up with the females playing 'objects' and the males playing the 'guardians' of their 'she objects'. Ewan subtly invited comparison between historicised behaviour and the present, provoking: 'We already have very different forms in the room. Maybe some things haven't changed'?[98] The actor exited and Ewan arranged the room, placing a male behind the door. Shortly after the actor entered she told him to close his eyes, and asked him to recall what he could see. He was immediately able to pick out the main threat of the male positioned behind the door. Ewan then repeated this improvisation, layering detail into the performative action of gender at play. She turned her attention to the females:

> So, females – you're going to be objects –The male can get you the chair – an object for an object. [To the males] You can look at them. They are there. They are the object. You can look with great respect ... For instance, you can look at them as if they were an intelligent object – encyclopedic.[99]

As the actors playing males walked around the room, looking at the seated actors playing females, the atmosphere changed from relaxed joviality to a distinct sense of unease. Ewan provoked:

> Look at one object at a time. You are allowed to look and I can see this is not comfortable. So, I sense this is feeling a bit real. Does it feel a bit familiar? Remember, in this 1950s context, when you are looking at the object you are not looking at them in a rude way – because you are a guardian. If we are 'doing' gender, here all the males are charged with being guardians, all the females are objects. Remember we are not 'doing' characters but a basic code that can define your difference when it comes to working on character.[100]

Here, gender is explored as an iterative technique to produce a Butlerian notion of 'doing gender'.[101] The female is de-humanised as an object and the masquerade is deconstructed to illustrate Butler and Rose's notion of socially constructed, inscribed and repeated acts. The female actors found this uncomfortable because, as they recognised in discussion, it felt rather too close to their reality. The restricted female body of the 1950s drew parallels with contemporary inscriptions of Botoxed faces, plastic surgery, tattooed eyebrows and body altering fashions. By asking them to perform their 'outline', the 'doubleness' of being, which Rose refers to as 'being as being divided', was made concrete.[102] The workshop produced a feminist reading of Lacan, with the females seeming to have the power as the guardians' gaze competes for the phallus, which the females possess. From this perspective, they performed their acts of femininity, their masquerade, in order to manipulate the male behaviour. However, the comparative invisibility of the males gave them the choice of visibility denied to the females. Ewan drew attention to this male freedom and their performed 'bravado' through physical 'gathering' activities, such as fighting or football. As the actors were invited to observe and then experience the cross-gendered playing, to see and feel the action from the other's point of view, they explored what it might be like to be in the other gendered body. In opening up this space between the 'natural' body and the cultural body Ewan enabled critical reflexivity. This sparked energetic discussion and some agitation, particularly amongst the female actors, one of whom, as a British Muslim, recognised the exaggerated masquerade she felt to be inherent in the structures of her community.

This workshop was pre-rehearsal for a production in which some actors were to play cross gender. In a class of sixteen there was only the opportunity to mix some of the casting as opposed to a full single-sex casting in two separate productions. Ewan bemoaned the loss of this opportunity for actors in their training, 'because it liberates several things and one of them is the clarity of actions and meaning because the stakes are different'.[103] She used the example of the act of kissing and how, in playing cross gender, the actor experiences the act of kissing as 'a political thing, as in who is in charge here'?[104] Through queering the action, power between bodies is reconstituted. This cross gendering of movement, as with Boston's cross-gendering voice in Chapter 3, asks actors to reflect on their unconscious bias to recognise how, when repetition inevitably produces difference, there is the opportunity to question and resist patriarchal frameworks.

Through her pedagogy Ewan looks for ways to empower both sexes to be better placed to deal with the industry's patriarchal structures. She gives the example of a female actor, tasked with performing a character described as 'buxom' by a male playwright for a male director, when she is not herself that body type. Faced with this challenge, it's vital that she approaches the character with detailed research to critically explore the gender discourse: how it emerges through the clothing, etiquette, social codes, family structures, work, dance, sport, eating, rituals, superstition and religion. She must interrogate the prevailing gendered behaviour of the time in order to question: why is this part written as female/male? How does gender affect her/his role in the piece? Does the character deviate from the expected roles of the time? What are the expected gender-based social responsibilities? What are the communication codes of flirting, relationships, fighting, emotion and linguistic patterning? This critical analysis of character enables her to move beyond objectification. This becomes vital if she is to resist the perceived norm of the time and it equips her with the knowledge she needs to discuss these choices with the director.[105]

Ewan also alerts movement teachers and directors to the ways that gendered behaviour can disadvantage them professionally. Many female MA/MFA Movement: Directing and Teaching students at RCSSD, with dance backgrounds, have developed habits of performing feminine aesthetics, and she coaches them to expand their communicative range, 'to play a deep note, do something loud, substantial in their movement' and to challenge their habitual behaviour.[106] In this way, Ewan guides her students to think about the power play of gender in relationships between movement director and director, and movement teacher/director and actor, so they might consciously resist perpetuating reductive appropriations.

### 'Doing' intimacy: Intimacy as technique

Ewan attends to the ways that the actor's body is vulnerable to exploitation and how the pressure to conform to industry stereotypes can be an ethical concern. In a section titled *Personal Safety in Movement* she highlights moments that can be considered to be a physical or emotional risk for the actor, looking beyond staged physical violence, which legally requires a fight director to highlight 'intimacy, ranging from the familiar touch of a friend, sibling or spouse to erotic touching, embracing, kissing, undressing, having sex or being raped'.[107] She arms actors with strategies to safeguard against the potential personal challenge, professional confusion or exploitation that might occur if tasked to perform such acts. She cautions that being 'open', a desirable quality in acting, should not make one vulnerable: 'Being available to discovery does not mean being sexually open, or open to unnecessary criticism or manipulation'.[108] Whilst required guidelines protect actors in fight scenes, it is only recently, notably through the work of movement director Ita O'Brien, a Central graduate who cites Ewan's influence, that intimacy guidelines have been recognised and adopted in film and theatre.[109] Ewan offers a practical methodology, with tools to guide the actor through the potential challenges including: setting provisos early on, halting the action and focusing on intentions and reactions.[110]

In a workshop with movement teachers/directors, looking at pedagogical approaches to scaffolding intimacy for actors in movement, Ewan returned to 'looking-at-being-looked-at-ness', through the task of sketching each other in pairs. This activity highlighted the necessity for movement teachers to equip actors with similar strategies that enable them to maintain their agency within the professional demands of exposure, particularly marked in scenes of intimacy. Two exercises, which sought to make the doubling of the actor explicit as a way to enable a distinction between the artistic body as object and the professional self, enabled scaffolding approaches. These exercises consciously constructed and legitimized the professional acting body, as another body existing alongside actor-as-self, actor-as-character. The gap between the professional acting body and actor-as-self can be used by the actor as a protective shield but this might easily become a space of harmful dissonance. Ewan's approach equips the actor to claim their agency in this space.

The first involved a mask. Ewan explained that many actors are familiar with the mechanism of mask work, whereby the actor puts the mask on, then turns to perform, and then turns away to take the mask off, becoming 'herself' again. Ewan translates this mechanism to explore the actor's agency in the workplace. She set up a technical score, demonstrating how to put on the mask with ones' back to the audience and then instructing pairs to perform an improvised exchange between a tutor and actor (the actor wearing the mask). The tutor instructed the actor in some simple task, the masked actor performed the task, and then removed the mask in order to receive critique. The act of removing the mask was a physical reminder of the shift between character/role and professional self. The use of the mask 'helps the actor as a 'non-human' to feel 'different' and this clearly offers a demarcation which highlights the space between where interaction between actor and director happens.[111] In moving between selves the professional self is established as a point zero, a safe space that protects the actor's agency. The second part of this example involved an improvisation exploring and challenging nudity, where actor, director and stage manager rehearsed a scene where the actor, imagined to be naked, crossed the stage as if walking into the sea. Ewan's introduction of a dressing gown echoed the previous function of the mask; after the task, the stage manager would pass the dressing gown to the 'naked' actor who would put it on before turning to the director to receive notes. The use of the mask and dressing gown made the implicit and instinctual knowledge of the actor explicit through the demarcation between the actor as professional and actor-in-role. Ewan coached the practitioners to think about how they might use their technical vocabulary to add value to movement direction in an intimate scene. She suggested that they 'up the science' in their movement vocabulary, in order to affect agency with directors. This becomes important in ensuring that intimate acts maintain the same technical mapping as any other complicated physical sequence. The second exercise coached the movement teachers/directors in how to support actors in staging a kiss. They worked in pairs on a physical score that would, through a smooth transition, lead into the moment of a kiss. Ewan demonstrated and set up this technical score, breaking down the sequence into three movements and encouraging the participants to speak the movements out loud as they did them, do them in slow motion and then to map the score with expression, stressing they should not 'fill in those gaps with the flow' but should work in shorter, distinct actions. Working to direct the actor to pay attention to all the technical aspects of the movement, for example, the breath as a journey, working with Laban keys or the ways that eye contact shifts moment to moment, allowed them to focus on technique rather than enter into the psychology of the intimate act. Once again, the professional self of the actor was foregrounded through explicit application of intimacy as technique.

One has the sense that Ewan's feminist pedagogy is operating from the eye of the storm. In her work with movement teachers/directors and with actors she equips them with ways to maintain agency whilst working in an aspectual profession where the body is objectified as part of a patriarchal system. Ultimately, decisions around movement should be everyone's responsibility, including the director. Ewan's approach is deeply pragmatic and, in its ideology and practice, I recognise feminist materialist constructs that position the female body as doubled, both object and subject, seeing and being seen, able to subvert gendered inscriptions, as through repetition, difference is inevitable.[112] The body is multiple, in states of becoming and relationally constructed. In the way that she utilises space, time and objects (drawing materials, chair, mask, dressing gown), Ewan's practice reflects new feminist materialisms, which challenge anthropocentricism, and foreground non-human agency. This critical pedagogy seems vital at a time when actors are recognising the need to take control of their professional status and, if necessary, to fight back. Her practice responds to Spatz's call for gender as technique in acting, seeking traction from within the industry, with the potential to re-shape mechanisms of control.[113]

## Niamh Dowling: The ecological body

Niamh Dowling is Head of School of Performance at Rose Bruford College in Kent. She has made a significant contribution to UK training practices through the development of international programmes of study – the first, at Manchester Metropolitan University 2002, was run in partnership with the Polish company Teatr Pieśń Kozla (Song of the Goat).[114] This initiative heralded a new wave of training in the UK, where universities collaborate with companies or international providers to provide multi-centre, intercultural training. In thinking through Dowling's practice, I consider the ways it brings Braidotti's theory into practice, producing a nomadic pedagogy.

Her early education played out during 'The Troubles' in Northern Ireland, where she represented her country internationally in cross-country running and was part of the Northern Ireland Mountain Rescue Team, later joining a mountaineering expedition to Iran, with the Young Explorers' Trust for the National Geographic Society.[115] This affinity for expeditions, running and climbing, developed as a formative feature of her pedagogic practice. On return, she completed a BA in Dance and Education in Cardiff, then an MA in Dance and Aesthetics at Goldsmiths and The Laban Centre, studying with Gill Clark and David Best. It was the study of aesthetics, with its focus on perspective and interpretation, that spurned an ongoing fascination for the role of language in dance pedagogy. Formative early work, developing movement and dance in an Oxford Further Education College, allowed Dowling to delve into the contemporary approaches of New Dance, fueled by the work of X6 collective, driven by feminist and queer politics and resisting the traditional structures and aesthetics of classical and contemporary dance practices.

As a self-taught practitioner, she sought out ways to school herself outside and beyond traditional notions of technique. It is perhaps this autonomous and organic process of learning, not bound to any particular school or to skills acquisition, that has driven her to seek out alternative pedagogic practices beyond the UK training ground. She shaped her own education, training with many seminal women practitioners: first, with Anne Bogart, through the Movement Research Network in New York; taking Alexander lessons with Eva Karczag in the U.S. (1990) and later with Don Burton in the Lake District; training with Monika Pagneux in Paris (1993–1995). As a result, four different strands cross fertilize within her practice: her BA experience with Laban (space, time, weight, flow); Pagneux's approach to play, the ensemble and the creative imagination;[116] Bogart's exploration of movement through Viewpoints (tempo, duration, kinesthetic response, repetition, shape, distance, topography, architecture, gesture); and Alexander Technique. Dowling reflects that the practice of Laban and Viewpoints have given her work structure and a vocabulary, and Alexander Technique gives a set of underpinning principles for the individual person in that structure, interacting through the play of Pagneux's ensemble. In the last decade, she has sought out therapeutic practices to better understand and support the developmental aspects of movement. She trained in hypnotherapy, to become more attuned to the ways that language can unlock the subconscious and in Systemic Constellation Therapy, a gestalt approach that facilitates a democratised therapeutic practice. I am drawn to the ways that, through the intersection between therapeutic practice and Alexander Technique, Dowling's practice operates as a nomadic pedagogy.

## *Foundational practices: Towards a nomadic pedagogy*

The ways that power is produced on, in and between bodies is, to my mind, at the heart of Dowling's pedagogy; a position informed by her leading performance projects in third-world counties. In 1998 in Africa, Dowling undertook a three-month project, *The Girl Child*. This led to the creation of *Three Sisters* in Tanzania, Zambia and Kenya where performers made a piece in one country, telling the story of one sister, and then performed it in the next country, where the story of the second/third sister was developed. The works responded to female circumcision and arranged marriage and were followed up with workshops in the local community, where the issue of agency and movement became paramount; for example, the women related movement exercises that explored accepting or blocking to issues of consent within a hierarchical gendered system. In 1997 in El Salvador, Dowling's movement work with widowed refugees opened up ways for them to take leadership roles in their community, to claim direction and to take space. From this, she learnt that somatic work will activate whatever is most useful for each individual and that, rather than asserting her own position, she needed to 'get out of the way', so that participants could discover their own ways to make it relevant.[117] The choice of pedagogical language was central in opening up or closing down this process and Dowling realised 'the less meaning that I give, the more meaning they get'.[118] I suggest that this position is a feature of *via positiva* in women's movement practices. Morris reflects a similar view:

> What is politically empowering is that you start with a group of bodies and they are all different and they all bring into the room completely different experiences and you work with the bodies that there are ... It's political because it's cross cultural ... It's a kind of metaphor for life because everybody is learning together but everybody processes it slightly differently. I think there's a lot of freedom in that. You just need to go on the journey and see what happens and I think that is quite female.[119]

This feminist pedagogy recognises the positivity of difference and guides each individual to work from their particular body, to be alert to and try to solve their specific blocks or inhibitions. From this perspective, notions of the neutral body seem obsolete.

The metaphor of 'life is a journey', reflecting Systemic Constellations, which I will go on to consider, is central to Dowling's approach which interrogates the source. As she explains, 'I'm really committed to the source. To go back as far as we possibly can to the origin in order to understand it'.[120] This idea of origin/source, where and how an idea or practice comes into being, opens up anthropological, sociological, political and psychological understanding. The MA Acting at Manchester Met in 2004, worked with Song of the Goat, travelling to and living with remote communities, and through this othering experience enabled participants to be better placed to understand connection to self, to community, to ancestry. In *Crossing Cultural Borders Through the Actor's Work,* Cláudia Tatinge Nacscimento considers the 'cultural border crossing' that an actor experiences when she learns and embodies a process that is foreign to her. Looking at the intercultural practices of Roberta Carreri and Ang Gey Pin, Nacsimento argues that, rather than being touristic, the ethical crossing of cultural borders is an empowering creative process.[121] The MFA International Theatre and Performance Practice at Rose Bruford College follows actor training and training approaches to Stanislavski's work from the UK to U.S. and finally to Moscow Arts Theatre School. The MFA Actor/Performer Training includes an expedition that creates the framework, conditions and impetus for students and collaborators to create an original ensemble theatre work. The initial research and the stimulus for this work is an expedition, a journey into the artistic heart of a different culture where the artistry – song, story, dance, ceremony, ritual – are integral to the health, wellbeing and continuance of community. Previous expeditions have journeyed into the Tusheti Mountains in Georgia; Roma enclaves in Extremadura Spain; the Maramureș and Bucovina regions of Northern Romania. These MA programmes move beyond training for the industry, and although many participants will go on to work as artists, this learning is underpinned by personal and social development, enabling 'every student to be the fullest of themselves ... to believe in themselves'.[122] In Dowling's development of a nomadic training experience I see the essential premise of Braidotti's new materialist theory. Braidotti's suggestion is that the oppressive structures of advanced capitalism, which inscribe borders and hierarchies, can be resisted when we work from our operative state of becoming, polymorphous, in constant flux, open to the positivity of difference. From this position we may be able to expand perceptions. She points to the scholarship of bio-feminists who 'fight matter with matter', drawing attention to nature's power to redefine constructs of self-ness and identity.[123] Dowling's nomadic practice opens up ideas of identity as students physically travel between countries and, through the development of an ensemble, intercultural exploration is facilitated. Participants are purposefully recruited as an intercultural cohort; on the MA Collaborative Theatre Making in 2020 the students came from the UK, UK/Jamaica, U.S., Spain, Turkey, UK/Hong Kong, Australia/Poland, Oman and Scotland. In this context, where intercultural exchange is operating through and within the matter of the bodies themselves, a shift becomes possible, moving exploration of the cultural body towards what Reeve calls the ecological body, 'situated in movement itself' perceiving 'the moving world through movement'.[124] This is embedded in the thinking of new feminist materialisms, which recognise relational construction beyond the human.[125] When a group is so diverse, the ensemble must establish a common language, moving beyond words, through movement, space, time, rhythm and vibration, where touch, observation and empathy are cultivated and fostered by the group.

The plurality that Dowling cultivates, where individual uniqueness and cultural difference is celebrated within the group, stems, in part, from the way that she utilises Alexander Technique to bring the individual into the structures of the movement. What is notable is that, whereas traditional Alexander is experienced one-on-one, Dowling facilitates a hands-on approach with a large group, teaching the tools that will enable performers to work on themselves or on another through release procedures. UK Drama Schools had to abandon one-on-one Alexander or Feldenkrais technique because of the cost but, through

Dowling's liberatory pedagogy, actors self-coach, to notice their habitual patterns of tension and to consciously release them. Dowling carefully scaffolds and supports this process, checking hands-on, correcting positions and giving coaching instructions. She breaks the practice up into separate body parts: head, spine, arms and legs, and then puts these parts together again to see how they work as one. In a three-hour session the same structure is offered: warm-up to sensitise and connect the group; floor work in pairs, which starts to identify the structure of that part of the body; anatomical instruction, using props (model, skeleton, diagrams); returning to hands-on pair work, with movement to activate and release that body area; work with image, where individuals open up their imaginations to activate the body part; then observation of an individual singing or speaking, with points of habitual tension noted by the observers; Dowling coaches the individual to notice and to release their particular points of tension through Alexander directions – widening, lengthening, up, down, side; finally, there is a plenary with group reflection. This foundational scaffolding structure offers the participant group a model to return to each time they explore a different body part, and because they know they are following the same schema, they can be more present in the work. There is a clear process of building the knowledge from outside-in, in the early stages of the workshop where the focus is on the anatomy and identifying habits through observation, then moving beyond seeing bodily patterns to hands-on work where, through touch, one becomes sensitised to feeling bodily patterns; finally, to an inner awareness where, through working with metaphor and image, one imaginatively feels the life-body within the release, working inside-out. In this way, the participants are guided to explore technique for inhabiting and embodying the process of release.

When, like Spatz, we consider bodily practices as technique, recognising that somatic work organically alters the bodymind, literally changing the way that you experience movement, we can accept that somatic approaches shift your experience in the world. Dowling is extremely conscious of her responsibility in supporting students through what can be confrontational transformations in the matter of the body: 'I am really conscious that something is changing [through the bodywork] that will never un-change ... I am really aware that what I am doing is intensely beneficial but also potentially traumatic'.[126] Through studying hypnosis in 2004 and training in Systemic Constellation Therapy (2013–2019), she has made space to better understand how to manage and caretake such personal change and to find a language through which to do this.[127] Systemic Constellations is a gestalt therapeutic practice developed by Bert Hellinger in 1978. This practice, particularly used in family therapy, seeks ways to solve particular relationship issues by reconnecting individuals with family members, both present and ancestral. Through a facilitated group process involving representatives and subjects, the subjects' stories are activated and representatives take the role of family members, past and present. The power dynamics of the situation are physically and spatially mapped, interventions facilitated and potential solutions suggested.[128] This practice uses history and the source as material through which to better understand the present; representatives take on the role of present and past family members, a grand-parent or great-grandparent. Space is given to represent the ancestral journeys that we carry through our own life journeys and to acknowledge that we stand upon the shoulders of those that have gone before us. Through this we can come closer to our personal truths, knowing that we are not alone but that we carry the spirits and the love of our ancestors as an inherent support structure, always in relation with others.[129] This moves beyond a 'talking cure' to engage all participants in an embodied and potentially transformatory process. When someone is supported by a group of mostly strangers to re-live and re-work essential and difficult truths, a heightened sense of democracy and plurality is generated, working with *via positiva* to support the individual to find solutions to their blocks.

Dowling intersects Systemic Constellations with Alexander-influenced release work, and explaining this process requires some thick description. In a movement session with MA International students focusing on the legs, she started with an exploration of anatomy, looking at a skeletal model to understand how the legs are located in the pelvis, the bottom of the spine and the coccyx. She introduced the image of a smile in the front of the pelvis to open and widen the lower back. Then, working in pairs, with one in semi-supine, they took it in turns to release the full movement of the legs, manipulated by the standing partner. Throughout her instruction, Dowling coached the ways that the participants should teach each other, through touch, through holding of weight, making the process explicit: 'It's not about pulling. It's about letting go'.[130] This encouragement to work with a more subtle force, to redirect the energy, like Ewan's call to 'do less', points to a feminist pedagogy that operates through a renegotiation of effort and power.[131] The group noticed the lengthening in the legs and the vital materialism of somatic work, where body chemistry changes, enabling it to open, widen, lengthen, take more space, is made manifest. When the participants move to explore walking, Dowling, directing the group to work with eyes closed, leads a visualisation exercise, informed by Alexander directions, shamanic journeying and her understanding of Systemic Constellations:

> Picture yourself standing at the edge of the ocean facing the land. In front of you there is an empty space and there's a space that represents time. We're going to walk through ages of time. Let's imagine you are walking through ages in ice ages and stone ages – centuries of developmental time. You're walking through and you are passing animals and evolution until you see the human in existence and walk into the centuries that that leads up until 2019. See yourself, travelling into these years – tunneling into the last 100, 200, 500, 600 centuries. Tunneling through those times. Heading to the start of the 1,000s, 1,500, 2000. So, coming into the time of people who are just dying in these days. Entering into the 2000s and now we're

moving through times where your generations have lived. Up until 2019. May 20th 2019. And as we stand here be aware of all the generations of people behind you. These generations of lives that go right back, some going right back to the time where the sea and the land met. Be aware of the people behind you – this whole world and the cultures that stand behind you. What does it do when you have that sense of it at the front? What are all the elements that bring you here in the fullest of yourself? Then, wherever you are, just say quickly to yourself any piece of text that you know – an old song, poem or even a speech – it can be in any language. It would be useful to think about something from your culture and something that your family has gone through. And as you have comfortably found *you*, in some areas of the room, just test out what you say.[132]

The room was filled with voices, with participants sounding and speaking text in their own languages. In discussion, some expressed surprise at the way that text that had come to them, often through a song that had been part of their earliest memories, or a story past down in their family. They commented on how their breath dropped and they felt deeply connected to the meaning of the text, through the relational constellation they had worked with through the visualisation. Working with image enables the imagination to be part of the process so the student works simultaneously from inside-out and outside-in. By using time and space as materials in the narrative of the image, re-enforcing the constellation of generational connection, and locating the present materiality within the wider cosmos, Dowling's pedagogy seems to ground participants, making invisible relational networks visible. To my mind, this produces what Reeve terms the ecological body, 'situated in movement itself and as a system dancing within systems, rather than as an isolated unit'.[133] The practice is working on many levels, anatomically, imaginatively, psychically, spiritually, and the ways in which language operates is key to this integration.

## *Mattering language*

Dowling's voice and language are dexterous and visceral, producing a type of somatic orchestration, a constant monologue, or stream of consciousness, persistent and often at high tempo. Her use of language is distinctly poised and pitched, not borne from habit or character trait, but a consciously tried and tested pedagogical tool with the voice operating as a material. With her lilting Irish accent, Dowling's voice generates a rhythm and melody that orchestrates the room through timbre, pitch, tone and volume to produce a diegetic underscore, which builds atmosphere and unifies a group. A signature exercise, one used regularly to start a class, operates through call and response where participants 'move faster than they can think. They are in the moment responding'.[134]

The group follows Dowling's instruction: 'Jogging ... dashing ... darting ... freezing ... creeping ... pairing ... grouping ... following ... stalking ... arriving ... leaving', shifting pace and focus, moment to moment and 'listening to the musicality of the group'.[135] Listening is heightened and bodies move with specificity and variety. Dowling's hypnotherapy training has taught her how language, tone, pace, volume and vocal energy enables a therapeutic experience: 'I'm speaking very quickly. I'm speaking to the part of you that will pick it up. I'm working on the subconscious level'.[136] One picks out and holds onto what one needs to know, editing the superfluous. In this way, she invites participants to select what to own, question or pass over.

In thinking through the ways that language matters in Dowling's practice I apply Milde's framework for rehearsal discourse alongside my framework for pedagogic analysis, to focus on her instructions, explanations and feedback.[137] Her language can be seen to operate in three distinct but mutually supportive ways: technical/anatomical language; practitioner focused terminology; metaphorical and imagistic language. This last category is particularly tuned and specific, honed over time through a careful refining and editing process. In this way, mattering language is an embodied feature of Dowling's professional knowledge, as fundamental as her Alexander expertise.

Metaphorical language is vital within the pedagogy of movement training because metaphor, in its many forms (primary, schematic, imagistic), is somatic in origin and therefore, as embodied metaphor theory identifies, inherently embodied. Evans notes the ways that 'images seem able to operate psychosomatically through emotional and physical associates, functioning far more effectively for students than objective description or instruction'.[138] Cognitive linguists, Lakoff and Johnson explain metaphor as different dimensions of experience, integrating perception and movement. Metaphor consists of two asymmetric experiential domains. The first is non-metaphorical and concrete (e.g. the experience of going on a journey) and the second, which is derived from the first, is metaphorical or conceptual (e.g. life is a journey). That means that, if we understand the source of the experiential domain, we are able to capture the meaning of the resulting experiential domain, but not vice versa.[139] As such, metaphor and imagistic metaphor are mattering languages, uniting experiential knowledge with conceptual knowledge. Although it is easy to place this in the realm of poetic language and thus inherently working differently from scientific or rational language, cognitive linguistics has recognised metaphor as essentially everyday embodied language, not restricted to a poetic domain. In a similar way to the performative language of speech acts (e.g. I pronounce you), metaphor performs its meaning through its perceived action. Returning to the earlier point about movement teaching working from inside-out and outside-in, metaphorical/imagistic language becomes a bridge or lever between the social body and the life body. In Dowling's practice certain types of images and metaphors dominate, associated with journeying and natural environments. Her practice produces a type of metaphoric worlding where the ecological body, always in flux, moves through and between landscapes, time zones and constellations. This ecology speaks to Systemic Constellations, placing the individual in relation to their past, present and future life journeys.

In a research orientated class, designed to explore the function and productivity of pedagogic language, Dowling tested her own linguistic habits, structuring the session into four parts and restricting herself to using particular types of language in each part. The class focused on the arms, one of the four body parts within her Alexander influenced release work. In the first part, Dowling limited herself to practitioner focused terminology. The students lay on the floor in semi-supine and explored 'constructive rest' through the five directions:'the neck releases, the head moves back and away and the back lengthens and widens, knees forward and up'.[140] Limiting herself to Alexander terminology, without the nuance of metaphor, imagistic and adverbial language, impeded Dowling's own ability to articulate and embody the instruction and consequently few students embodied it. She instinctively turned to hands-on, touching the head or neck to enable the required release in the body. In discussion, the students identified the disconnect that they felt in this section and their relief when Dowling brought them through touch into the release. Observing Dowling operate, without the richness of her nuanced and subtle language, her expertise was stripped back in the struggle to communicate the functional pedagogy. In the second part, she restricted herself to using technical anatomical language, showing diagrams of the rhomboid and explaining its connections to the pectoral muscles and the trapezius. Working in pairs through floor work she led participants to aid release in the trapezius, applying light touch under and on top of the shoulder. After this, they worked from standing to move the arm and reveal the full flexibility of the muscle to their partner, who had to resist her immediate instinct to help, allowing herself to be moved and 'to let the interference out of the way'.[141] Once again, through the restricted choice of language Dowling recognised the distinct lack of embodiment *she* felt through the instruction: 'It feels really stilted. With the reduction in the richness of language – using words like pour, spill – I notice a big difference when I talk and I'm *not* embodying it and when I *am* embodying it'.[142] One of the marked features of Alexander practice, traditionally one-on-one, is that the teacher is both giving and receiving through the transactional exchange of touch. Dowling recognised that language, more than anything else in her practice, 'touched' in the teaching/learning exchange.

When she worked with her accustomed imagistic and metaphorical language in the third part of the class, the instruction and explanation started to be embodied by the participants and by herself. She explained the movement of the arm, the trapezius and the latissimus, like the movement of a wing asking, 'Does the image change the way that you understand it?'[143] They looked at the difference between the right and the left arms with Dowling elucidating, 'It's wide and expansive. The wing goes beyond the fingertips. We create a presence with it that is bigger than the body'.[144] Working with the wing image enabled participants to make a link between the outer, physical description of the body and their embodied experience, explored through the final extended visualisation task. With eyes closed the students explored the image through a narrated journey:

> Explore the width, shape, movement of the wing. The wing moving from the feet, not just the pelvis. Work on the image – maybe it is like a cloak? We are going to let these wings take you on a journey. You are going to find a way for the wing to take you up high. You are seeing Toynbee Studios, Shoreditch, Kent, the South East coast, moving over-seas, forests, rivers, mountains, places that you know and your ancestral connection to those places and to places you haven't known. Waterfalls, paths, mountains. You see a beautiful, perfectly framed mountain that you are going to land on. As you land you notice all the colours and a person is on the other side waving. Your center rises. There is the need to be seen and you wave back. You look down the valley, down the middle flows a river. Put your hand in the water of the river. Feeling your hand in the water at the perfect temperature you find an object. It represents or is something that you'd lost a long time ago. You lost it and you'd forgotten it. What age were you? Does it represent a person? A feeling? It's something you recognise you had but now it's lost. In the remembering that you'd lost it, touch where you lost it from and hold the object to that place so it begins to fold back into the body. It travels into the whole of that area somehow filling it up. So, it travels to the rest of the body and somehow goes to that place. You are going to leave that place. You can choose what it is that you want to do with that object. Do whatever you have to do to integrate it into the fullness of your body. You wave to the person and you use your wings to take you back up. Sometimes you are free, falling, collapsing, lifting and soaring back down. You fly back over the beaches, villages, town and cities, and that island that is England, Scotland, Wales. You circle round Toynbee Hall, Toynbee Studios, fall back into Studio 2 and feet back as you land so you are aware of the space you are in. You have a moment where you take each person in the room in to your attention.

This image work activated the Alexander release of the rhomboid and trapezius whilst operating on a number of psychological, imaginative levels. The anthropomorphic image, beyond human, liberated the senses and enabled the imagination, shifting away from the social body, yet returning to it at the point of the wave to reconnect with 'being seen-ness'.[145] The lost object connected directly to psychology, taking the person to a point of emotion through a memory but without forced retrieval. A number of students reflected on the level of emotional release working *beside* embodiment they experienced in this exercise. Although the lack of any technical vocabulary proved destabilising for some, they agreed that the image work enabled them to embody the Alexander directions more than the vocabulary of the directions and anatomical language alone.

Dowling enables the ecological body through her language use, a body in relation with time, space, human and non-human. She harnesses the neutral body as process, a way of seeing what one is not, to work on the vital materialism of body and imagination. This approach, in its form and content, produces a nomadic pedagogy where the diversity of the participant group, the ways that the natural body is explored *beside* the neutral body working through *via positiva* enables *jouissance*, through relational release. Nomadic pedagogy offers actors ways of coming to know themselves *in relation with* a constellation of connections, resisting inscription, in states of becoming and working with the positivity of difference. Like Braidotti's theories, this pedagogy is an antidote to inward looking, individualistic practices, moving beyond skills/techniques to open up the epistemic scope of movement for actors. Dowling and Ewan's practices examine movement as a mode of being, something *we are* as opposed to something we do.[146]

## Notes

1 Mark Evans, *Movement Training for the Modern Actor* (London & New York: Routledge, 2009).
2 I presented an argument for *via positiva* as an antidote to the foundational, male constructed, pedagogy of *via negativa* in Chapter 2.
3 There is an MA in Movement Directing and Teaching at RCSSD and previously at Guildhall. One should note that the cost of MA training is a barrier for some to enter the profession and many movement teachers, including Shona Morris at RADA, Liana Nyquist at Drama Centre and Jackie Snow at Manchester Met, worked as actors first and were then trained by other movement teachers.
4 For example, Shona Morris was Head of Movement and Movement Director at the Shakespeare Festival Theatre Ontario, The Globe Theatre, Chichester Festival Theatre. She is Creative Associate at Watford Palace Theatre.
5 Merry Conway, *Tea with Trish: The Movement work of Trish Arnold* (2008) http://www.teawithtrish.com/[accessed 11.1913].
6 Evans, 69–119.
7 Evans, 78–99.
8 Litz Pisk, *The Actor and His Body* (London & New York: Bloomsbury Methuen Drama, 2018), Annie Lou, *The Physical Actor* (London & New York: Routledge, 2009), Dymphna Callery, *Through the Body* (London: Nick Hern, 2001), Lorna Marshall, *The Body* Jackie Snow, *Movement Training for Actors* (London & New York: Bloomsbury Methuen Drama, 2012), Vanessa Ewan and Debbie Green, *Actor Movement: Expression of the Physical Being* (London & New York: Bloomsbury Methuen Drama, 2015), Niamh Dowling, *Alexander in Performance 1–4* (Routledge Performance Archive) https://www-routledgeperformancearchive-com.ezproxy.sussex.ac.uk/search?searchString=niamh+dowling# [accessed 01.03.20].
9 Evans comments, 'Whilst the key international innovators in the history of movement training for actors were almost entirely male, those who created individual if

more anonymous careers teaching their skills in drama schools were, and still are, mostly female'. Evans, 8.
10 In Chapter 2 I explain critical pedagogy as an umbrella term encompassing feminist, queer or engaged pedagogy, concerned with empowering the learner in different ways. This approach stems from the work of Paulo Freire and Henry Giroux: Paulo Freire, *Pedagogy of the Oppressed* (New York & Great Britain: Continuum, 2000), Henry Giroux, *Schooling for a Democracy: Critical Pedagogy in the Modern Age* (London & New York: Routledge, 1989).
11 Vanessa Ewan with Kate Sagovsky, *Laban's Efforts in Action: A Movement Handbook for Actors* (Bloomsbury, Methuen, 2019) 23.
12 Shona Morris, email exchange 23.04.20.
13 Ayse Tashkiran, 'British Movement Directors' in *The Routledge Companion to Jacques Lecoq*, ed Rick Kemp and Mark Evans (London & New York: Routledge, 2016).
14 Ayse Tashkiran, *Movement Directors in Contemporary Theatre: Conversations on Craft* (London: Methuen Drama, 2020)
15 Ibid.
16 Ludus Dance https://ludusdance.org/ is a portfolio organization, funded by Arts Council England serving the North of the UK.
17 Lloyd Newson (DV8) and Nigel Charnock both worked with Extemporary Dance.
18 In 2020, at Cell Project Space in London there was an exhibition *X6 Dance Space (1976–80) Liberation Notes*.https://www.cellprojects.org/exhibitions [accessed 01.03.20].
19 More information about The Diorama is available: https://database.theatretrust.org.uk/resources/theatres/show/428-diorama-arts-centre. [accessed 17.04.20]. Libby Worth references Natural Dance Workshop in *Dancing Naturally: Nature, Neo-Classicism and Modernity in Early Twentieth-Century Dance*, ed. Rachel Fensham and Alexandra Carter (London: Palgrave MacMillan, 2011) 161.
20 In Chapter 2 I argue this position.
21 Somatics is a field within movement studies and bodywork. The term was used by U.S. movement therapist and philosopher Thomas Hanna in the 1980s to describe experiential movement practices.
22 In relation to movement for actors, I am particularly thinking of Alexander Technique, Feldenkrais and Yoga.
23 Mabel Ellsworth Todd's 'ideokenisis' is considered in Sondra Fraleigh, *Moving Consciously: Somatic Transformations through Dance, Yoga and Touch* (University of Illinois Press, 2015), 26. Gerda Alexander's 'Eutony' is considered in Claire Thomas, *Bodywork: What Type of Massage to Get and How to Make the Most of It* (New York: William Morrow and Co., 1995) 40–56. Irmgard Bartenieff's 'Bartenieff Fundamentals' is considered in Martha Eddy, 'The Ongoing Development of "Past Beginnings": A Further Discussion of Neuromotor Development and Somatic Links Between Bartenieff Fundamentals, Body–Mind Centering and Dynamic Embodiment', *The Journal of Laban Movement Studies*, 3: 55–79.
24 Rachel Kaplan and Anna Halprin, *Moving Toward Life: Five Decades of Transformational Dance* (Weleyan University Press, 1995), Sally Banes, *Democracy's Body: Judson Dance Theatre 1962–64* (Ann Arbor, Michigan, 1983), Sally Banes 'Trisha Brown; Gravity and Levity' in *Terpsichore in Sneakers: Post-Modern Dance* (Connecticut: Wesleyan University Press, 2011) 77.
25 Ruth Zaporah, *Action Theatre: The Improvisation of Presence* (Berkeley, AC: North Atlantic Books, 1995), Anne Bogart and Tina Landau, *The Viewpoints Book: A Practical Guide To Viewpoints and Composition* (Theatre Communications Group, 1st Edition, 2004).
26 Interview with Shona Morris, RADA (14,02,20).
27 Ibid.

28 Evans (2009) 20.
29 The *Me Too* or #Me Too movement, started by Alyssa Milano in 2006, a global campaign to speak out about sexual violence which garnered huge attention in 2017 was prompted by the public accusations from many high-profile female actors of sexual harassment and assault by Harvey Weinstein, an influential U.S. film producer, who was found guilty in 2020. Black Lives Matter was founded in 2013 in response to the acquittal of Trayvon Martin's murder. Black Lives Matter Foundation, Inc. is a global organization in the U.S., UK and Canada, whose mission is to eradicate white supremacy and to intervene in violence inflicted on Black communities by the state and vigilantes. The murder of George Floyd by a white policeman on 25.05.20 ignited global support for Black Lives Matter.
30 Anon, 'Drama School's Former Principal Apologises for Racist Remarks', BBC News, (12.06.20) https://www.bbc.co.uk/news/entertainment-arts-53027976 [accessed 17.06.20].
31 Georgia Snow, 'Drama Schools Commit to Ethical Guidelines to Tackle Sexual Harassment,' *The Stage* (19.04.18) https://www.thestage.co.uk/news/2018/drama-schools-commit-ethical-guidelines-tack [accessed 15.04.20].
32 Evans (2009) 134.
33 Rosi Braidotti, *Nomadic Theory: The Portable Rosi Braidotti* (New York & Chichester: Colombia University Press, 2011) 17.
34 Luce Irigaray posits that 'Women are concerned with a corporeal geography whereas men establish new linguistic territories', in Luce Irigaray, *Sexes and Genealogies* (New York: Columbia University Press, 1993) 175.
35 This pedagogy reflects the *via negativa,* where the actor is brought to an awareness which allows her to work to eliminate her physiological blocks.
36 Evans, email exchange (11.03.20).
37 Morris (14.02.20).
38 Snow, 24.
39 Vanessa Ewan and Debbie Green, *Actor Movement: Expression of the Physical Being* (London and New York: Bloomsbury Methuen Drama, 2015) 65.
40 Frankie Armstrong and Jenny Pearson (eds), *Well Tuned Women: Growing Strong Through Voicework* (London: The Women's Press, 2000) 109.
41 Equity https://www.equity.org.uk/, the UK trade union for creative practitioners and Tonic Theatre's 'Advance' initiative http://www.tonictheatre-advance.co.uk/ continue to agitate for gender equality.
42 The Act for Change Project https://www.act-for-change.com/# continues to agitate for diversity in the arts.
43 Elizabeth Grosz, *Volatile Bodies: Towards a Corporeal Feminism* (Bloomington and Indianapolis: Indiana University Press, 1994).
44 Grotz elucidates three feminist approaches to the body: egalitarian feminism, where the biology of a woman's body (menstruation, pregnancy etc.) is seen as both a constraint, stopping women from achieving equality, whilst enabling special qualities of insight. As seen in the work of Beauvoir or Wollstonecraft, biology itself both entraps and exonerates the female condition. The second category, social constructivists, such as Kristeva and Butler, includes Marxist and psychoanalytic feminists. These positions maintain a mind/body dualism where the body and images of the body, including notions of biology, are socially and culturally constructed. The body is at the whim of the effects of attitudes and beliefs and values. Grotz terms the third group of feminists of sexual difference, including Irigaray, Cixous, Butler, Spivak and Gallop. Here, the specificity of the body is crucial to understanding women's psychic and social existence, a lived body where 'instead of seeing sex as an essentialist and gender as a socially constructionist category, these thinkers are concerned to

undermine this dichotomy. The concept of the social body is a major strategy in this goal'. Grosz (1994) 3–24.
45  Ibid. 14.
46  Ibid. 13.
47  Ibid. 23.
48  Eve Sedgwick, *Touching Feeling: Affect, Pedagogy, Performativity* (Durham: Duke University Press, 2003) 8.
49  I overview this position in Chapter 1.
50  Iris Young, 'Throwing Like a Girl: Self-Objectification Predicts Adolescent Girls' Motor Performance', *Journal of Sport and Social Issues*, 29(79), (2005): 79–101.
51  I unpick this idea in Chapter 1.
52  Judith Butler, *Bodies that Matter: On the Discursive Limits of Sex* (London: Routledge, 1993) 234.
53  Evans (2009) 158–167.
54  Jane Gallop, 'Beyond the *Jouissance* Principle,' *Representations*, 7 (Summer, 1984): 110–115.
55  Julia Kristeva, *The Kristeva Reader* (Oxford: Blackwell Publishers, 1986).
56  Hélène Cixous, 'The Laugh of the Medusa,' *Signs*, 1(4), (1976): 875–893.
57  Luce Irigaray, *This Sex Which Is Not One* (Cornell University Press, 1985).
58  Rosi Braidotti, *Nomadic Theory: The Portable Rosi Braidotti* (New York & Chichester: Colombia University Press, 2011) 17.
59  Kristi Lempiäinen, 'With You but Different: *Jouissance* and Feminist Writing,' *Nora, Nordic Journal of Women's Studies*, 5(2), (1997): 105–118, 112.
60  Evans (2009) 159.
61  Ibid. 171.
62  Sandra Reeve, *Nine Ways of Seeing a Body* (Devon: Triarchy Press, 2011).
63  Bonnie Bird (1914–1995) was a member of the original Martha Graham Dance Company and was Director of Dance at Laban from 1974. Marion North (1925–2012) was Principal of Laban from 1973 to 2003. Jean Newlove (1923–2017) was Rudolph Laban's assistant when he first came to England and was Movement Director at Joan Littlewood's Theatre Workshop. Maggie Bury joined Theatre Workshop in 1946 and started East 15 in 1961.
64  Ewan (15.11.13).
65  Vanessa Ewan and Debbie Green, *Actor Movement: Expression of the Physical Being* (London & New York: Methuen, Bloomsbury, 2015) 205–243. A detailed practical methodology for her teaching of Laban is set out in Vanessa Ewan with Kate Sagovsky, *Laban's Efforts in Action: A Movement Handbook for Actors* (London & New York: Methuen, Bloomsbury, 2019).
66  Ewan (15.11.13).
67  Ewan, email exchange (30.05.20).
68  Ibid.
69  Ibid. X1.
70  Ibid. 68. The square brackets used here and in future references citing this text point to the move away from using the pronouns he/she to the neutral term they/their in the second edition (pending).
71  Elin Diamond, *Unmaking Mimesis* (London & New York: Routledge, 1997) 52.
72  Kristine Landon-Smith (07.03.13).
73  Interview with Vanessa Ewan, Zoom meeting (28.05.20).
74  Interview with Imogen Hale, Bristol (30.01.15).
75  For Ewan, 'Every movement is motivated with an inner driving force and an outer manifestation. For the actor to experience total transformation, the work must be both internal and external'. Ewan, 2015, 121–122.

76 Bertolt Brecht, *Brecht on Theatre: The Development of an Aesthetic* (London: Methuen, 1978) 196.
77 Ewan (2015) 101.
78 Wangh, op.cit.
79 Murray, op.cit.
80 Ewan (2015) 102.
81 Ewan (15.11.13).
82 Ibid.
83 Noelle McAfee, *Julia Kristeva: Routledge Critical Thinkers* (London & New York: Routledge, 2003) 98.
84 Ewan (2019) 51–78.
85 Ibid. 83–171.
86 Interview with Vanessa Ewan, Zoom meeting (28.05.20).
87 Ewan (2015) 229.
88 Sandra Reeve, *Nine Ways of Seeing a Body* (Devon: Triarchy Press, 2011) 43.
89 Ewan (2015) 229–243.
90 Interview with Hale, Bristol (30.01.15).
91 Ewan (2019) 25.
92 Observation of gender workshop with second-year BA actors at the RCSSD (06.06.14).
93 Elin Diamond, *Unmaking Mimesis* (London & New York: Routledge, 1997).
94 A thick description is a type of research common in social science, where context and behaviour is observed and analyzed. I open up the theory in more detail in Chapter 1. Joan Riviere, 'Womanliness as a Masquerade', in *Formations of Fantasy*, ed. Victor Burgin, James Donald, Cora Kaplan (London & New York: Routledge, 1986), Judith Butler, *Bodies that Matter: On the Discursive Limits of Sex* (London: Routledge, 1993), Jacqueline Rose, *Sexuality and the Field of Vision* (London: Verso, 1986).
95 Ewan (06.06.14).
96 Ibid.
97 Ibid.
98 Ibid.
99 Ibid.
100 Ibid.
101 Butler (1993).
102 Rose (1986) 62–64.
103 Ewan (15.11.13).
104 Ibid.
105 Ewan (2015) 250.
106 Ewan (15.11.13).
107 Ewan (2015) 247.
108 Ewan (2015) 250.
109 Ita O'Brien, 'Best Practice when Working with Intimacy, Simulated Sex Scenes and Nudity', https://www.itaobrien.com/intimacy-on-set-guidelines.html [accessed 05.09.19].
110 Ewan (2015) 245–259.
111 Vanessa Ewan, 'Intimacy and Movement Teaching', RCSSD (29.09.19).
112 Butler explains this as the 'hiatus of iterability' in *Bodies that Matter: On the Discursive Limits of Sex* (London: Routledge, 1993) 234.
113 Ben Spatz, *What a Body Can Do: Technique as Knowledge. Practice as Research* (London & New York: Routledge, 2015).
114 To date Dowling has set up the following: MA Acting with Song of the Goat in Poland, MA/MFA Actor/Performer Training with expedition at Rose Bruford College, MFA International Theatre Practice and Performance with National

Theatre Institute in Connecticut, USA (Three-year programme across three continents: UK, U.S., Moscow), MA Devised Theatre Practice with LISPA in Berlin, MFA Advanced Devising Practice with LISPA in Berlin, MA/MFA Integral Movement Performance Praxis with Thomas Prattki Centre for Integral Movement and Performance Studies, Berlin, Foundation Acting programme in Belfast, Northern Ireland. Dowling also worked with nuns in El Salvador 1998. Ran an 18-month movement training programme in Singapore 2001/2002. Ran a three-year theatre training programme for voice and movement teachers in Uzbekistan between 2015 and 2019. Ran a three-year Erasmus plus programme in Georgia with MA Acting programme.
115 This was an ethno-nationalist conflict that began in the 1960s and ended with The Good Friday Agreement in 1998.
116 Pagneux's work also draws on Feldenkrais, Gerda Alexander and Mary Wigman.
117 Ibid.
118 Ibid.
119 Morris (14.02.20).
120 Interview with Niamh Dowling, Toynbee Studios (14.11.19).
121 Cláudia Tatinge Nacimento, *Crossing Cultural Borders Through the Actor's Work: Foreign Bodies of Knowledge* (London & New York: Routledge) 10.
122 Ibid.
123 Braidotti (2011).
124 Reeve (2011) 47.
125 Here, I am thinking of the works referenced in Chapter 1: Karen Barard, 'Posthumanist Performativity: Toward an Understanding of How Matter Comes to Matter', *Signs*, 28(3), (Spring, 2003), Donna Haraway, *Simians, Cyborgs and Women: The Reinvention of Nature* (London & New York: Routledge, 1991) 127–149, Rosi Braidotti, *Nomadic Theory: The Portable Rosi Braidotti* (New York: Columbia University Press, 2011), Jane Bennet, *Vibrant Matter: A Political Ecology of Things* (Duke University Press, 2010), Elizabeth Grosz, *Volatile Bodies: Towards a Corporeal Feminism* (Indiana University Press, 1994).
126 Dowling (14.11.19).
127 Dowling trained at the Atkinson Ball College of Hypnotherapy and Hypno-healing in 2004.
128 Dowling came upon this form of therapy in 2013 and trained in it for four years to became a qualified practitioner in Organisational Constellations with a foundation year in Family Constellations in 2019. In order to better understand the intersections with Dowling's practice and this therapeutic processes I participated in two days of Systemic Constellations in London. That weekend there were about fifty people acting as representative and eight people who were the subjects. The therapy focused on the stories of the subject with the group acting as one to help the subject discover potential solutions or strategies in dealing with their problems. The practice operates through narrative therapy principles where, through telling of the story, the subject is able to revisit and reposition themselves within the situational narrative of their problem. The guiding principle is about coming closer to a point of truthfulness as, often in life we are unable to be completely truthful with ourselves and with others. As a result Systemic Constellations promotes the need to return to natural orders and to find our way back into truthfulness. In practice each constellation took around an hour and moved through the following stages. First, the subject sat next to the therapist in the circle and recounted his/her story. Then, facilitated by the therapist, she 'cast' her story from the representatives sitting in the circle. At any time in any constellation one could find oneself representing someone's father, child, ancestor or thematic tension (e.g. class, money, war). The representatives found their position in the room in the centre of the circle, in relation to each other within the context

## 132 Considering Practice

of the story. The therapist questioned the representatives about how they felt in this situation and they would answer 'in character'. The subject stepped into the spatial configuration and the therapist gave her lines to say to particular characters. Then, through guided conversation and exchange the subject moved towards finding ways to move from pain to open heartedness, often through a process of forgiveness. The therapist asked the subject to reflect on how she felt now. Finally, the subject would bow and receive applause from the representatives.

129 When we think about similar approaches in Drama in Education, Augusto Boal's theatre of the oppressed, most notably image theatre, comes to mind. Here a constituent group create images, which demonstrate specific forms of oppression and then, through the participant groups' re-imagining, and often with the help of a facilitator, or 'joker', the image is re-shaped to offer possible solutions. Augusto Boal, *Theatre of the Oppressed* (London: Pluto Press, 1979).Equally, Dorothy Heathcoat's 'mantle of the expert' approach invites the participant group to become the experts in forming an enterprise base through which to improvise solutions to specific problems. These practices operate through bodies in space and a collective interrogation of agency and power through proxemics and re-imagining narratives. Dorothy Heathcote, *Drama for Learning: Dorothy Heathcote's Mantle of the Expert Approach to Education* (Portsmouth: Heineman, 1995).
130 Observation of MA International Theatre and Performance, Rose Bruford College (20.05.19).
131 I consider ideas around female authority in Chapter 2.
132 Observation of MA International Theatre and Performance, Rose Bruford College (20.05.19).
133 Reeve (2011) 48.
134 Dowling (28.11.19).
135 Dowling (14.11.19).
136 Dowling (28.11.19).
137 I introduced Milde's framework for rehearsal discourse analysis in Chapter 2. She points to 10 different ways that language operates in the rehearsal room: 1. using a script, scripting text; 2. providing feedback; 3. providing explanations, providing background information; 4. Using improvisations; 5. Providing instructions and using keys as a way of providing instructions; 6. framing one's own activity; sharing ideas, thoughts, stories and anecdotes; 8. acting out/performing a version of; 9. providing/asking questions; providing/making suggestions. In Peck's framework for pedagogic analysis, again introduced in Chapter 2, I consider 9 points: how the hidden curriculum of personal and social knowledge is delivered; how an atmosphere of trust and relationality is built; how vulnerability is supported; how authority operates in the room; how choice and action are scaffolded for the actor; how instruction, explanation and feedback are given; how individual and group progress is managed within time constraints; how gender and/or ethnicity operates within the learning; how non-human materials, space, time and objects function in the learning exchange.
138 Evans (2009) 88.
139 George Lakoff and Mark Johnson, *Metaphors We Live By* (Chicago & London: The University of Chicago Press).
140 Observation of MA Collaborative Theatre Making, Toynbee Studios (28.11.19).
141 Ibid.
142 Ibid.
143 Ibid.
144 Ibid.
145 Dowling (31.10.20).

146 Evans refers to Royona Mitra's scholarship on Akram Khan, which proposes six themes to generate a new inter-culturalism in dance. From this, he identifies eight elements for a progressive movement training, which I return to in the Conclusion. Mark Evans, *Performance, Movement and the Body* (London: Macmillan International, Red Globe Press, 2019) 142–143.

# 5
# WOMEN AND THE MATTER OF ACTING

One of the ways to notice inequities is to count. As outlined in the Introduction, the absence of women in accounts of actor training is striking. Indeed, in *The Actor Training Reader* voice practitioner Kristin Linklater is the only female to be represented amongst thirteen international pedagogues.[1] In the second edition of *Twentieth Century Actor Training,* Alison Hodge increased the number of female practitioners from two to six out of fourteen: Monika Pagneux, Stella Adler, Anne Bogart, Joan Littlewood, Maria Knebel and Arianne Mnouchkine.[2] Although scholars are starting to address the dominant patriarchy, it seems important to question the particular nature of this absence. Is it that women are marginal in this field or have they avoided documenting their practices as methodologies? What might a gendered reconsideration reveal about the knowledges of acting?

One possible reason that women's work has remained relatively hidden is the way that practice is branded. Actor training is dominated by familial apostologies or tribal 'belonging' to a certain practice, where an actor might be described as being a Lecoq, Stanislavski or Meisner trained actor. The value economy of the acting industry is built on reputation and fame and although the UK tends towards a more heterogeneous 'tool-box' approach, practitioners bank on the provenance of their training as capital and actors become commodified, evolving into a brand to sell certain institutions.[3] The relative absence of women in the training lineages might suggest that they have been less concerned or successful in branding their practice. Di Trevis, the first female director at the National Theatre in the 1980s, considers how she resisted the commercialisation of training, finding the idea of a 'Trevis trained actor' abhorrent. She reflects that the notable disparity in branding practice might be considered to be a gendered trait.[4] Likewise, Catherine Alexander, a founding member of Complicité, suggests that the 'untouchable arrogance' of being able to set down your ideas and pass them on to future generations is perhaps a male domain, borne out of societal practices operating beyond the training of actors.[5] However, as we saw in Chapter 3, this is not reflected in voice training where women have similarly branded their work.[6] Voice practice, with its liberatory pedagogies and self-help formats is process driven and concerned with the politics of the unique voice. Thinking back to Chapter 1 and the feminist epistemologies that underpin acting, might it be that definitive notions of linear, product focused, one-size-fits-all acting methods alienate women who are more process orientated and attuned to personalised learning?

UK actor training methodologies have tended to come from male acting teacher/directors such as: Declan Donnellan (2002),[7] John Wright (2006),[8] Mike Alfreds (2007),[9] John Abbot (2010)[10] and Nick Moseley (2016).[11] The absence of women's practices offering alternative approaches in training perpetuates male dominated curriculums, which continue to ignore gender within practice. This is curious when we consider that so many UK drama schools were founded by women. During the early 1900s there was a flowering of training establishments in the South of England. Elsie Fogerty (1865–1945) was an English teacher of speech and drama who trained at the Paris Conservatoire and in 1889 taught at the Crystal Palace School of Art and Literature. In 1906, she founded the Central School of Speech and Drama, a school dedicated to the training of actors, which operated from Albert Hall, before moving to Swiss Cottage in 1967. At Central, drama teacher training courses, actor training and voice training ran alongside each other.[12] Another vocational drama school, the Italia Conti Academy of Theatre Arts, was founded by Ruth Conti (1874–1936) and grew out of a production at the Savoy Theatre in 1911, when Ruth, an actor, was employed to help direct the children. The Arts Educational School was first founded in 1939 and was originally known as the Cone–Ripman School. It was formed as a result of a merger between the Cone School of Dancing, founded in 1919 by Grace Cone, and the Ripman School, founded in 1922 by Olive Ripman. These pre-war London drama schools enabled developmental approaches to education and vocational actor training to develop beside each other.[13]

After the war years, this trend continued with women setting up a number of prestigious schools. In 1950, Rose Bruford, an actor and voice teacher who taught at the Royal Academy of Music, founded a unique drama school in Kent that aimed to unify theatre practice and drama education under one curriculum. She fought to actively foster the interdependency of teaching and acting and 'aimed to train actors who could teach and teachers who could act and foster a spirit of collaboration'.[14] This recognition of the education inherent in a vocational training led Rose Bruford to become the first college in the UK to offer a degree in Acting and Theatre Practice in 1976. Margaret Bury and Jean Newlove, an assistant to Rudolph Laban, founded East 15 in 1961 in Essex. Both women were long-time members of Joan Littlewood's Theatre Workshop and directed the students in the style of the company, drawing on Littlewood's collaborative practice. The Theatre Workshop was based in the Theatre Royal, Stratford, part of the East 15 postal district from which it took its name.[15] These women were formative in establishing and developing UK actor training, their pioneering work placing pedagogical enquiry at the forefront of practice.

Perhaps it is an orientation towards pedagogical processes that has precluded documentation, as few UK women have documented their approaches. Contrastingly, American practitioners have successfully branded their practices as methods: Uta Hagen (1973); Stella Adler (2000);[16] Ivana Chubbuck (2004); Mary Overlie, Anne Bogart and Tina Landau's *Viewpoints*;[17] Tanya Gerstle's *Pulse Training*[18] and Susana Bloch's *Alba Emoting*.[19] One could speculate that the U.S. encourages a more commodified training culture. In the twenty-first century, UK women who teach acting tend to deliver their interpretation of European, American or Eastern methodologies inherited through their own training. In many cases, teachers have been students at the same institutions and so a familial apostology is maintained – this is most clearly evidenced by Dee Cannon, acting tutor at RADA, whose Stanislavski teaching methodology was passed down from her mother, Doreen Cannon (1930–1995), who was Head of Acting at RADA for many years.[20] In the UK, the result of this pass-it-on acting tradition is that it is the institution itself that becomes a brand, as an in-house style is maintained, which creates a 'RADA actor' or an 'East 15' actor. Occasionally, female practitioners have documented their approaches, particularly when it offers an integrated methodology and liberatory process, for example Dorinda Hulton's *The Creative Actor*,[21] and more recently Experience Bryon's *Integrative Performance*[22] and Amanda Brennan's *Energetic Performer*.[23] Some have made significant developments to curriculum design: Catherine Alexander has developed and run the Collaborative and Devised Theatre Degree (CDT) at RCSSD since 2006, to redefine traditional understanding of conservatoire actor training and to position the actor as theatre-maker. However, although women are better represented as course leads in the fields of voice and movement there are comparatively few women leading acting programmes and in positions to shape curriculums.[24] It is curious that, when females significantly outnumber males in drama school applications, acting seems to remain a male dominated terrain. If a female actor trains in a UK institution it is likely that she will be taught from a canon dominated by male lineages, with a male head of acting, mostly performing in plays written by men, where the majority of challenging roles are for men. This continues to affirm systems of male privilege as the way to pass on knowledge. One practitioner described this as: 'An old fashioned cabal of patriarchs setting an agenda that is no longer relevant'.[25] Such a response reflects the frustration at the sluggish movement in actor training towards gender equality and progressive pedagogies.

Although male lineages dominate the landscape, when we widen our field of vision the significant contributions of female practitioners to acting pedagogies are brought into sharp relief. When we think about acting, not as a method but as a politicised process of coming to learn we can re-invigorate the knowledges of acting technique. In order to survey the broad UK training landscape, and to consider what a gendered re-framing might reveal, I consider the work of two practitioners who, at the time of writing, were working in different contexts: the industry and university and drama school training. Each example of practice offers a snapshot of the practitioner's work and looks at how they try to solve particular problems: Kristine Landon-Smith develops an intra-cultural practice, teaching the actor to work through their multiple cultural identity and Alison Hodge develops a relational core training, where the actor examines coming into being through the other.[26] Both practitioners produce Critical Acting Pedagogies, where techniques of race, gender and acting intersect. My concern is to better understand how learning to act enables the personal and social knowledge, which I term 'the hidden curriculum' of acting and my focus is the way that they scaffold, or structure learning through moments of interaction. In observing rehearsal practices I apply the fluid analytical methodology explained in Chapter 2.[27] I'm interested in how these pedagogies intersect with new feminist materialisms to foreground the matter of acting.

## Kristine Landon-Smith: Intra-cultural acting

Kristine Landon-Smith is the joint founder of Tamasha, one of the longest running multicultural theatre companies in the UK, which brings contemporary work of Asian influence to the British stage. As part of the Black, Asian and Minority Ethnic (BAME) community, born to an Indian mother and Australian father, Landon-Smith acknowledges her marginalised position. She explains: 'I am conscious of my own mixed heritage background because I position myself as "the other", so I'm already "the other" with "the others"'.[28] Cultural theorist Rustom Bharucha coined the term 'intra-cultural' as a way to describe how different communities and cultures exist alongside one another in the same country.[29] Bharucha was concerned with the 'cultural tourism' he perceived in the work of Barba, Brook and Grotowski, the ethics of representation underlying cross-cultural exchange and the social relationships that constitute it.[30] Landon-Smith's praxis responds to these concerns by enabling multi-ethnic actors in the UK to work with their multiple, hybrid identities as a powerful asset for performing.

In 1977, Landon-Smith trained as an actor in Australia at the National Institute of Dramatic Art (NIDA), but left after a year to complete an acting degree at the Royal Scottish Conservatoire. It was her own negative experience of training that led her to teaching and directing. She explains: '[W]e had a lot of teachers who, in my mind, didn't help me as an actor. I mean we all sort of had to get on with it'.[31] In 1987, she taught at the National School of Drama in Delhi, directing *Untouchable*,[32] cementing her role as a director, and in 1988, she trained and subsequently worked with Philippe Gaulier in Paris. She returned to the UK and with the playwright and actor Sudha Bhuchar set up Tamasha, a training and production company, with the remit to provide opportunities and development for British Asian artists. Tamasha operates in three distinct ways: firstly, it provides a platform for new writing by BAME artists in the UK, thus making the stories of under-represented communities central to the work; secondly, it builds new audiences; thirdly, it provides intra-cultural training for actors, directors and writers and outreach work in schools and communities. Tamasha has now been operating since 1989 and has 'played a key role in driving the crossover of Asian culture into the British mainstream',[33] with a mixture of new writing and adaptations, achieving success with *East is East* in 1996. Between 2013 and 2016, Landon-Smith taught at NIDA whilst completing an MPhil investigating her practice as research. Currently, in 2020, she is Head of Acting at Drama Studio UK. Since 2013, I have observed her lead five day-long intra-cultural training workshops, including a live transcontinental exchange between the UK and Australia, and three weeks rehearsal for the production *The Arrival*, based on the illustrated novel by Shaun Tan, co-created with Sita Brahmachari, which toured the UK in 2014.

Landon-Smith's intra-cultural practice illustrates what I term a Critical Acting Pedagogy (CAP), which considers the blurred space between the performative and performance as a critical form of enquiry.[34] By learning to recognise our performative behaviours, by which I mean the repeated bodily and speech acts that inscribe ideas of race, age, gender and class on our bodies, we might challenge and resist their forms of production in performance. Landon-Smith's practice opens up the space between the lived body and the social body as a reflexive space for the actor to utilise the political potential of her/his intra-cultural identity. As such, this practice can be seen to challenge limiting notions of sameness, where actors acknowledge their multiple selves to work with the positivity of difference. The foundational features of this pedagogy re-orientate gendered power to work with the *via positiva*.

Landon-Smith's own training and teaching with Philippe Gaulier means that she situates constructs of 'le jeu' (play) as central to her teaching.[35] She begins any workshop or rehearsal with games, or *paida*,[36] designed to help the actor 'play well', such as 'keepy uppy', where the group work as a team to keep a ball in the air for the longest time possible, name tag or musical chairs. Using games at the start of any rehearsal or workshop establishes a culture of learning through play and flattens hierarchy, as Landon-Smith plays with and referees the actors, enabling a dynamic of shared risk taking. The games allow her to quickly diagnose the qualities and habits that actors bring to their practice. She can identify who might be holding back through fear, who is playing 'too hard' and where individuals hold their energy (high or low). She makes 'playing well' explicit, asking people to identify when they observe this behaviour in others. 'Playing well' is when the actor is able to give all their attention outwards, whilst being relaxed and open in their attitude and physicality. Landon-Smith uses humour to engage and cajole, whilst instilling a sense of competition in the play to energise and sharpen the actor – praising, gently teasing, encouraging or challenging. She invites actors to reflexively question their own responses and guides them to observe performative habits.

In Gaulier's clown practice, the experience of 'flopping' is central to the pedagogy where, in order to find her clown, the actor is put in situations where she becomes foolish and 'flops' in front of the audience. Through this exposure, she discovers the ways in which she is funny. As previously examined, learning by confronting one's blocks, *via negativa*, is a formative pedagogic process in actor training.[37] The actor independently diagnoses and finds a solution to their own performance problems and through this experience becomes their own teacher – an autodidact. Landon-Smith guides the actor to diagnose her own habits through flopping and then to *re-learn* how to play well. However, she re-orientates Gaulier's pedagogic approach, to facilitate a shared problem solving – a joint experimentation.[38] The autodidact process through *via negativa* is a particularly impactful pedagogy in actor training but it requires a robustness from the individual and can be a hit-or-miss approach.[39] Because the teacher withholds explicit explanation, the actor can be left feeling exposed, vulnerable and humiliated.[40] Chapter 2 problematised the oppressive affects of this guru/apprentice approach to learning, which has characterised the male dominated training lineages and, which I suggest, can disempower and, at worst, damage the actor.[41]

Landon-Smith's pedagogy has developed in response to two aspects of Gaulier's practice she felt were lacking: explicit and direct feedback, where the actor is given strategies to solve their problems and a kinder, more supportive approach, which does not leave them feeling vulnerable and belittled. She recognises that, whilst she personally benefited from Gaulier's pedagogy, some actors struggle with it and she reflects on her preference for affirmative learning:

> I do ultimately feel it is better for people to work from the crest of a wave with a level of confidence and feel good. And I must say, I personally am uncomfortable when people flop for too long. I've got an empathy for that, so maybe, naturally, I do move people beyond that in a session or in a rehearsal room. I don't let the actors leave the floor and feel bad. I'm interested in helping people.[42]

Landon-Smith's pedagogy recalls Braidotti's affirmative approach as an antidote to a negative value system where one can only advance through pain or suffering.[43] She is not naively suggesting that struggle can be avoided, but believes that in adopting an affirmative position and working from the positivity of difference, development is supported and sustainable.[44] In this way endurance is viewed as a positive process, pleasure as opposed to pain is privileged and there is a joint experimentation between teacher/director and actor, driven by intrinsic motivation as opposed to extrinsic sanction and fear of failure. This pedagogical approach illustrates the *via positiva* in practice.[45]

Landon-Smith's authority as a teacher is built on transparency. She is, 'quite happy to have a very open rehearsal room' and positions herself as a diagnostician with inclusive, direct and incisive observation, rejecting Stanislavskian psychological terminology for the simpler terms of somatic 'felt sense'.[46] Andrea Milde, a linguist whose work was discussed in Chapter 2, has researched Landon-Smith's practice and identifies key terms as forming part of the dialogic scaffolding structures, where learning happens in the moments of interaction between actor and teacher.[47] Terms such as being 'open', 'soft', 'full', 'fluid', 'forward' are used to explain the quality of 'playing well' in contrast to 'playing too hard', 'being too heavy' or 'inward'.[48] These material descriptors recall the imagistic and metaphorical language of movement teaching explored in Chapter 4, which foregrounds the somatic felt sense of the lived body as opposed to the psychological state. As Landon-Smith establishes herself as both participant and adjudicator, there is a sense of working for and with the group, allowing her to pick up on actors' habits or defense mechanisms from the start with coaching such as, 'Don't play too hard'!; 'Listen more carefully'!; 'Lighter'!'[49] This dialogue is immediately transparent and direct. For instance, fear, which is acknowledged as a primary obstacle, is openly discussed and strategies offered. As a result, an atmosphere of trust is established, with Landon-Smith explicitly explaining the learning: 'What I'm doing with you is I'm helping you to explore what it is that happens when you are open'.[50] This openness establishes a shared responsibility for each other's progress, where actors can learn 'from the crest of a wave'.[51]

## 'All these little parts of yourself'[52]

Landon-Smith's approach has developed to help actors, in particular BAME actors whose first language is not English, solve the disconnect that can happen when working with text. She explains that for her, 'Chapter 1 is the actor ... normally chapter 1 is the text, which is very problematic'.[53] As seen in the work of Jane Boston and Nadine George in Chapter 3,[54] destabilising the tyranny of the text and giving the power back to the somatic self can be viewed through a new feminist materialist lens, in the way that it fights matter with matter. Actors are brought to discover the multiple voice, where the symbolic formal structures of speech (*langue*), work beside the language and word (*parole*).[55] Julia Kristeva genders these forms when she positions the symbolic (text) as belonging to a male domain and the semiotic (voice) to the female.[56] This theoretical construct is made manifest in Landon-Smith's practice as the semiotic and symbolic, text and voice, are interrogated in their beside-ness and made explicit for the actor.

A disconnect can result from feeling alienated or intimidated by the text, particularly when working with Shakespeare. This is exacerbated for BAME actors who are trained to deny their accent or dialect and perform a homogenised self that obscures their heritage. English, as spoken by multi-ethnic communities, is seen to have 'impurities'[57] and by accessing their multiple voices actors, 'think of themselves as particular rather than neutral, to play with difference in the rehearsal room'.[58] This is facilitated through various stages of improvisation, where the actor uses her first language in order to connect to the space between self and text, to inhabit the space between the symbolic and semiotic. In this way, she moves to connect speech with voice as a bodily felt experience. The power hierarchy shifts from serving the law of the text to taking control of it. Adriana Cavarero's theory of 'multiple voices' critiques how the agency of the voice is sidelined when compared to speech, when it is through the voice that relationships are created, which in turn enables political power.[59] Thinking of voice in terms of identity, Cavarero's multiple voice points to a vital materialism, where the body, in its essential hybridity and between-ness, can claim its agency, resisting and re-shaping cultural inscriptions. Landon-Smith, who originally considered becoming a voice teacher, helps actors rediscover the positive potential of their hybridity and, as the layers of text and speech are peeled away, the self emerges in a constant state of becoming.

The exposure of multiple selves occurs through a form of Active Analysis, where the actor moves behind the text, to explore her own responses in the given circumstance.[60] Once the logical sequence of actions and intentions is discovered, the text is layered on the top. In this way the actor's self is the starting point, rather than any constructed notion of character. This enables the actor's double consciousness, where she is connected both to her 'self' and to herself being in performance. In an acting master-class, where actors came prepared with a speech to work on, Landon-Smith states the aim of the session (to resolve any disconnect that occurs when working with text) and, after enabling the state of 'playing well', she offers a simple structure such as counting consecutively as a group from one to twenty. When she claps her hands, she asks an actor to move into their text. Through this, the group is able to witness how there is an immediate tendency to disconnect one's own voice to perform an appropriation of oneself, with an inscribed 'Britishness' and Received Pronunciation. In doing so, the direct connection to an inner self in the situation is lost and the actor becomes 'closed', explained by a participant as, 'You can hear your own voice lying. You can feel your physicality lying'.[61] This fascinating reflection acknowledges a moment of reflexive self-surveillance, where performative action is critically felt.

Landon-Smith's skill lies in her ability to spontaneously diagnose what is the most useful and, most importantly, pleasurable improvisation for each individual to play to locate their multiple voice. Her approach is diagnostic and relational, 'I totally just respond to what's in front of me'.[62] By observing and talking to each individual about their cultural heritage and background, she is able to frame an improvisation that either directly, or obliquely, reflects the circumstance of the text. At no point does she analyse or discuss the text itself.

In her diagnosis of each individual's needs she will strip back language, asking some to improvise in their first language, others to work with a strong accent and some to imitate the accent of a family member. Other actors and sometimes the whole group are part of the improvisation. She side-coaches where necessary, stepping into the improvisation to raise the stakes and provoke a 'fuller', imaginative connection to the situation. Once the improvisation is fully underway and the actor is open to the impulses and relationships that have emerged, she will direct her to move to the text, sometimes still in her first language and eventually in English. The text falls lightly over the top of action and the actor maintains a connection to her 'natural' voice.

Although ostensibly Active Analysis is a common method of working with text, the way that layers of speech and language are peeled back to expose the multiple voice reveals the body/voice as an expression of hybrid identities. The dismantling of language, speech, dialect, accent, voice, illuminates the different tempo rhythms of different selves.[63] As actor Antonio Harris explains:

> For example, often in English you assume a certain tone. So I am much more relaxed when I speak in English, I am much more one tone. Yet if I speak in Italian, all at once I will become more articulate, for instance my voice goes a lot louder, I use my body expression much more. I can often forget that because I have learnt to speak English so well. But by allowing me to speak Italian you bring all these little parts of yourself out, which you could forget if you are just speaking in English.[64]

The breath, tone, pitch and inflection create a distinct vocal and physical rhythm and the imposition of different rhythms changes the psychophysical experience. Landon-Smith leads the actors to navigate the space between these different rhythms and identities. For the white actor this might be the space between themselves and themselves playing text; for the BAME actor this may be themselves as an actor working in the UK industry and their cultural identity inherited from their parents, for as Landon-Smith points out, 'Everything you learn from your parents is just in you, without you realising it is'.[65] This connection to family through their first language can provide an emotional release. Jackie Le, an actor in *The Arrival* acknowledged, she felt more confident and 'full' as she only spoke to her parents in Vietnamese, so the rhythm of the language immediately tapped into her most vulnerable self. She explained: 'It feels more natural when I have to express emotion. I feel that I can express it with assertiveness or directness. So I try to channel them [my parents] when I speak'.[66] By helping the actor gain access to the space between multiple voices, Landon-Smith guides her to access her vulnerability. Actors talk of the 'pride' they feel when bringing their cultural heritage into the process of their learning.[67]

## *'Doing' race*

Elise Pineau makes a distinction between Performance Studies as a kinetic process, which interrogates notions of power, choice and agency and the 'mimesis' of acting.[68] From this perspective, acting is seen to perpetuate normative assumptions and values, which negates its political potential. In Landon-Smith's practice the space between the performative and the performed self of the actor enables a critical acting pedagogy, which challenges Pineau's reductive view.[69] In 2014, a cross-continental training workshop, where a live feed enabled six multiethnic Australian actors to simultaneously undertake training with six multiethnic UK actors, brought notions of space between into sharp focus.[70] This event asked actors to improvise with each other through the live broadcast and initiated a provocative inter-continental debate about commonly experienced problems of homogenising cultural identity and appropriating racial stereotypes in acting. Paradoxically, Landon-Smith utilises performative actions that inscribe stereotypes as the lever to liberate the actor to work from her 'cultural self', and to reconsider notions of difference as positive. She uses the term 'cultural self' to refer to the actor's inherited culture and reflects on her experience of working with an Aboriginal actor at NIDA. At first, the actor was resistant to the idea of playing from her Aboriginal self, as she saw it as limiting her potential casting by being forced to play a negative racial stereotype.[71] When she attempted this approach, she performed '[A] mimic of her own culture. She presented what she thought the cultural authority wanted to see of her, the Aboriginie'.[72] In other words, the actor was 'quoting' race in the way that she drew on the repeated performative action, which inscribes the enthic type. Judith Butler in *Bodies that Matter* refers to such actions as 'doing' race, where through repetition, assumptions about gender or race become assimilated.[73] Looking at Landon-Smith's practice we can see how by 'doing' race the actor gains awareness of the positive power, *potencia*, that her difference allows. Landon-Smith reflects on the way that this enables the multiple voices of her ancestry to be heard. She explains, 'When she allows herself to tap into her own personal narrative, she brings this echo of her history. It's extraordinary and you can hear the history in her performance'.[74] Only by experiencing the difference between performative action and performed action could the actor at the NIDA workshop start to recognise her choices.

Performing the stereotype as an anti-model is used in Boalian performative pedagogy to critically expose the social constructions that subjugate minorities. By modeling the negative stereotype in a role play, you then re-model, repeating the performance in different ways and working with different choices to reflexively challenge limiting representations.[75] This approach frames acting as a kinetic process of discovery that opens up a site of resistance in performance. Actors might be asked to appropriate 'Chinese Man' or 'African woman' as a way to get them to connect with their inherited culture and so explore this part of themselves through an-other.[76] Rather than seeing these as stereotypes, Landon-Smith prefers the term 'cultural sign-posts', or in other words, 'archetypes'. She explains:

> [T]he Indian mother and the Indian son relationship, it's a cultural signpost. The person who is playing that will have some knowledge of that and so they can be the expert and they'll know how to play the Indian son and the Indian mother and whilst it might be a stereotype to start with, we can keep modeling it and then end up with the nuance. So I do subconsciously go to cultural signposts.[77]

In improvisation, Landon-Smith uses situations where a tension is built around an imbalance of power. For example, waiter and customer, nanny and employer or king and servant. In this way she uses a structure of anti-model, where a negative and oppressive power structure is revealed in order for the imbalance to be critiqued and possible solutions found. The cultural context is approximated, but through this comes an awareness of 'the difference between appropriating yourself and being yourself'.[78] By placing actors in situations, whether bound by racial stereotypes or by the circumstances of failing (not getting the job, losing the boyfriend), she invites them to defend their position and raises the stakes, which is the hook to engage full commitment to the situation. Once a clear objective is being played at high stakes, the actor moves beyond the stereotype. The shift in confidence and ownership brought to the playing of the text is palpable and transformative. It can appear as if Landon-Smith is unpeeling the layers of socially constructed behaviour.

In her summary of the key features of postmodern performance, Harris considers that all performance is always already inevitably within quotation marks and it is the visibility or loudness of the citation that determines the style and effect of performance.[79] The actor shifts between mimicry, mimesis, appropriation and presentation to reveal the choices available and to locate herself within this citation gauge. For Landon-Smith, the concern that modeling might be seen as reductive shuts down the transformative positivity of difference and results in race being homogenised. Only by being open to questioning can stereotypes and ignorance be challenged as 'you cannot censor in an intra-cultural practice'.[80] She uses the performativity of their 'cultural self' to guide the actor to experience the tempo rhythms in voice and body that are deeply embedded in their cultural psyche, to 'use that cultural power to find the unpredictable rhythm'.[81] Butler mentions the way in which 'a hiatus of iterability' interrupts normativity and allows for the potential of difference.[82] By enabling actors to work through iteration with the multiplicity and differences within themselves, as well as between each other, Landon-Smith's critical pedagogy makes space for these discoveries.

## Alison Hodge: The relational actor

Alison Hodge, who passed away in November 2019, has been described as 'one of the most original actor trainers'.[83] She was artistic director of The Quick and the Dead, a European ensemble that began in 2005 with postgraduate students at Royal Holloway University, where she taught from 1996 to 2013 whilst leading actor training workshops in UK drama schools and internationally. Her scholarship, *Twentieth Century Actor Training*[84] and *Core Training for the Relational Actor*[85] have made an important contribution to the field. From 2013, she worked freelance and continued to develop Core Training with her company of five female performers from Spain, Italy, Turkey, Greece and the UK. Hodge's first company, Theatre Alibi, travelled to Poland in the 1990s to train with Gardzienice and her collaboration with Wlodzimierz Staniewski is a well-documented formative influence.[86] Less considered are the female influences on Hodge's teaching, which can be traced through a genealogy of Scaravelli yoga trainers (Diane Long, Sophie Hall and Caroline Lang)[87] and through the legacy of Joan Littlewood.[88] Built on principles of Merleau-Ponty's phenomenology,[89] Hodge's practice helps actors develop their relational awareness and their capacity for reciprocity.[90] During five days of workshops at RCSSD between 2013 and 2015, I experienced her work as participant researcher. Before I examine key aspects of her approach in relation to feminist materialisms, it is useful to consider the ideological underpinnings and foundational features of her pedagogic practice. One of the first things to note is the way that she examines gender as technique, responding to ideas around female-ness.

In part, Hodge's practice developed as an antidote to the male dominated Polish lineages of actor training. She reflects on the dominant masculine body in the laboratory theatres of the 1960s and 1970s and how, whilst women such as Anna Zubryzcka, Iga Rodowicz-Czechowska, Dorota Parowska and Krz Mazeika were part of the company, 'Gardzienice's work is extremely dominated by men ... it was a masculine world ... it's a male director talking about his perspective on life. That was for me possibly the hardest thing to connect with'.[91] Hodge left Poland to address a number of 'silences' she perceived in the landscape of actor training: the absence of the female body, the neutralising of gender and the lack of women in the lineages of training. She elucidates:

> The thing that I was really interested in is how the female body and the notion of the female actor is incredibly under researched and under celebrated. I was really sure when I'd seen it in drama schools here [in the UK], that there were sort of quite clichéd notions of what a female actress is, whether it's the old crone or the character actor or whatever ... [T]here was an absence of the female body and female presence in a lot of actor training.... I think it's very interesting, the space for women and that needs to be looked at. One of the impulses for the work was to celebrate the

female body, female ugliness, female imperfections, the non-traditional archetypical female stuff and try to find ways of exploring femaleness in artistic ways that are not traditional.[92]

Although inspired by the female condition, Hodge didn't want her practice to be ghettoised as a solely female training, recognising that its central features – touch, breath, physical contact and rhythm – are universal.[93] Inevitably, working with a company of women orientated the concerns. One of the actors in the company, Daniela García Casilda, reflects, 'Ali pays a lot of attention to femininity. The training is useful to everybody, men and women, but it embraces the feminine universe'.[94] Another company member, Tatiana Bre, sees the practice not so much as a 'feminine universe', but one that enables the actor to connect to their personal and cultural landscape. 'So, in that sense, all sorts of preconceptions or stereotypes related to sex are questioned'.[95] For the actors, the work has enabled an extended investigation of gender and acting techniques as intersected and embodied.

Hodge's *Core Training for the Relational Actor* reflects a new feminist materialist ideology. She foregrounds the body to explore how the sense of self comes into being through its encounters in a constant state of becoming. Likewise, she resists naming her practice as a 'methodology' but explains it as an organic process, constantly in flux, fluid and liminal. Bodies are not to be 'trained' through a set regime to display a particular skill. As she says, 'We don't want to perfect, or correct our bodies, or hone a particular aesthetic body but to celebrate their uniqueness and the particularity of each encounter'.[96] This encounter is different each time the company meet, as individual lives have moved on. 'We always start from where we are and who we are'.[97] Hodge teaches actors to experience how consciousness exists in relation to others, as opposed to an individual sense of self, which, she suggests, dominates traditions of Western actor training.[98] Reflecting Gardzienice's practice of mutuality,[99] where the state of being exists through the inter-relational action with the other(s), Hodge works on the self as 'a fundamentally relational understanding'.[100] This moves beyond dualistic notions of the self and other, to focus on the space between, the inter-relational connection among the self, space, human and non-human.

Hodge has gone some way to theorise her approach through socio-scientific paradigms, referencing the three E's of cognitive consciousness – embedded, enactive, embodied.[101] She dismantles dualisms to present a lived body as an integrated organism and explains how the definition of self 'is becoming more porous, more fluid, that we are less easily divisible from each other and our environment'.[102] In this, I see traces of the agential realism of feminist scientist Karen Barad,[103] and the 'thing-ness' of Jane Bennet,[104] who have 'mattered' consciousness, drawing attention to the agency of non-human objects, atoms and molecules. In training, Hodge works to develop an actor's relational awareness to all elements of 'other' including space, time and objects. She explains:

> [T] here isn't such a thing as an object. They each have their own quality and presence so nothing is finite. We are all in relation to things that are changing. That's a much bigger conversation about capitalism and about products and how we choose to see the world, but actually it's all alive ... things are in a process as we are.[105]

Working with the materials of space, time and non-human objects – sticks, chairs, veils, skirts – allows the actor to investigate the object's agency and its ability to affect and transform her body. Casilda recalls,

> I remember at some point working with skirts as if they were a mask, almost a mask of femininity. You had to feel the skirt and work physically with it. And of course it was bringing many issues, physical and emotional about being a female.[106]

Working with non-human agents looks beyond the psychophysical towards what Frank Camilleri explains as a *bodyworld*, responsive to advancements in materialist paradigms.[107] Whereas scientific thinking pervades Hodge's practice, at its roots, perhaps through its Polish lineage, is an interconnectedness to nature, life and humanity. Sandra Reeve might describe this as the ecological body: 'a system dancing within systems, rather than an isolated unit'.[108] This spiritual quality, reflecting its Polish Catholic foundations, works beside the scientific to ignite the empathetic and emotional affect of this practice, which develops the hidden curriculum of acting.

In particular, the work advances listening, impulse, instinct, sensitivity and empathy. Hodge cites Evan Thompson to assert: 'One's consciousness of oneself as an embodied individual in the world is founded on empathy'.[109] Empathy has been situated as a gendered behaviour, with females tending to show more development in the neurological connections of the right brain.[110] The right and left sides of the brain offer different types of attention with the left more focused and the right more holistic, responsible for the capacities that help us form bonds with others, emotional intelligence and empathy. Ian McGilchrist, a psychiatrist who observed The Quick and the Dead in 2011, recognised in this practice, 'a distillate of between-ness, in enabl[ing] the actors' practical engagement of right and left brain activities'.[111] Hodge explains this type of attention as 'polyphonic', which allows single-minded attention, where we are thinking about ourselves, to work beside double-minded attention, where we also keep someone else's thoughts in mind. This 'thinking beside',[112] attention, is both empathetic and political, as it ignites responsibility for the other; as Hodge explains, 'The individual is dead. It's all about the relationship'.[113] This moves towards what Phelan describes as a 'reciprocal gaze',[114] which develops empathy through a critical shared somatic pedagogy. When one thinks of the term 'Core', the association of core muscles tends to direct thinking towards the body; however,

Hodge points to the etymological meaning of the term, which has the double referent to body and emotion. Learning how to feel places the body as the 'locus for one's feelings'.[115] This awareness of interdependency and co-creation enables a critical somatic pedagogy. Observing Hodge's work, the atmosphere and dynamic changes in the room. People appear to become more careful with each other, more caring, with a potential for greater understanding.

Hodge's practice enables a Critical Acting Pedagogy, reflecting a number of feminist traits, including the inclination towards empowering participants and encouraging their ownership of the training process:

> I'm not sure you can teach anything to anybody. If I said do it in a precise way, you would never take ownership. Work with it until you find the way that it makes sense, the way that it works for you.[116]

Like other female practitioners, Hodge is wary of branding training as a method or product, encouraging actors to 'Try to think about how it really works'.[117] This situated pedagogy enables people to learn through each other, which 'depends on the group of people'[118] and Hodge, like Landon-Smith, explains her approach as diagnostic:

> The more you see who is in the room, the amount of bodies you have looked at, after a while you begin to understand what people need or what needs encouraging. I am very instinctive. I work with who's in the room. I work with what I see.[119]

In practice, Hodge establishes a calm and respectful space and she does not present herself as having the answers. She works with a 'follow me' structure, where she models an exercise, but the action is always in relation to another, she is never presenting an individual technical score to be perfected (unlike Eastern training structures).[120] Whilst she demonstrates the technical way to do an exercise, *how* you do it depends on who you are working with and what qualities you bring to the task together. The structure of learning is through 'follow me' and then 'joint experimentation' and Hodge talks throughout the class, coaching and questioning.[121] She partners when needed, moving around the room and touching the bodies to shift positions, or pointing to where attention should be. The language is encouraging and specific, for example: 'Notice people – don't just glaze – really notice – that's the energy you want'; 'Don't get heavy – lift your centre'; 'Use the energy from your partner'; 'Keep the space alive between you'; 'Don't be polite, just negotiate'.[122]

In this work, the challenge is less about an individual confronting psychophysical blocks through the *via negativa*, but the subtle psychophysical possibilities investigated together. Hodge enables discussion throughout and, just as she helps people attend to the moments of pause (sats),[123] between breath and impulse, she scaffolds the learning through moments of reflection, following the practice of educationalist Schön,[124] allowing for regular mini plenaries. Enabling time and space for reflection is a key pedagogical feature as she explains:

> I'm a great believer in immersive work and then reflection, because I think it can become either precious or one particular note if you don't allow for pauses. Sometimes people do need to let off a little steam. They want to share it and if you silence it … making notes an hour later is no good, sometimes you have to name it at the time.[125]

Unlike Staniewski, Hodge welcomes discussion into the room, encouraging critique and comment to enable a liberatory pedagogy where actors take ownership of their learning.[126] Working through the body as a way to better understand our relationships allows participants to consider possible sites of resistance, to seek more inclusive ways of being in the world.

## Foundational practices: Sensuality, touch and feeling

Hodge identifies four strands operating through her work: Attention and Attending; The Porous Body; The Feeling Body; Working with Time and Space.[127] Here, I focus on the Feeling Body and consider how Hodge works with touch to scaffold a number of skills including: polyphonic attention, tempo-rhythm, breath, voice, impulse and caretaking.[128] She acknowledges that sensuality, touch and feeling have been starting points in her practice, noting that 'One of the big things in training that we neglect is touch. Touch forces you to connect with sensation and rhythm [and has] enormous capacity to open feelings in the body'.[129] Restoring touch as central to a sensory engagement with the world presents the body as 'porous', the skin not as a boundary, but as a place where one makes contact with the other. Anthropologist Timothy Ingold repositions touch as being as important as sight and hearing, as a bodily attitude that helps us make sense of the world.[130] Touch unlocks sensuality and feeling, which have been essentialised as a more female domain.[131]

Hodge and participants work barefoot and the practice recognises that tactility is not just through the hands, but also, most importantly, through the feet. Touch through the feet, hands, spine, body is the reciprocity that teaches an actor to move beyond the complex language of the social space to listen to 'the quieter areas of the body'.[132] Neuroscientist Damasio points to how 'physiological responses are what initiates an emotional reaction'.[133] As such, emotion and feeling are embodied with a biological core, and physical experience shapes our thoughts. Hodge identifies two key influences on her work with touch: the first, Christian Jaker, who practised on her whilst training to become a Shiatsu master practitioner, prompting her understanding of touch as a pedagogical tool; the second, the somatic touch practised by Gardzienice. The pedagogical use of touch recognises that what is felt is not subordinate to what is heard or made visible, the immediate forms of communication, which can cut us off from the relational nature of ourselves. Heidegger suggests that touch is a type of language, rooted in thinking, that extends human consciousness.[134] When we attend to touch we can recognise it as more than one single sense, enabling a complex range of understandings, involving a number of different skin sensations such as pressure, temperature or pain. 'Haptics', meaning the active affect of touch from the Greek *haptein* 'to touch', is 'an umbrella term for a variety of sensory perceptions'.[135] When vision is taken away, haptic sense takes over and unlike vision and hearing, which correspond to memory and certain geometric principles, haptic sense is always read as an experience of the now, arguably more live and responsive than the other senses.

Touch enables sensation, proprioception, kinesthetic learning and importantly affect. In this way 'touching' and 'being touched' exist beside each other with 'being touched by something' pointing to the emotional connection between the act and the affect. Eve Sedgwick, in her seminal collection of essays *Touching, Feeling: Affect, Pedagogy, Performativity* positions texture and affect, touching and feeling as types of hidden knowledge, irreducibly phenomenological, which enable a deeper form of perception.[136] Through touch we can move from questions about action and affect, to focus on the process and to ask 'How did it get that way and what can I do with it'?[137] Actor, Martin Welton, questions the modality of touch he experienced in performance where both actors and audience were in the dark.[138] He says

> If touch (in a joint haptic–affective sense) becomes as important to acting as visual appearance, then the condition of the actor's self becomes as important a consideration as the condition that she or he enacts upon or within the spectator. Touch then, in both haptic and affective senses, tells us both how and where we are, and, as such, provides an experiential base for a wider sense of being.[139]

This points to the central tenet of Hodge's relational practice, where actors, through the experience of touching and being touched, experience a wider sense of mutuality.

Hodge uses touch to explore the body in time and space, with others and with objects. At a foundational level the actor is coached to attend to the connections the body makes to surface and space. Whether lying on the floor, running, or touching another, Hodge draws attention to the spaces between: the space behind the ankle; behind the knees; between two spines; between hands. An awareness of weight, gravity and connection to the floor extends from the self, to giving one's weight to another and meeting through the spine. The spine is the starting point for connection between actors as it goes behind the social space of vision to a more subtle form of seeing through listening. Actors encounter each other in meeting spine to spine, giving and receiving the weight of their partner. In practice, Hodge coaches through questioning: 'What do you notice'; 'How can you speak to each other through the spine'; 'How does your body fit with this body'; 'What's the presence of this body in relation to you'; 'What's the temperature of the body'; 'How soft is the spine in relation to yours'?[140] The connection between spines extends into exploring weight and balance where two actors work in constant flow of giving and receiving weight. The actors listen to each others' tiny shifts in movement and breath to discover a shared tempo rhythm where they are communing through impulse with responsibility for the other, where the feeling of being off balance demands you support and adjust to and for the other. This touch through the spine extends to the hands, the arms and then the whole body. Two exercises illustrate this. The first, 'Flying', involves two actors supporting a third in the centre with their arms and taking their weight. The actors on the outside hold the arms of the third very carefully. Their job is to enable the actor in the middle to move as freely as they want in whatever way, listening and reading their breath, impulse and rhythm. It offers freedom for the actor in the middle who almost has a sense of flying. In the other exercise, 'Caretaking', one actor, wearing a veil, gives their weight to those around them, freely exploring impulse, space and rhythm by allowing herself to be fully supported by the group. They work with a veil to remove facial communication, and the transaction of the social body. Each actor brings a totally unique personality to the exercise and everyone adjusts to the individual. On the outside, the actors are always on the edge of movement, not crowding the actor in the middle, but caretaking her: catching, guiding, lifting, directing, balancing and supporting. 'Her freedom and risk is made possible by the group'.[141] In practice, there is a shared responsibility to the other and the touch and attention generate a feeling of empathy and plurality.

Extending haptic understanding to include breath reflects the 'felt sense' of Scaravelli yoga. Hodge positions breath as key to connecting with feeling:

> I have found that working with my breath helps me access emotions more easily ... It is the breath that is leading the actor and is teaching them about their experience. The feeling of the breath affects you.[142]

The connection between breath, touch and empathy recalls Luce Irigaray's essay 'To Begin with Breathing Anew' introduced in Chapter 3, which insists that we give 'more breath to meaning and more meaning to breath' in order to generate 'a culture of love for the other, as well as for ourselves, in respect for our difference(s)'.[143] In Hodge's practice breath and touch enable relationality.

In the first stages, the actor focuses on her own breath through somatic breathing where she feels the tempo of the breath throughout the whole body, allowing the breath to release the emotion. In rhythmic breathing, the actors work with connection and find a shared rhythm and working in pairs they breathe into hands, one actor holds the other's rib cage, to feel the rhythm, the pause between inbreath and outbreath and the quality of the breath.[144] Another exercise asks one actor to support the other through the lower spine, whilst listening to the rhythm of the breath. At the point of the pause between inbreath and outbreath, the partner gives a direction to the other through the pressure of their hand on the spine, which offers an impulse for movement. This connection among touch, breath, weight, rhythm and impulse sets concrete technical demands for the actor and enables a heightened polyphonic listening.

The use of touch in relation to objects is another aspect of *Core Training*. Actors work with a broom handle to manipulate the object in space, keeping the space between themselves and the stick alive and dynamic, allowing it to fall, catching it and maintaining flow and energy. Extending from this, actors pass the stick to each other, allowing each throw and catch to exchange a particular question and answer. Hodge warns that: 'The conversation is more precise when the questions are clear'.[145] Working with rhythm, breath and connection with object the space between becomes alive and this work extends to exploration of chairs, costumes and props. The touch and affect enable the actor to create a responsive and relational score where they animate the inanimate. This work then extends into theatre-making processes where actors can generate powerful images and archetypal patterns. Welton considers how the relationship between objects can become as real as the objects themselves, as it is these 'behavioural units' that give meaning to the object.[146] Consequently *how* one sits on the chair or throws the stick affects how one is moved and touched by it. Like the heightened awareness of touching the floor at the start of the practice, the possible connections to a chair can offer the actor an endless variety of choice, impulse and feeling.

Because the company is all female and because touch is foregrounded as a learning process, female sensuality becomes a feature of the practice. This is most noticeable when watching film footage of Hodge's company, with its artistic framing, fragmented screens, dual perspectives, close ups of body parts and intermittent sounds of breath.[147] The shots and edit present a sensual effect as moments of touch are highlighted with moments of silence. In practice, working with touch in the pair work inevitably changes depending on whom you are working with and is affected by the gender of your partner. In a mixed gender partnership, one immediately sees and feels the power play of gender, sexuality and the clichés of representation, recalling Phelan's observation that seeing is gendered.[148] When working with the same gender the archetypal images are more open, nuanced and contradictory. Impulse work connects to desire and this, in itself, is inevitably read as gendered. Shapiro explains desire as lacks, gaps or needs, felt to complete our subjectivity and linked historically to modes of production.[149] The representation of gendered desire affects how we observe a sexed encounter, but this reading of desire opens up when the group is the same sex. In Hodge's view, female desire is complex and her work enables the female body to move beyond issues of objectification to an expression of female consciousness.

The foundational practice of touch and breath offers actors a way to connect into feeling through their relation to the other. Two things are particularly striking when observing or participating in this work – firstly, the focus generated through the technical challenges. Participants wear the same expression – a kind of intensity, which is immediately emotionally involved – whilst maintaining a whole body openness to the other. This work is orientated to awakening the senses of the impulse and of the emotion, described by Bre:

> [C]ultivating a sensitive body and body/mind awareness by keeping contact with all sorts of impulses that give rise to spontaneous, direct reactions and generate feelings at the same time.[150]

Secondly, there is a palpable shift in the way that participants embrace touch. They start to touch themselves more, as well as others, which changes the dynamic in a room.

## *Queering acting*

> Real 'acting out' occurs when the man is able to break through the limitations of his male conditions and assumptions to reach the secret and the enigma of the female body. Of course you cannot get it without identifying with the female soul and vice versa. This is the old knowledge of Eastern theatre and of ancient Greek theatre, but now it is extremely difficult to reach it. Through transcending your own state and culture, you have much more knowledge about what you have just broken through.[151]

Returning to Wlodzimierz Staniewski's allusion, which prompted consideration of the female ontology of acting in Chapter 1, it is interesting to consider how Hodge has re-interpreted this knowledge. She sees, in Staniewski's statement, the gender transcendence of Eastern performance, such as Mei Lanfang who inspired Brecht.[152] The vulnerability of the male actor when playing female 'shows you the possibility of being human, be that masculine or feminine'.[153] The potential for transformation and vulnerability is at the heart of Hodge's practice, and in this respect her understanding aligns with Gilson's notion of vulnerability as a 'gift of changeability' with 'force in fragility'.[154] Referring to her most recent work, *The Rego Project*, she considers the intersection between vulnerability, transformation and female-ness that characterise the piece:[155]

> So I wouldn't want to be pigeonholed that this is female training and feminine. I'm interested in that liminal space where you are becoming and where you see vulnerability and possibility. I just think that women have

not always had the opportunities to break through the clichés and stereotypes into something more liminal, like these wonderful male actors who play female. It is that possibility that seems to be a little bit limited, so I'm not looking for 'femaleness' per/se. I'm looking for opening the door on that possibility.[156]

Hodge's is a queering practice, resisting reductive representations and seeking spaces of transformation and change. The Quick and the Dead's first work, a response to *The House of Bernarda Alba*[157] allowed for an investigation of female power and desire. In *The Rego Project*, Hodge wanted to investigate the female body without 'confining women to the usual categories'.[158] She found her source in Paula Rego's paintings, where women become 'something other, which isn't any notion of "femaleness"'.[159] In Rego's work, women are depicted as confined in different ways, such as in their dress or through their behaviour. Their response is sometimes to transform into the non-female and non-human. Hodge explains:

> [W]hat's so beautiful in Rego's work is that she shows you the contradictions. So she shows you the powerful woman in the vulnerable position, or the child that has grown up too quickly. She's always looking at these wonderful, truthful contradictions of the external image of the female body and what is actually going on inside that woman's feelings. She's talking about submission, not just aggression. She's talking about all sorts of states that women find themselves in.[160]

The transformative and transgressive subject matter enables Hodge and the company to investigate what Braidotti terms the 'vital materialism' of the body – its constant state of becoming.[161] The female body is both inscribed and inscribing, able to change, mutate, evolve and become other.

The Rego Project consists of four films, devised in response to four paintings that Hodge chose with each actor, who worked to find a score where they responded to the painting and, during the course of the score, transform into *Dog Woman* and then back into the world of the painting. Each film was shot in The Master Builder's House in Deptford on a hand-held camera by Molly Dineen and then edited by Hodge and archivist Peter Hulton. The work premiered in London in 2014 and was shown in Lisbon in January 2016. Each film is presented on a huge projection screen in one room and played simultaneously, with the audience experiencing their own encounter as they move between the rooms. In Lisbon the original Rego painting was hung in each room in conversation with the film. The only sound in each film, which spills between the rooms, is breath, the sound of heels on the floor, chairs scraping, skirts rustling and the women barking. The training practice is immediately recognisable in the aesthetic of the performance:

We applied the training exercises as we began to inhabit the images. You can see how the actor uses her breath, the sensory encounter with her environment whilst she is holding the images of the painting in her mind ... a wonderful tension between the social body and the response to the environment. Part of this is that the camera and the actors are starting to confront the images of the paintings, just as the characters in Rego's paintings confront the viewer in the frame.[162]

At moments in each film, the actor directly looks at the camera, defiantly confronting the male gaze, even though in practice she is looking at Dineen. Hodge wanted the actors to explore an awareness of the audience and did not want the audience to be 'let off the hook' through the experience of viewing these women. In this way she aims to give the power back to the actor and to enable a 'reciprocal gaze'.[163] The images show women in surprising positions: *Dog Woman* shows a woman being a dog, *The Little Murderess* shows a girl about to murder a cat, *The Salmon Coloured Dress* shows a girl at various stages of sliding down a wall in a party frock. *The Rego Project* brings all the aspects of Hodge's practice together, in the way that you can see the training within the work as an ongoing part of the process. It challenges clichéd representations of the female body to examine the social body *beside* the life body, its inherent tensions, unruly transformations and vital possibilities. In this way Hodge's practice with her company queers notions of female-ness through a critical acting pedagogy.

Conrad Alexandrowicz, problematising the culture of self-objectification, which pervades the acting industry and particularly oppresses female bodies, cautions:

> We need, as theatre practitioners and instructors, to ask ourselves whether we are training artists and citizens with the capacity for critical thinking, or crop after crop of willing, able and enthusiastic consumers.[164]

Exploring the work of two practitioners who seek to challenge reductive and homogenising representations of race and gender and placing these practitioners in conversation with one another reveals the hidden curriculum in training practices and the critical imperative. Both Landon-Smith and Hodge have reinterpreted male practices and pedagogies from their gendered position. Although their pedagogies are distinct and particular to their respective context, aesthetic and the specific issues they are working to solve, they share a concern to build 'dispositional qualities',[165] develop 'transferable skills'[166] and attend to notions of difference and identity. Qualities of relationality, empathy, impulse, vulnerability and transformation are made explicit in the learning process, and it is fascinating to note the ways in which different sensory approaches emerge as dominant scaffolding structures. Landon-Smith works to help the actor explore her hybrid cultural identity with a focus on voice and Hodge develops an actor's capacity to feel through touch. Although specific and unique, certain commonalities emerge from these practices. Both practitioners work somatically and diagnostically to respond to the needs of the individual and the group. They orientate the acquisition of learning towards pleasure and affirmation – *via positiva* – as opposed to pain and failure, to establish authority based on a shared responsibility. Their pedagogies enable the actor to explore her/him self from a position of the positivity of difference, making learning explicit through reflective and reflexive discussion. They both investigate the vital materialism of the body through biopolitics and the body's multiple possibilities. These approaches can be seen to illustrate Critical Acting Pedagogy in practice, where the personal and social knowledge of the actor is privileged. In this way acting can, either explicitly or more implicitly, politicise the actor.

## Notes

1 Jonathan Pitches notes how issues of gender in training are 'too often overlooked' in *The Actor Training Reader,* ed. Mark Evans (London & New York: Routledge, 2015) 56.
2 Pitches, citing Alison Hodge, *Twentieth Century Actor Training* (London: Routledge, 2010) 57.
3 The steps to the entrance of The Royal Central School of Speech and Drama (RCSSD) are engraved with the names of famous graduates, who are claimed as the professional currency of the school.
4 Interview with Di Trevis (09.08.13).
5 Ibid.
6 I consider this at the start of Chapter 3, 'Women and the Matter of Voice' when pointing to the work of Berry, Linklater, Rodenburg and Fitzmaurice.
7 Declan Donnellan, *The Actor and The Target* (London: Nick Hern Books, 2002).
8 John Wright, *Why Is That So Funny? A Practical Exploration of Physical Comedy* (London: Nick Hern Books, 2006).
9 Mike Alfreds, *Different Every Night: Freeing the Actor* (London: Nick Hern Books, 2007).
10 John Abbot, *The Acting Book* (London: Nick Hern Books, 2012).
11 Nick Moseley, *Actioning and How to Do It* (London: Nick Hern Books, 2016).
12 The Royal Central School of Speech and Drama, 'History', http://www.cssd.ac.uk/about-central/history [accessed 11.11.13].
13 Arts Educational, 'History', http://artsed.co.uk [accessed 11.11.13].
14 Rose Bruford College, 'History', https://www.bruford.ac.uk/about/our-history/ [accessed 11.11.13].
15 East 15, 'History', http://east15.ac.uk [accessed 11.11.13].
16 See Rosemary Malague, *An Actress Prepares* (London: Routledge, 2011), for a feminist reading of Hagen and Adler's approach.
17 Anne Bogart and Tina Landau, *The Viewpoints Book: A Practical Guide to Viewpoints and Composition* (New York: Theatre Communications Group, 2005).
18 Tanya Gerstle, 'Pulse: A Physical Approach to Staging Text', http://www.doubledialogues.com/in_stead/in_stead_iss03/Gerstle.html [accessed 10.07.15].
19 Susana Bloch, 'Alba Emoting: A Psychophysiological Technique to Help Actors Create and Control Real Emotions', *Theatre Topics*, 3(2), (1993): 121–138.
20 Jane Boston, 'Teaching Stanislasvki: An Investigation into How Stanislavski Is Taught to Students in the UK'. A project initiated by SCUDD (the Standing

20 Conference of University Drama Departments) in conjunction with PALATINE (the Higher Education Academy Subject Centre for Dance, Drama and Music), 2008. http://www.heacademy.ac.uk/assets/documents/subjects/palatine/teaching-stanislavski.pdf [accessed 16.19.13].
21 Dorinda Hulton, 'Creative Actor (Empowering the Performer)' in *Theatre Praxis*, ed. Christopher McCullough (London: Macmillan, 1998).
22 Experience Bryon, *Integrative Performance: Practice and Theory for the Interdisciplinary Performer* (New York & London: Routledge, 2014).
23 Amanda Brennan, *The Energetic Performer: An Integrated Approach for Stage and Screen* (London and Philadelphia: Singing Dragon, 2016).
24 In 2016, I surveyed the seventeen institutions that were members of what was then Drama UK (now The Federation of Drama Schools). At the time there were only two women holding course lead roles in Acting, Joyce Deans at the Royal Conservatoire of Scotland and Caroline Lesley at LAMDA. In 2020, this has risen threefold to include: Danièle Sanderson at Royal Birmingham Conservatoire; Julie Spencer at Arts Educational; Aly Spiro and Jayne Courtney at Alra; Kristine Landon-Smith at Drama Studio.
25 Acting practitioner at a London conservatoire (1.11.13).
26 Alison Hodge, *Core Training for the Relational Actor* (London: Routledge, 2013).
27 The nine-point methodology is: how the hidden curriculum of persona and social knowledge is delivered; how an atmosphere of trust and relationality is built; how vulnerability is supported; how authority operates in the room; how choice and action are scaffolded for the actor; how instruction, explanation and feedback are given; how non-human agents operate within the teaching/learning; how individual and group progress is managed within time constraints; how gender, sexuality, class, ethnicity and able-ism operate within the learning.
28 Landon-Smith (17.01.15).
29 Rustom Bharucha, *Theatre and the World: Performance and the Politics of Culture* (London & New York: Routledge, 1993).
30 Bharucha, 4.
31 Landon-Smith (07.03.13).
32 This is an adaptation of the novel by Mulk Raj Anand, following a day in the life of an Indian latrine cleaner. It was the company's debut production in 1989 at London's Riverside Studios playing alternative nights in English and Hindi.
33 Tamasha, http://www.tamasha.org.uk/about/history/ [accessed 15.05.15].
34 Critical Performative Pedagogy (CPP) is a term used by Elyse Pineau to describe a politically engaged somatic approach to teaching and learning, which she claims as the domain of Performance Studies. CAP develops this form of learning to include forms of critical pedagogy and the intersection between performance and performativity; I explain CPP in relation to acting in Chapter 2. See Elyse Pineau, 'Pedagogy: Fleshing Out the Politics of Liberatory Education' in Nathan Stucky and Cynthia Wimmer (eds), *Teaching Performance Studies* (Carbondale, Illinois: Southern Illinois University Press, 2002) 41–54.
35 Ibid.
36 Lynne Kendrick, 'A Paidic Aesthetic: An Analysis of Games in the Ludic Pedagogy of Philippe Gaulier', *Theatre, Dance and Performance Training*, 2(1), (2011): 72–85.
37 The term *via negativa* is used by Grotowski and attributed to Lecoq to explain how an actor learns by confronting her blocks and then working to solve her own solutions. I explore this in Chapter 2.
38 I refer to this approach as examined by Donald Schön in Chapter 2.
39 Simon Murray, *Jacques Lecoq* (London & New York: Routledge, 2003) 49–51.
40 Maggie Irving, 'Clown Training: Preparing for Failure'. Un-published paper presented at TAPRA in 2010.

41 This approach has also been noted in the practices of Meisner and Strasberg. Whilst not taking an explicit pedagogical perspective, Rosemary Malague examines this in *An Actress Prepares: Women and 'The Method'* (London: Routledge, 2011).
42 Landon-Smith (07.03.13).
43 Rosi Braidotti, *Nomadic Theory: The Portable Rosi Braidotti* (New York: Columbia University Press, 2011) 299–314.
44 Ibid. 268–298.
45 The *via positiva* as a feminist intervention is explained in Chapter 2.
46 Intracultural Actors' Masterclass, Kings Place, King Cross, London (17.09.13).
47 Andrea Milde, 'Spoken Language and Doing Drama', *Working Papers in Urban Language & Literacies,* Paper 89, (2012a), http://www.kcl.ac.uk/sspp/departments/education/research/ldc/publications/workingpapers/the-papers/WP89.pdf [accessed 23.04.14].
48 Taken from observation notes: Actors Workshop. The Rug Factory, Brick Lane, London (28.11.12), (19.02.13).
49 Landon-Smith (28.11.12), (19.02.13).
50 Ibid.
51 Landon-Smith, op.cit.
52 Antonio Harris, Circus Space (08.03.13).
53 Landon-Smith, interviewed in London (17.01.15).
54 See Chapter 3, 'Women and the Matter of Voice'.
55 *Langue* (meaning language) and *parole* (meaning speaking) are linguistic terms, used by Ferdinand de Saussure in his *Course of General Linguistics* (London & New York: Bloomsbury Revelations, 2013).
56 Julia Kristeva, *The Kristeva Reader*, ed. Toril Moi (Oxford: Blackwell Publishers Ltd. 1985) 94.
57 Ibid.
58 Intracultural Actors Masterclass. Kings Place. King Cross. London (17.09.13).
59 Adriana Cavarero, *For More Than One Voice: Towards a Philosophy of Vocal Expression* (Stanford University Press, 2005) 134.
60 For an overview of Active Analysis see Bella Merlin, *Konstantin Stanislavsky: Routledge Performance Practitioners* (London & New York: Routledge, 2003).
61 Actors Workshop. The Rug Factory, Brick Lane, London (19.02.13).
62 Landon-Smith (07.03.13).
63 Stanislavski explains the tempo rhythm of an actor's body on page 466 in Jean Benedetti, *An Actor's Work* (London & New York: Routledge, 2008).
64 Harris (08.03.13).
65 Landon–Smith: Intracultural Actors Masterclass, London (17.09.13).
66 Jackie Le, Circus Space (08.03.13). This connection to parents recalls the influence of Systemic Constellatios on Dowling's movement practice examined in Chapter 4.
67 (17.09.13) Intracultural Actors Masterclass. Kings Place. King Cross. London.
68 Pineau, 44.
69 Geraldine Harris offers an overview of the problematic blurring of these two terms in *Staging Femininities: Performance and Performativity* (Manchester & New York: Manchester University Press, 1999) 172–175.
70 Intracultural Actors Masterclass. Kings Place, King Cross, London (17.09.13).
71 Landon-Smith (17.01.15).
72 Ibid.
73 Judith Butler, *Bodies that Matter: On the Discursive Limits of Sex* (London & New York: Routledge, 1993) 12–18.
74 Ibid.
75 Augusto Boal, *Games for Actors and Non-Actors* (London & New York: Routledge, 1993) 173.

76 Intracultural Actors Masterclass. King Cross, London (17.09.13).
77 Interview with Landon-Smith (17.01.15).
78 Ibid.
79 Harris, 77.
80 Interview with Kristine Landon-Smith (17.01.15).
81 (17.09.13) Intracultural Actors Masterclass. Kings Place. King Cross. London.
82 Judith Butler, *Bodies that Matter: On the Discursive Limits of Sex* (London: Routledge, 1993) 234.
83 Ibid., Front piece.
84 Alison Hodge: *Twentieth Century Actor Training* (London & New York: Routledge, 2010).
85 Hodge, 2013.
86 Wlodzimierz Staniewski and Alison Hodge, *Hidden Territories: The Theatre of Gardzienice* (London & New York: Routledge, 2004).
87 Hodge (21.03.15).
88 Ibid.
89 Phenomenology explores the inter-relational experience of being in the world. See Merleau-Ponty, *The Visible and the Invisible* (Eranston: Northwestern University Press, 1968).
90 Hodge, 4.
91 Hodge (21.03.15).
92 Ibid.
93 Since 2015, Hodge has led sessions internationally in 'Women and Leadership'. Working with a specifically gendered pedagogical focus outside of actor training and theatre-making has enabled an objective observation of certain traits that she essentialises as female such as 'the use of touch, learning to take your space and feel alright about it, being supported by other women and making that easier'. Interview with Alison Hodge (21.03.15).
94 Casilda (16.04.15).
95 Bre (20.04.15).
96 Hodge, 28.
97 Ibid.
98 Here I am thinking of the 'Work on the Self' in Konstantin Stanislavki, *An Actor's Work* (London & New York: Routledge, 2008).
99 Staniewski, 74.
100 Hodge (16.01.13).
101 Phillip Zarrilli, Jerri Daboo and Rebecca Loukes, *Acting: Psychophysical Phenomenon and Process* (Basingstoke: Palgrave Macmillan, 2013) 1–50.
102 Hodge, 4.
103 Karen Barad, 'Posthumanist Performativity: Toward an Understanding of How Matter Comes to Matter', *Signs*, 28(3), (Spring, 2003) 801–831.
104 Jane Bennet, *Vibrant Matter: A Political Ecology of Things* (Duke University Press, 2010).
105 Interview with Alison Hodge (21.03.15).
106 Casilda (16.04.15).
107 Frank Camilleri, *Performer Training Reconfigured: Post-Psychophysical Perspectives for the Twenty-First Century* (London & New York: Methuen, 2019) 57–83.
108 Sandra Reeve, *Nine Ways of Seeing a Body* (UK: Triarchy Press, 2011) 48.
109 Hodge, 3, citing Evan Thompson, 'Empathy and Consciousness', *Journal of Consciousness Studies,* 8(5–7), (2001): 1–32.
110 Nicole Karafyllis and Gotlind Ulshofer, *Sexualised Brains: Scientific Modelling of Emotional Intelligence from a Cultural Perspective* (Cambridge, Massachusetts & London: The MIT Press, 2008) 1–13.

111 Hodge, 10.
112 Eve Sedgwick, *Touching Feeling: Affect, Pedagogy, Performativity* (Durham and London: Duke University Press, 2003) 8.
113 Hodge (16.01.13).
114 Peggy Phelan, *Unmarked: The Politics of Performance* (London & New York: Routledge, 1993) 17.
115 Hodge, 7.
116 Hodge (16.01.13).
117 Ibid.
118 Ibid.
119 Hodge (21.03.15).
120 Here I am thinking of Phillip Zarrilli's practice with Kalari Piat see Phillip Zarrilli, *Psychophysical Acting: An Intercultural Approach after Stanislavski* (London & New York: Routledge, 2009).
121 In 'Follow me' the teacher models and the student copies; 'joint experimentation' has teacher and student working out solutions together. Both are explained in Chapter 1.
122 Taken from observation notes: Hodge (21.03.15).
123 Eugenio Barba and Nicola Savarese, *The Secret Art of the Performer* (London & New York: Routledge, 1991) 236.
124 Donald Schön, *Educating the Reflective Practitioner* (San Francisco: Jossey Bass, 1987).
125 Hodge (21.03.15).
126 In interview Emma Rice notes how Staniewski preferred silence during training. (29.01.15).
127 Hodge,7.
128 Caretaking is when the actors work with absolute attention to the others' needs and this scaffolds impulse work.
129 Hodge (21.03.15).As previously noted, the introduction of critical codes of conduct around consent in UK drama schools has, since the time of this research, shifted the ways that practitioners can work freely with pedagogic touch. Georgia Snow, 'Drama Schools Commit to Ethical Guidelines to Tackle Sexual Harassment', *The Stage* (19.04.18) https://www.thestage.co.uk/news/2018/drama-schools-commit-ethical-guidelines-tack [accessed 15.04.20].
130 Hodge, 19.
131 Studies have examined the relationship between touch and gender and identified certain types of touch, notably empathetic touch, as being more prevalent in female communication. See Matthew Hertenstein and Dacher Keltner, 'Gender and the Communication of Emotion Via Touch', *Sex Roles*, 64(2010): 70–80. Published online.
132 Hodge, 20.
133 Ibid. 22.
134 Shelly Shapiro, *Pedagogy and the Politics of the Body: A Critical Praxis* (London & New York: Routledge, 1999)35, citing Heidegger (1968) 16.
135 Martin Welton, 'Once More With Feeling', *Performance Research: A Journal of Performing Arts*, 10(1), (2005): 100–112.
136 Sedgwick, 21.
137 Ibid. 22.
138 Welton, op.cit.
139 Welton, 108.
140 Taken from observation notes RCSSD (21.03.15).
141 Ibid. 16.
142 Hodge (21.03.15).
143 Luce Irigaray, 'To Begin with Breathing Anew' in Lenart Skof and Emily A. Holmes, *Breathing with Luce Irigaray* (Bloomsbury, 2013) 224, 226.

144 This work with touch and breath presents similarities to Nadine George's voice practice examined in Chapter 3.
145 Ibid.
146 Welton, 111.
147 Hodge (2013).
148 Peggy Phelan, *Unmarked: The Politics of Performance* (London & New York: Routledge,1993) 17.
149 Shapiro, 44.
150 Tatiana Bre (20.04.15).
151 Staniewski, 97.
152 Bertolt Brecht, *Brecht on Theatre: The Development of an Aesthetic* (London: Methuen, 1964) 99.
153 Hodge (21.03.15).
154 Erinn Gilson, *The Ethics of Vulnerability: A Feminist Analysis of Social Life and Practice*. (London and New York; Routledge, 2014) 88.
155 A recording of this work was shown to the author by Hodge (21.03.15).
156 Hodge (21.03.15).
157 *The Quick and The Dead*, archive recording.
158 Interview with Hodge (21.03.15).
159 Ibid.
160 Ibid.
161 Braidotti, 161.
162 Interview with Hodge (21.03.15).
163 Phelan, 18.
164 Conrad Alexandrowicz, 'Pretty/Sexy: Impacts of the Sexualistaion of Young Women on Theatre Pedagogy', *Theatre, Dance and Performer Training*, 3(3), (2012): 298.
165 Simon Murray cited by Maria Kapsali, 'Training for a Cold Climate: Edited Transcript of Roundtable Discussion', in *Theatre, Dance and Performance Training*, 5(2), (2014): 2019–232.
166 Stephen Wangh, *The Heart of Teaching: Empowering Students in the Performing Arts*. (London & New York: Routledge, 2013)139.

# 6

# WOMEN AND THE MATTER OF DIRECTING

Most formative actor training approaches have come from directors. There are many similarities between the roles of teacher and director, as both take responsibility for leading a group of people through a process of discovering a language together to create something new. As such, I position the director as pedagogue, an educator in a vocational context, and I'm interested in the ways that a critical pedagogy operates in theatre-making practices. When women directors remain a minority, it is unsurprising that male lineages dominate the field.[1] Whereas a number of male UK directors have specifically authored their practice as a training for actors,[2] no female has documented their approach in this way.[3] This chapter considers how the practice of women directors has shifted the pedagogies of acting. I focus on the work of Katie Mitchell and Emma Rice, directors whose work has made a significant impact on theatre in the UK and internationally. In providing a context for their work, whilst recognising that this can only be a snapshot of the landscape, I posit three questions: In what ways have women's directing practices in the UK developed feminist actor training approaches? Who has made key contributions to this field? What might a gendered consideration of women's directing pedagogies reveal?

When we look outside of the UK, we see that female directors have made vital contributions to the development of actor training through the ways in which they have built communities of practice. For example, in the U.S. Anne Bogart (1951–) and her Saratonga International Theatre Institute (SITI), which she founded with Japanese director Tadashi Suzuki in 1992, continues to experiment with a performance style that unites Viewpoints training and Suzuki. In France, Ariane Mnouchkine (1939–) founded Theatre du Soleil in 1964 and, through the influence of an Eastern aesthetic, developed a company dedicated to exploring the essential qualities of being in the present.[4] Although Mnouchkine has described any theory of acting as 'somewhat imperialistic and pretentious',[5] she has asserted that it is the duty of every director to invest in the pedagogy of actors to ensure their ongoing training.

In the UK, this investment can be seen most clearly in 1970s collaborative women's theatre practices, which radically shifted the ways that theatre was made and, consequently, refreshed acting pedagogies. Michélène Wandor, in her overview of UK women's theatre during this decade, *Carry on Understudies: Theatre and Sexual Politics,* identifies the dominant influences as: social materialist feminism, the women's liberation movement and Theatre In Education (TIE).[6] Women's theatre was fueled by a desire to politicise and to educate with a commitment to a collective collaborative practice, which flattened traditional writer/director/actor hierarchies and de-centralised the text. Alex Merkimedes identifies the radical practices of companies like Sphinx Theatre Company, Split Britches, Gay Sweatshop and Monstrous Regiment as re-defining theatre-making processes through what she terms 'The Collective and the Devising Playwright'.[7] Women worked to flatten hierarchies in organisational practice through collective discussion, democratic decision-making and fluid power structures, working with their personal and shared experiences in the spirit of resistance. In the development of devising processes, feminist theatre companies radically changed the ways that actors worked.[8]

Women directors also worked to destabilise the conventional power dynamic, for example: Annabel Arden, co-founder of Complicité; Anne Jellicoe (1927–2017) and her development of the Community Play;[9] and Annie Castledine (1939–2016), described in her obituary as 'a modern Joan Littlewood'.[10] Any mapping of UK practitioners must recognise Littlewood (1914–2002) – described as 'the Mother of Modern Theatre'[11] – as a pioneer, trying to reach a working-class audience. Littlewood founded Theatre Workshop in 1945 to re-awaken British theatre after the Second World War, developing an aesthetic and a way of making work which was both anarchic and poetic, highly politicised and democratic.[12] Clive Barker identifies the important contribution she made to the development of actor training, citing one company member who claimed that 'he learned more from one afternoon with Littlewood than in all the other time he spent at Drama school'.[13] She privileged the shared learning process, and worked with research, games and improvisations to develop the actor's spontaneity. Whilst she never documented her process, and her contribution is often sidelined in favour of her male contemporaries, many cite Littlewood's theatre-making practice as an inspiration.

It is important to note the inextricable influence of Shakespeare on UK actor training.[14] Theatre researcher Elizabeth Freestone holds Shakespeare's legacy responsible for the gender inequality in acting employment traditions in the UK theatre, as he wrote only 155 female characters, heavily outweighed by 826 male roles.[15] Contributions by women directors in this field are important to acknowledge. Buzz Goodbody (1947–1975) was the first woman to direct at the

Royal Shakespeare Company (RSC), and was pioneering in her development of pedagogy in theatre-making, setting up The Other Place in 1961 in Stratford-upon-Avon, with a commitment to engage a wider audience demographic. Goodbody was noted for 'the incredible freedom she gave her actors to bring their ideas to the fore'[16] and she applied the same Marxist approaches and resistant politics of fringe theatre to work at the RSC. Goodbody's death by suicide in 1975 was a catalyst for the next generation of women directors. In the 1980s, actors at the RSC, including Fiona Shaw, Lyndsay Duncan and Juliet Stevenson spoke up about the lack of female directors and their comments were taken up by the media as part of a wider feminist backlash. When Deborah Warner directed *Titus Andronicus* in 1988, she was the first woman to direct on the main stage, and half of the eight directors that season were women.[17] In 1991, a landmark production of *Richard II*, directed by Warner, saw Fiona Shaw playing the title role, which opened the floodgates for female directors to give opportunities to female actors with gender blind or cross-gendered casting. This enabled training opportunities for female actors to develop their skills through the complex protagonist roles previously denied to them. Over the last two decades, a growing number of cross-gendered Shakespeare productions continue to challenge convention.[18] In 2012, Phyllida Lloyd directed a trilogy of all female productions at the Donmar Theatre, with Harriet Walters playing the title roles in *Julius Ceasar, Henry IV* and *The Tempest*. In 2016, Emma Rice, whose work forms a case study in this chapter, became the first female appointment as artistic director of The Globe theatre and pledged her commitment to a 50/50 gender split in casting asking, 'How can we change the mould'?[19]

Although women continue to challenge patriarchal structures, developing acting pedagogies through alternative theatre-making processes and cross-gendered casting, it is perhaps in re-thinking the very notion of directing that a gendered practice becomes most pertinent. At a panel discussion in 2012, entitled *Renaming the Director*, eight directors considered how the role might be re-articulated for the twenty-first century.[20] The three female directors aligned themselves with the role of 'facilitator', whereas the males were more comfortable with the role of 'controller', with one asserting, 'actors want directors to tell them what to do'.[21] This appeared to indicate a gendered approach to directing, with connotations of instruction or command pointing to a more male approach. Although such essentialism might be considered to be reductive, it is interesting to question the ways that gender operates in the rehearsal room. At a workshop in 2015, entitled 'Women as Artists', Katie Mitchell guided fifteen female directors to consider the ways that their gender impacted in their practice and how they might define the role.[22] Certain autocratic ways of thinking about directing such as 'driver, author, controller', were seen to perpetuate a traditional patriarchal understanding and to be unhelpful in practice. A preference emerged for terms such as, 'artist, precise coordinator, analyst, facilitator'.[23] If directing practices are more gendered than we have previously considered how might this impact acting pedagogies?

Through the pedagogic practices of UK directors Katie Mitchell and Emma Rice we can identify feminist acting pedagogies, which foreground and challenge considerations of gender and sexuality. These case studies draw on three years of rehearsal observations and interviews between 2011 and 2014. Both identify as feminist directors and both have created significant bodies of work, which have changed the face of UK theatre. The feminist form, content and orientation of their work is central to their creative teams' pedagogical experience as they, albeit implicitly, act as feminists in its joint creation. Moreover, I suggest that the learning exchange continues for the audience who, in receiving work invested in confronting patriarchy, may be provoked to act as a feminist.

The nine-point methodology outlined in Chapter 2 helps me to evaluate the feminist potential of the pedagogic exchange. This considers: how the hidden curriculum of personal and social knowledge is delivered (where, in a theatre-making process, the content of the material is a determining factor); how an atmosphere of trust and relationality is built; how vulnerability is supported; how authority operates in the room; how choice and action are scaffolded for the actor; how instruction, explanation and feedback are given; how non-human agents operate within the teaching/learning; how individual and group progress is managed within time constraints; how gender, sexuality, able-ism, class and ethnicity operate within the learning. As feminist director pedagogues, Mitchell and Rice develop pedagogies rooted in feminist materialisms.

## Katie Mitchell: Schooling actors

Katie Mitchell has been described as 'the closest thing Britain has to a genuine auteur',[24] with some critics describing her experimental work as 'genre defining'[25] and others dismissing it as 'wacky'.[26] Although there is plenty of scholarly interest in her productions and processes, there has been no specific focus on her pedagogical practice. In this section, I consider how Mitchell's self-proclaimed feminist concerns intersect with her pedagogy. Drawing on rehearsal observation between 2011 and 2013 across four productions, including two large-scale classical texts, new writing, 'live cinema',[27] a week's training workshop, 'Women as Artists',[28] and extended interviews with Mitchell and her actors, I unpick the ways in which she re-thinks mimesis, to highlight the vital contribution she has made to the development of theatre-making pedagogies.

Mitchell's trajectory in the UK theatre industry illustrates the extent to which, despite recent improvements, directing remains a gendered field. This is made manifest in the tone adopted by theatre critics when they write about her work, a strand of analysis pursued by Ben Fowler.[29] Critics have used Mitchell's 'auteur' status as a criticism, with Charles Spencer pointing to the 'overweening arrogance ... of a group of mostly female directors such as Katie Mitchell, Deborah Warner and

Emma Rice'.³⁰ The ways that both Mitchell and Rice have been positioned as 'other' highlights the deeply ingrained value systems at work in British theatre. Mitchell reflects,

> It would be very interesting to analyse the tone of the reviews of my productions. The tone is very different from the tone adopted when writing about male directors and the reviews often give the impression that the critics are chastising me as if I were a very naughty little girl or a bad daughter who should really be doing something else. The mixture of radicalism, pro-Europeanism, feminism and my gender is clearly a challenging cocktail for the patriarchal status quo.³¹

Mitchell's route into directing and theatre-making was rapid and followed the tradition of Oxbridge educated male directors. She was President of the Oxford University's Drama Society and, after graduating, gained an assistant directorship at Paine's Plough and then with the RSC. During the 1980s, she assisted directors Di Trevis and Deborah Warner and directed Emma Rice. This network points to a genealogy of female directors in the UK learning from each other.³² In response to a feeling that 'there was something absent'³³ in the British theatre tradition, Mitchell used a Churchill fellowship to study how directors were trained in Russia, Poland, Lithuania and Georgia. In Russia she saw a greater emphasis on constructing behaviour accurately, with a focus on bodily action, to consider issues of 'time, place, intention and obstacle';³⁴ in Poland, the physical ensemble practice of Gardzienice became a formative influence, which confirmed her sense that British representational acting was lacking.³⁵ She brought this learning to her practice with actors and, from 1990 to 1993, she directed her company Classics on a Shoestring to great acclaim. In the decade that followed she was appointed as an Associate Director to the Royal Court, the RSC and the National Theatre, where she has directed eighteen productions under four different artistic directors.³⁶

Over the last decade Mitchell has made work in Germany, Austria and France, countries which champion experimental theatre.³⁷ This period, which she labels 'the feminist phase', prioritises female concerns and she reflects:

> I have a commitment to putting women's experience at the heart of everything I direct. I used to hide my feminism because I thought it wouldn't help my career, but having experienced patches of quite intense sexism, which in some cases stopped me from doing the work that I wanted to do, I realised that there was no point hiding it, so I decided to really investigate it.³⁸

She cites Pina Bausch, Liz LeCompte, Jane Campion, Marion Jerez and Francesca Woodman as formative influences.³⁹ These are artists who, in various and particular ways, focus on the female body and gender politics. Mitchell's work engages with writers who attend to the marginalised female position: tragedies by Euripides, early-twentieth-century European naturalism, adaptations of feminist literature such as Virginia Wolf's *The Waves* and Charlotte Perkins Gilman's *The Yellow Wallpaper*. These works foreground the suffering enacted on and embedded in the bodies of women.[40] Feminist theorists and writers such as Simone de Beauvoir, Hélène Cixous, Hannah Arendt and Friederike Mayröcker[41] influence her thinking, their writing sometimes directly appearing in scripts.[42] The work of female writers often appears as commentary or counterpoint to extant texts, an example of which can be seen in the way that Inger Christensen's poetry in *Fräulein Julie* colours Strindberg's sparsely used original text.[43] In this way Mitchell's 'feminist phase' of experimental work excavates and exposes a female consciousness in both form and content, even from within problematically 'male' and sometimes misogynist texts, to produce a feminist schooling for actors.[44] Mitchell's production of over one hundred works over the last three decades has made a seminal contribution to twenty-first-century theatre and, through her experiments with form, she has shifted the pedagogies of theatre-making.

## Feminist director pedagogue

The pedagogical imperative of Mitchell's work is evidenced in a number of ways: in her commitment to lifelong learning; the education of early career directors;[45] the creation of a community of practice; her early investigations into how to work with actors; her ongoing exploration into how to affect audiences. In these last two points, Mitchell is attentive to the potential pedagogic exchange that occurs in performance, between the actor/audience. As such, in considering the scope of her feminist pedagogy, we need to recognise these constituents.

Throughout her career she has pursued opportunities to develop her craft, in the 1990s with experimental European practices and between 2001 and 2003, supported by a grant from National Endowment for Science, Technology and the Arts (NESTA), exploring interdisciplinarity (art, film, dance) and the biology of emotions. Mitchell has an aptitude for teaching, which I noticed from my first observation.[46] Actor Benedict Cumberbatch states that she offers 'a schooling in acting' which is like an 'acting gym'.[47] Although Mitchell prefers the term 'translator' to 'teacher', she acknowledges her consistent commitment to 'translating professional theatre-making tools for people who are either amateurs, in education or starting out in their careers'.[48]

Over time Mitchell has built a community of practice, which enables artists to learn together over extended periods. This has particularly facilitated women who tend to dominate her production teams, which Mitchell describes as a 'matriarchy',[49] acknowledging the influence of Pippa Meyer who has stage-managed over thirty shows with military authority and huge presence. Long-standing relationships between female collaborators, including set designer Vicki

Mortimer who has worked with Mitchell since the 1980s, produces a magnified female authority where trust and directness is central to an analytically demanding process. Younger actors learn from 'veterans' and this familial apostology is 'a really nice shorthand'.[50] Like Cumberbatch, many actors acknowledge that Mitchell's practice offers them a training at whatever stage they happen to be in their career. Esther McAuley describes it as, 'the drama school experience that I never had',[51] and veteran Sandy McDade explains, 'Actors who try really hard to put their ego to one side and enjoy the creative discovery get to do things they haven't done before'.[52] Mitchell's ongoing commitment to developing ways of working with actors is symptomatic of her formative experience in Russia, which shifted how she viewed naturalistic acting to reposition mimesis, looking beyond representation towards a presentational form, focused on task and action. She believes that UK directors are significantly disadvantaged by a lack of structured training in how to work with actors. Consequently, in *The Director's Craft*, I suggest that directing and acting pedagogies are developed beside each other.[53] She has consistently supported women directors: at the Young Vic in 2015 she led a week's workshop for fifteen female directors, 'Women as Artists'; and in 2016 she led the 'Women Opera Makers Workshop' in Aix en Provence. From 2018, Mitchell has continued to refine her pedagogy in the training ground, contributing to the MA in Theatre Directing at Royal Holloway, University of London.

Mitchell can be seen to work with critical pedagogy, empowering learners, be they directors or actors, with alternatives to received knowledge and hierarchical learning processes.[54] Features of critical pedagogy can be summarised as: recognising that *how* you teach something is as important as *what* you teach; flattening power structures; individualising learning with a commitment to develop political, personal and social awareness; recognising the complexities of problems as opposed to seeking conclusions; taking notions of difference and particularity as productive sites for potential resistance and change. These strategies are evident in Mitchell's feminist pedagogy with actors which foregrounds the position of women and uses gender as a tool for analysis. I'd like to focus on three aspects of her work that emerged from observing rehearsals: the ways that power operates; the scaffolding structures or 'constructions' that lead the actor through a materialist investigation of bodily action[55] and the dialogic practices.

The way that power operates in Mitchell's theatre-making practice is subtle and complex. Her formative experiences of Russian director training 'and the attendant master–teacher relationship that underpins that history'[56] have influenced her agency as pedagogue, where there is no notion of flattened hierarchy within a collaborative process. In fact, Mitchell maintains that because of the complexity of performance-making she is 'into clear roles … You don't want to have discussions about job descriptions'.[57] It would be easy to see this as replicating patriarchal structures; however a closer consideration of Mitchell's authority from a feminist perspective illuminates the empowering collaboration that

Schenkar describes as operating less like a pyramid and more as interceptive spheres, with each person 'responsible for her or his special circularity'.[58] In practice, clear roles and a rigorous structure allow power to be shared, so that she simultaneously facilitates and leads. Sarah Davey-Hull, a director who trained with Mitchell reflects: 'I'm not there to tell an actor what to do, but to lead an actor'.[59] This idea of leading as opposed to controlling is a subtle but important shift in power produced through the teaching/learning exchange. 'Control' suggests that the actor is told what to do and is passive in the process. However, the clear and explicit scaffolding structures that Mitchell has developed, whether giving an actor feedback, developing the ideas structure of a play, or pinning down action, offers choice within defined parameters and facilitates a Critical Acting Pedagogy. The actor is liberated to take command of the process, because the process is made absolutely explicit from the point of audition. As such, there is a shared and transparent contract, where both director and actor commit to rigorous interrogation of the text in action.

Mitchell has had to learn how to delegate. In the workshop 'Women as Artists' she considered authority from a gendered perspective, stressing the importance of establishing a shared goal with the company and an agreement about what that means; to find a 'lightness of touch'; a 'cool, calmer location'; less of 'a close-up relationship; and more of a long shot'. These terms suggest the need to remain objective and measured in communication. Mitchell relayed how an actor had once described her authority as 'Blow, blow, blow, push'.[60] This alludes to the nurturing imperative of female labour, touched on in Chapter 1 and recalls Tristan Sturrock's observation that female directors 'push softer but harder'.[61] In this way, Mitchell can be seen to 'lead from behind',[62] which evidences a reflexive practice where she is able to conserve her emotional and physical stamina, moving to 'full frontal energy' when needed.[63] The pedagogic structures that underpin the foundations, architecture and fabric of the work, allow the company to progress with clarity and direction without her physical presence. This became apparent when, during rehearsal for *The Cherry Orchard,* Mitchell was ill for a week and I observed how her authority functioned in her absence. The stage management, assistant directors and actors were able to run rehearsals with precision, due to the shared ownership of the ideas structure and the established dialogic practice. Mitchell was able to watch recordings of rehearsal at home and then send notes on each act/section. In her absence her pedagogy was most present, as the company embodied it.

Mitchell's theatre-making is structured differently depending on the form of the piece, whether play, devised or 'live cinema', but it can be broadly divided into two stages: pre-rehearsal preparation with the whole creative team, where the aim is to discover the 'ideas structure' of the work and later, rehearsal with actors. Throughout her career Mitchell has sought ways to help actors achieve the hyperrealism and mutuality that she experienced in Russia and Poland. In *The Director's Craft* she explains each stage of her methodology, breaking down specific tasks with actors, but these practices are worth re-considering through the lens of new feminist materialism intersecting with her pedagogy.

Mitchell's process facilitates the actor with all the information s/he needs to make an informed action choice; to reflexively consider 'the three-dimensional structure of the play and the character, so that they 'play everything, not just one little muscle of it'.⁶⁴ Playing 'everything' means that bodies are politicised and action responds to a complex network of power structures. Every action is seen as bodily data, information through which one might read socially/culturally constructed action (inscribed *on* the body), and biologically/psychologically constructed action, (inscribing *through* the body).⁶⁵ As such, Mitchell teaches actors to interrogate the materiality of the body, where nature operates *beside* culture; to be alert to patriarchal structures and the possibility of feminist acts of resistance.

Learning is scaffolded through two stages: the first, a detailed investigation and construction of time and place, biography, past pictures (shared memories); and an analysis of action choices, through mapping the events and intentions throughout the text. Every action choice is the result of a democratic negotiation, with action analysed as socially, historically and politically constructed. The company creates a unified understanding of the place and period, through identifying facts and questions, which are researched and shared, enabling the group to become the experts. In rehearsals for *The Cherry Orchard* in 2014, Mitchell first shared her timeline, which charted key events and their relationship to the politics and context of the period. This allowed facts and questions to be noted, researched and shared by the company to build a detailed and comprehensive through-line of action for the events in the play. The list of facts and questions was exhaustive, with as many as 400 to be shared amongst the actors as homework. The ensemble located the Gayev estate accurately in Russia, to map the geography of the estate itself, the building and the layout of the rooms, the distance and position of the lake where Grisha drowned in relation to the cherry orchard, the train distance from Suni to Moscow and the distance from the village when walking or travelling by carriage.⁶⁶ Physical maps were created and, along with images of locations and portraits of secondary characters, this information was pinned around the rehearsal room. At the end of each day individualised or group homework tasks were set. Setting homework is a pedagogic feature of Mitchell's practice, which enables the actors to educate each other to construct a shared understanding of the world of the play. For example, actors created detailed autobiographies and timelines, which enabled a collective mapping of networks to create a common history. The shared construction of the play-world allows time and place, the social domain and habitus, to be accurately played through the material body. The script is then analysed to map the events and intentions which drive the action.⁶⁷ Recalling Loukes' situational en-action theory, these actions are responses to the situation, time, place and the other characters, and so are both externally (culturally) and internally (naturally) drawn.[68] In this way, Marxist notions of inscribed power *on* the body collide with phenomenological states of being *in* the body and this is made explicit for the actors who play this through the agreed actions. The second stage is to get the piece 'up on its feet' by improvising the events and intentions in each section, receiving notes and testing their logic and accuracy in relation to each other. Once tested in practice, the text is 'laid on top' of the action and, in this way, the ensemble moves through the whole text, from analysis to improvisation, working with text, receiving direction, repeating and so forth.

Through these 'constructions', Mitchell's theatre-making pedagogy enables a democratised and critical learning process. Members of the company are supported and guided to negotiate, navigate and take responsibility for every action decision, which results in shared ownership of the project. Sandy McDade, an actor who works frequently with Mitchell, explains the plurality of this learning:

> I think if you accept you're a fish in a shoal or a bird in a flock you are absolutely fine, but you mustn't try to move away from that image ... Actors are often cast because they have a certain charisma. Katie doesn't do that. You are there for the group.[69]

Mitchell's work, whether classical naturalism, theatre for children, large-scale operas or 'live cinema' celebrates and develops the power of the ensemble, no doubt referencing the heightened state of mutuality that she experienced through the practice of Gardzienice. The rigour and challenge of the group learning process flattens hierarchical divisions. The actor finds it harder to retreat into their own imagination or psychological tendencies, which Mitchell terms 'affinities',[70] because every decision has been negotiated with everyone else. Mitchell leads this process, questioning and guiding to reach a shared interpretation and 'by fixing certain aspects of the character, the actor is freed to do their own work'.[71] Once the 'ideas structures' have been decided, actors can play within these parameters, which Mitchell necessarily monitors.

Some actors dislike the pinning down of decisions. As Rebellato observes, 'It is very demanding; bad theatrical habits are dismantled, approximations and short cuts are exposed'.[72] However, actors repeatedly reflect on how this rigorous rehearsal structure paradoxically allows for greater freedom. Nick Fletcher explained, 'I've felt much more suffocated and controlled by other directors, mainly because there's not proper communication between us. But it's a unified understanding and it's the result of a detailed discussion'.[73] The detailed research, discussion and off text improvisations allow the actors to share the same imaginative picture of the world they inhabit. McAuly reflects, 'You don't ever have to make anything up. You've just done it all'.[74] Every aspect of time, place and circumstance has been questioned and answered, including the temperature, weather, function and history of objects. For example, McAuly, in her role as a maid in *A Woman Killed With Kindness*, had researched and practised every aspect of her domestic duties, working with specific materials.[75] Kate Duchêne observes: 'Sometimes I've felt that working with other directors I tend to flail about and resort to doing things I've done before, whereas all the improvisation means you know what your reactions to things are'.[76] The detailed architecture of back story and given circumstance built through the ensemble process supports the actor to 'play every little muscle' and to be spontaneous within the themes and ideas put forward by the play.[77]

It is useful to recall Milde's structure for rehearsal analysis or spoken artistic discourse as we consider the ways that Mitchell's liberatory pedagogy operates through dialogic interactions.[78] Milde breaks down modes of exchange as: providing feedback; providing explanations; using improvisations; providing instructions and using keys (meaning spontaneous coaching or 'side coaching'); framing one's own activity; sharing ideas, thoughts, stories, anecdotes; making suggestions; asking questions.[79] This final strategy is central to Mitchell's critical pedagogy. The constant application of guided questions, in homework tasks building time and place or in defining intentions, foregrounds choice for the actor, who is invested in the multiple construction of ideas. The specificity that characterises Mitchell's pedagogic dialogue is partly the result of two years of training with Ellen Bowman at Living Pictures[80] to identify 'things that stood in the way of me clearly organising lots of people'[81] and to refine and sharpen her feedback. Duchêne notes, 'Katie doesn't like words like "good" or "bad" and that is liberating'.[82] It is the absolute clarity of feeding back through the constructs of events, intentions, time and place that is instrumental to her authority. In discussion, certain phrases emerge, which might be seen as the second order of rehearsal dialogue. Mitchell cautions actors against playing 'affinities', imaginative leaps not drawn from evidence within the text; she avoids choices that she describes as 'blurry' or 'muddy' and guards against 'acting clichés', striving to anticipate 'acting corners' and to 'land' or 'park' an action choice. 'Acting corners' refer to difficult moments for the actor where she might find herself without a logical action choice and resorting to a clichéd appropriation. The need to 'land' a 'simple' or 'clear' action choice is at the heart of the process as Mitchell guides actors away from purely psychological interpretation to focus on the behavioural action of 'data'.

Although Mitchell steadfastly claims her allegiance to Stanislavski's methods, in certain respects her approach, with its inner and outer attention, places Brechtian practice *beside* Stanislavski, or enables the two approaches to intersect. Playing on the Stanislavskian terminology, 'Method of Physical Action', which influences Mitchell's process, I position her work as a 'method of feminist action', which interrogates the materiality of the body. As we shall see, this moves acting beyond representational ideas of mimesis, which feminist scholarship has reviled for its inherent phallocentric structures, to insist on the forensic analysis of action as 'data'. Elin Diamond's seminal project, *Unmaking Mimesis*, which re-figures representation through the Brechtian inspired approaches of feminist theatre-makers, can be re-considered through Mitchell's post-Stanislavskian/Brechtian approach, which enables actors to *re-make* mimesis for the contemporary stage.[83]

## *Re-making mimesis: Vital materialism*

The ideological roots of Mitchell's pedagogy can be seen in new feminist materialisms, which draw on developments in science and technology to recognise bodies as vital, relational and in states of becoming. Rosi Braidotti explains: 'a new brand of "materialism" is current in our scientific practices, which reinstates the vital, self-organising capacities of what was previously seen as inert matter'.[84] This 'matter realist feminism' offers an alternative to limiting post-structuralist linguistics and 'fights matter with matter'[85] to recognise nature operating *beside* culture. As explained, Mitchell's pedagogy teaches actors to read the data of bodies with these two strands operating beside each other. Stanislavski's interest in looking 'behind psychology at biology'[86] was an early revelation, which led her to research bodily conditions, working with neuroscientist Mark Lythgoe to explore the biology of emotions and with psychiatrist Dr Neil Brener to interrogate psychological conditions. In the process of character development in rehearsal for *The Cherry Orchard*, actors mined the body as material, exploring the conditions of: narcolepsy (Pishchik), the autistic spectrum (Gaev), depression (Varya), post-natal depression (Ranevskaya), stroke (Fiers) and agoraphobia (Pishchik's daughter).[87] These conditions were researched and the minutiae of physical symptoms examined. In this way 'mimesis' necessitates the forensic deconstruction and reconstruction of corporeality, moving beyond representation towards something altogether more nuanced, complex and layered – in short, something more real.

In *Reconsidering Stanislavski: Feeling, Feminism and the Actor*, Rhonda Blair draws attention to how feminist scientists have questioned cognition, behaviour and sexuality and how these might be embodied in the brain.[88] She cites Antonio Damasio, a neuroscientist who has also influenced Mitchell, to highlight how the self is actualised through relational action.[89] Like Mitchell, Blair works at the intersections of theory, practice, history and science, and she challenges 'feminist actors and acting teachers to be more rigorous in their understanding of bodies, consciousness, and feelings … with the awareness that these processes are reflective of brain structure and function'.[90] This post-Stanislavskian approach strives to teach acting in a more precise and accurate way, combining phenomenological theory of embodiment with Marxist and post-structuralist considerations of bodies and power. Working in this way, the female actor recognises how, through detailed analysis, she might author her action within the constructs of realism. For example, in rehearsal for *The Cherry Orchard*, Duchêne, playing Ranevskaya, discovered that her legs literally gave way when she was in a heightened state of emotion. This unbalancing gave physical expression to her grief at the loss of her child to recognise Ranevskaya as a victim of her social circumstance *and* her maternal body.

Such heightened psychophysical awareness was sharpened in 2003, when 'The Emotion Workshop' enabled Mitchell and Lythgoe to work with actors to interrogate the phenomenology of emotion, action and cognition, exploring seven dominant emotional states to investigate the body/brain response. The actors explored the delay that happens in between an event and the corresponding emotional reaction. In this moment, unless the actor is clear about what is happening, the action she communicates can be 'muddy' and the audience is not able to read it clearly. Central to Mitchell's hyper-realism is acting that interrogates the minutia of unconscious behaviour. For example, in rehearsals for *The Cherry Orchard* actors shared 'slice of life' improvisations on unrequited love. They worked with a partner to re-enact a moment from their life when they had been rejected sexually or romantically. The improvisation was observed 'not for judgment' but 'as scientists' and Mitchell led the analysis. She was careful in her framing of this exposing exercise, ensuring that the veterans performed first, and prompting the actors to notice information in unconscious physical behaviour.[91] This personal sharing, apart from offering a framework for analysis, was bonding for the group. Obviously, each individual body experiences and performs emotional states in different ways, but by teaching actors to observe physical data accurately, Mitchell develops a reflexive awareness and specificity in her performers. She is not leading the actor to *experience* the emotion, but to accurately *show* it, so that the audience can feel it, referencing a post-Brechtian approach. She explains this:

> Any investigation of emotion as it is etched on the body, is an investigation in order to re-construct the shape of that emotion so that the audience can feel something – it's not about the actor feeling the emotion, because sometimes when the actor feels something inside themselves, what we see on the outside is quite opaque.[92]

However, as we will see, this directorial intention does not necessarily correspond with the actor's subjective experience.

In its determined preoccupation with the female consciousness and the affect of bodily data, Mitchell's work has opened up opportunities for female actors to interrogate the unruly female body in extreme states of trauma, transformation and endurance. The preoccupation with female suffering has earned her the self-imposed title 'Queen of Despair',[93] where bodies are simultaneously vulnerable and powerfully enduring, performing their sexed materiality whilst impacted by patriarchal violence. Female bodies are the material transactions of war, marriage and prostitution, and in their trauma they are visceral, leaking, messing, spoiling.[94] Actors mine the physiological states of the sexed female body through thematic strands of reproduction, mothering, sexuality and suicide: *Small Hours* investigates postnatal depression;[95] *Iphigenia at Aulis* tackles genocide; *Women of Troy* child murder;[96] *The Cherry Orchard* foregrounds Ranevskaya's grief at her son's drowning; *Cleansed* sees the body no longer intelligible in terms of sex or gender but, in its becoming, a site of resistance.[97] One could argue that feminist resistance is most forcibly produced through the pervasive theme of female suicide. During 2016–2017, three works playing in London had suicide at their core: *The Forbidden Zone,* which combined science, women and war through the dual suicides of Clara Immerwahr, whose husband developed poisonous gas and decades later her grand-daughter Clair Haber who discovered her grand-mother's story;[98] *Ophelias Zimmer,* a portrait of the psychological damage that preceded Ophelia's suicide;[99] and *Anatomy of a Suicide,* which places the lives of three generations of women, two of whom commit suicide, the play ending with the third requesting sterilization, with the controversial suggestion of an inherited suicide gene.[100] Mitchell's daughter has challenged her mother about this recurrent theme, asking why women can't, 'go forward and do something more positive in the world?'[101] However, Mitchell is clear that while her work foregrounds 'the effects of women inside patriarchal structures, their attempts to cope with them and fight them', it doesn't attempt to offer 'alternative structures'.[102] Perhaps, through this collective feminist act of creation, all involved – director, creative team, actors and audience – are called to account, to act as feminists, to seek out these alternative structures.

In the creation of a body of work that foregrounds the vital materialism of female bodies, Mitchell allows female actors, too often restricted in roles, to flex their muscles in her acting gym. How then is the body of the actor transformed through this schooling? 'Veteran' Kate Duchêne has repeatedly played 'weeping women' who face death, the loss of a child and suicide: Clytemnestra in *Iphigenia et Aulis,* Hecuba in *Woman of Troy,* Ranevskaya in *The Cherry Orchard,* Maria Handke in *A Sorrow Beyond Dreams.* In interview, she reflects that it may be the extremity of female emotion that alienates male critics or the dismantling of female representations, where the unruly body expels, transforms and destroys. She considers the habitual vulnerability she has confronted in these roles and the essence of Mitchell's process:

> She wants me to go much further in what we know to be real emotions that women experience. And not only about simply suffering, I mean there's a culpability to these women too. Katie wants precision, accurate intellectual analysis and the emotion to go as far as it needs to, which is often extreme.[103]

This feminist method of physical action, which places nature *beside* culture in its rigorous insistence on specificity, has allowed director and actor to mine the possibilities of female-ness together. However, reflecting on her process in *Women of Troy,* Duchêne admits that, on this occasion, she failed to work with Mitchell's approach. She found it impossible to objectively construct the emotion through physical action when embodying a theme as cataclysmic as genocide. She said, 'It was a bit of a nemesis for me ... I'm not very good at pretending to feel things'.[104] We are reminded that, however objective the analysis, Duchêne's own body matters, reveals itself, belying any system. Mitchell offers actors a process but ultimately individuals will experience this in their own way.

## Agential realism and cyborgs

It is perhaps in Mitchell's 'live cinema' that she has most transformed acting pedagogies and altered the relationship between actor and audience. Mitchell describes this work as being, 'on the edge of theatre',[105] where theatre and cinema exist beside each other and the space between the two becomes a third productive medium. Mitchell was influenced by the work of seminal New York experimental theatre ensemble the Wooster Group[106] and when she saw them in 2002, she had already been experimenting in ways that might allow the audience a closer connection to the physical body of the actor. Her adaptation of Virginia Woolf's novel *Waves*, at the National in 2006, was seen as radical in its genre-defying approach and she has continued to refine and develop the complexity of this genre in her 'feminist phase' over the last decade.[107] Most of these works are adaptations of period novels or short stories,[108] either devised by the company or by a writer, sometimes drawn from feminist literature or re-orientations of male authored works to a female centered perspective. Citing Hélène Cixous, the form and aesthetic invites the audience into the consciousness of the female protagonist as a kind of *écriture feminine,* with a fragmented and multi-sensed reality.[109]

This inter-medial form develops a new feminist materialist approach as Mitchell and actors interrogate the body in relation with technology. Duchêne reflects, 'I love the multi-media stuff because I am interested in different ways of acting ... I like the feeling of construction around it in a different, more technical way'.[110] The interface with technology exposes the hybridity of the individual, with 'being' presented as division, to resist the limiting structures that inhibit and oppress women in particular. *Waves* had actors sitting at tables with microphones, narrating Woolf's fragmented novel whilst constructing and filming shots, which were projected on a huge wide screen above the stage. Lehmann describes this doubling, which separates voice from presence, as 'resulting in the creation of a kind of voice mask that "ghosts the character" and renders him/her a spoken "it" as opposed to a speaking "I"'.[111] This work enables actors to produce a democratised stage where their bodies have no more agency than the technology they struggle to work with. Louise Le Page observes how, in *Waves,* identity is not defined by psychological type but 'according to what the body *does,* not what it is'.[112] The focus is on the labour of production and by separating character and human elements – body, voice, sound – 'a *schizo* subject'[113] emerges that offers actors an alternative to phallocentric notions of truth and ideas of fixed identity. Bodies appear in shifting states of becoming and possibility. By ... *some trace of her* at the National in 2008, a company devised adaptation of Dostoyevsky's *The Idiot,* the fragmented narrative moved out from behind tables, to be more fluid and physical. In rehearsal and in performance actors danced around the stage, as camera cables weaved in and out of each other, one-minute acting in character within a shot, the next creating the Foley sound, narrating the text or setting up and filming the image. In this work, actors doubled their roles to create a second role as camera operators, constantly switching between worlds; the 'real' world of filming and the constructed temporality of the fragmentary narrative.[114] For the actor, working in these small constructions, moment to moment, moving from task to task with specificity, offers another level of challenge.

The actor's doubling makes the authoring of performance the subject of performance, as they present themselves as both subject and object. Gendered assumptions are shattered as dialogue is passed between ensemble members and, through the manipulation of the camera, the actor is seen to take charge of the constructed image of representation. When the camera is in the hands of a female actor, costumed in restrictive period clothing, setting up her own shot or setting up the shot and filming another, the female gaze and women's shifting historical agency is foregrounded.[115] In Mitchell's doubling strategy, women author 'looking at being looked-at-ness', to be the agents of their own production. In 'making the canvas fair' Mitchell decentralises attention from humans to the power of thing-ness,[116] to achieve what Karen Barad describes as an 'agential realism'.[117] The performance of the apparatus – film screen, camera, tripods, cables, properties – is no less vital than human performance. This moves from a reflected mimesis to a refraction, a *re-making of mimesis*, where in the liminal space between 'watching' an image or a sound being constructed and 'seeing' the effect, room is made for mis-seeing and mis-hearing. For example, in the work with Foley sound, the space between absence and presence is phenomenologically felt. When we hear the amplified sound of footsteps accompanying the image on the screen of a man walking, whilst simultaneously seeing the Foley artist crunching an empty shoe onto a tray of gravel, and the actor being filmed walking on the spot, a type of synesthesia occurs and we work harder to reconstruct the de-constructed sensory elements. Human and non- human (camera, tripod, screen, shoes, gravel, tray, microphone) performatively construct the image. Paradoxically, in the space between construction and deconstruction this produces a more radical form of realism, phenomenologically changing the bodies of the audience.

In 2014, I observed the making of one of Mitchell's 'live cinema' pieces *A Sorrow Beyond Dreams*.[118] The production was an adaptation of Peter Handke's harrowing short novel recording his own reaction to his mother's suicide. It was a collaboration among UK, Austrian and German artists. Like many of Mitchell's more recent works the set was highly complex, consisting of a four-room three-dimensional apartment, with two pods either side of the stage, one for a Foley artist and the other for voice artists. It was fascinating to observe a re-imagined theatrical ensemble through this form where the rehearsal room becomes a film set. Time as a material seems to become thicker in the making of this work, where there are up to thirty people working simultaneously in a confined space to construct a perfectly timed choreography relying on technology, which inevitably fails at different points and so halts the process. The highly pressurised matter of timing is taken on by the stage management, who co-ordinate the different parts of the team and move the project steadily forward, second by second. The shared human endeavour to master and control the technology is palpable, a post-human way of being with 'flatter structures of mutuality'.[119] The cameras are extensions of the actor's body and this blurring between human and technological matter recalls Haraway's post-feminist cyborg.[120] Haraway's cyborg feminism questions what it means to be embodied in a high-tech world without gender divisions where the blurring of boundaries and borders might dissolve phallocentric structures. From this perspective, Mitchell's vital materialist position can be seen to extend beyond the matter of the body to interrogate the mattering of technology. The camera lens allows for a microscopic gaze, as the actors manipulate the tripod, wires and focusing, moving over and under each other to perform their score. The cables, which must be successfully threaded in and out of each other in order to achieve the journey through the piece, start to resemble the tendons and veins of the body of the work. When the technology stops, all motion stops, like blood clotting. The technology is part of the corporeal structure and becomes the eyes of the actor and the audience. As the gaze of the camera is the gaze constructed by an actor filming another actor, the power of the acting position is shifted from 'looking at' to 'looking at being looked at'. Like the de-gendered voice, the gaze is neither male or female as the camera passes between actors producing, what Phelan calls, a 'reciprocal gaze'.[121] This work 'shifts culture' in the way that it challenges the idea that there is one (male) privileged point of view to show that perception is shifting, relational and that we exist together in states of becoming.

Mitchell's hugely varied body of work has made a seminal contribution to the development of actor training and theatre-making pedagogy more broadly in the UK and in Europe. For over three decades she has explored the ways that actors, directors and audiences can make work together through approaches that foreground her feminism. Her work seeks to understand the female condition and in its intersections with new feminist materialism it challenges actors to re-think and refine their work with human and non-human matter. As feminist pedagogue, Mitchell can be seen to have shifted the culture of theatre-making in the ways that she re-makes mimesis to challenge artists and audiences to perceive acting, theatre and constructs of gender differently.[122]

## Emma Rice: A school for wise children

Emma Rice's body of work is story-telling at its most theatrically exhuberant, pursuing concerns that reflect her own life-experience, her hopes, losses, dreams and fears. These stories are often adaptations of myths (*Tristan and Yseult*, 2003, *The Bacchae*, 2004),[123] folk/fairy tales (*The Red Shoes*, 2000, *Wooden Frock*, 2003),[124] or Shakespeare plays dealing with wonder (*Cymbeline*, 2006, *A Midsummer Night's Dream*, 2016).[125] She positions her work as feminist, citing Angela Carter, Tracey Emin, Louise Bourgeois, Pina Bausch and Joan Littlewood as key influences.[126] Like Mitchell, she has been dubbed a female 'auteur' and suffered vitriolic reviews from male critics.[127] However, unlike Mitchell, Rice maintains a commitment to make theatre that is 'uncynical ... without any barrier of cleverness and intellect coming between the performance and the audience' infused with 'vulnerability and foolishness'.[128] The quality of high-art/low-art that characterises her work produces what Duska Radoslavljevic refers to as 'subversive populism' as opposed to 'explicit radicalism'; through appealing to the audience with commercially successful adaptations that are then re-authored, the work becomes a 'continuous political act that has provoked and challenged some established models of theatre-making'.[129] Rice has moved between the subsidised and commercial sectors of British theatre, producing crowd-pleasing shows whilst pushing at the boundaries of theatrical form. In this section, I consider the ways that Rice's work, as a feminist act, has developed the pedagogy in mainstream UK theatre. In analysing her approach, I draw on rehearsal observations between 2014 and 2015 across two shows, *Tristan and Yseult*, a new adaptation of Daphne du Maurier's *Rebecca* and interviews with Rice and actors from the ensemble.[130]

Rice's career trajectory differs from the majority of directors (male and female) who have come through Oxbridge channels. She was born in Oxford in 1967, trained as an actor at Guildhall and from 2005 worked with Mike Shepherd as the joint Artistic Director of the internationally renowned Kneehigh, a company originating and based in Cornwall. In May 2015, the Globe Theatre announced her appointment as the first female Artistic Director, and Rice took up the post in April 2016, positioning herself at the vanguard of the UK's cultural landscape. Her first 'Wonder Season' broke box office records and was described as 'a feminist makeover', as Rice committed to gender equality in casting.[131] However, within two years she resigned from the post, citing irreconcilable differences around 'personal trust and artistic freedom' between herself and the governing board who objected to the use of technology on the Globe stage.[132] Her premature exit prompted questions about the purpose of the Globe, as heritage industry or theatre, with Kim Solga asking who 'owns' Shakespeare?[133] In 2018, Rice secured Arts Council funding to start a new company based in Bristol, Wise Children. Its inaugural production, of the same name, was an adaptation of Angela Carter's novel. Its remit is to develop and tour new work and to establish a theatre school offering training courses and mentoring for actors, musicians, directors, designers and writers. The artists that Rice works with are also expected to teach, and 50% of the places are free for disadvantaged groups. Now in her fifties Rice, like Mitchell, is actively exploring her role as feminist director/pedagogue, passing on her knowledge to the next generation of theatre-makers. She reflects, 'The next chapter has to also be about what you can put back in'.[134]

Rice's theatre-making pedagogy developed as an antidote to her own training experience. Her most seminal creative training took place before drama school studying for a BTEC in Performing Arts at Harrington Further Education College. Here she credits her teacher, Marielaine Church, as a formative influence, recalling how each week they would take turns to direct, light, design, act or run sound.[135] Actor training at Guildhall School of Music and Drama, which she describes as 'a skills camp',[136] taught her 'how to deliver to the industry, not really to be creative ourselves'.[137] In the early 1990s she joined Theatre Alibi, the Essex based company founded by Alison Hodge and Tim Spicer. Touring schools with a theatre-in-education programme allowed Rice to shift from drama school constructions of character and fourth-wall naturalism, to focus on the story as 'Children care about what happens next and whether it's interesting or not, the two basic principles of storytelling'. These parameters continue to define her work.[138]

Theatre Alibi brought Rice into contact with a different set of references than those she had previously encountered, including Kantor, Grotowski, Wilson and Gardzienice. Most importantly, it put her in a position where she was developing a creative voice, 'discussing the work as well as doing the work'.[139] In 1993, Alibi received an education grant to develop their training practices with Gardzienice in Poland. Rice was subsequently invited to join the company as an actor and, as with Mitchell and Hodge, her experience with Gardzienice is formative, 'We all had an unspoken bond. It was like a survivors' group'.[140] She returned to the UK, working with Mitchell as an actor and choreographer in the mid-1990s and her collaboration with Hodge and Mitchell extends a genealogy of UK women practitioners learning from and with each other.

The contradictory experience of training Rice received in Poland instilled an almost spiritual engagement with theatre-making. Rice comments, 'As a performer I felt cracked open by Gardzienice in a way that three years at drama school had not touched me. I feel that I was sort of borne out there in many ways'.[141] However, the masculine, 'authoritarian' training regime, which was 'punishing', 'controlling', 'full of fear which gets results',[142] cemented Rice's own ideas about the ways that she did and did not want to work. Unlike Hodge and Mitchell, who experienced the training with the agency of visiting collaborator and director, Rice received it as an actor and found it overwhelming, at times oppressive and often disorientating:

> Everything about it disarms you … It's a very physical, European, autocratic system. Staniewski, the leader of the troupe, is amazing but he does shout at you and some things you can never get right … It was terrifying.[143]

When Rice first joined Kneehigh in 1994 and then committed herself to the company in a full-time capacity in 2000, she found a way of making theatre through affirmation and pleasure as opposed to failure and anxiety. She reflects, 'It was a bit like being in Poland because it was rural and people ate together, but it was happy. Instead of creating pain to make something beautiful there was laughter creating something beautiful'.[144] This recalls the positive imperative of the *via positiva* explained in Chapter 2, a condition that defines Rice's process. Kneehigh's aesthetic is borne from rough theatre and storytelling practices, anarchic, often in the open air, responding to the geography, myths and folkloric traditions of Cornwall. Kneehigh founders Mike Shepherd and Bill Mitchell encouraged Rice to direct, and in 2000 she won Best Director in the Barclays Theatre Management Association awards for *The Red Shoes*. Following this, there was a run of successes, with Rice making up to three shows each year,[145] establishing an aesthetic of highly visual and musical storytelling, total theatre, which is irreverent, passionate and populist.[146]

Rice acknowledges that she offers 'something a bit different from other directors, where you come in and you get your script. I train actors in the way that I like to make theatre, building an ensemble'.[147] Unlike Mitchell, she has not documented her own practice as an educational tool but she has explained her methodology as a form of training in interview.[148] Her most recent venture, to create a 'School for Wise Children' demonstrates her commitment to prioritise theatre-making pedagogies.

## *Pedagogy for the collective imagination*

> So all I can do is take my team marching alongside me and I'm a little bit in front and I'm absolutely telling them which way to go, but I'm picking them up if they fall, not leaving them, so none of it particularly feels like a choice. I feel I've built a process around my experience, my personality and my aesthetic, that results in what I know best.[149]

Katie Mitchell's comment, 'Emma leads from the front and I lead from behind'[150] offers an interesting perspective from which to think about how these two pedagogues broker their authority and facilitate collaboration. Rice explains her practice as harnessing 'the collective imagination', yet her use of the term 'collective' is perhaps misleading when it comes to understanding her authority.[151] The idea of the 'collective imagination' suggests equally shared decision-making; however, as Shepherd explains, 'The notion that we are all chipping in with ideas and that there is a sort of woolly, collaborative process is not the case'.[152] Rice uses the term 'collective' to indicate a plural imagination, where power is passed among the ensemble who take a collective responsibility in the creative process, which she leads. This approach reflects Peggy Phelan's call for a pedagogy where power is 'less monolithic, more local and in perpetual motion'.[153] No doubt this reflects Rice's formative theatre-making with Gardzienice and Kneehigh, where a community of practice is produced through living together in an isolated rural location,[154] built on a shared ideology, which Hannah Arendt explains as the 'force of mutual promise or contract'.[155] For Kneehigh, the mutual promise is made manifest in a collection of words written on a wall in their rehearsal space, which appear as a type of creed or contract – 'generosity, wonder, joy, naughtiness, irreverence, anarchy'.[156] These dispositional qualities define this community whose way of being is familial through dwelling together. The notion of 'family' is repeatedly used by Rice to explain the nature of a company, its relationships and its structures. Maddy Costa, in her description of Kneehigh's process, describes Rice as 'not the matriarch, but the elder sister, aware that someone needs to exercise a modicum of responsibility'.[157] Sisterly, as opposed to maternal authority, points to a more equal relationship.

Through Kneehigh, Rice has established a core group of collaborators including Shepherd, sound designer Simon Baker, writers Carl Grose, Simon Harvey, and Anna Maria Murphy, composers and musicians Stu Barker and Ian Ross, choreographer Etta Murfitt, lighting designer Malcolm Rippeth, photographer Steve Tanner and puppet maker Sarah Wright. Due to their long associations they share an aesthetic, dialogue and knowledge of each other's ways of working and these relationships have developed beyond theatre-making so that the ensemble resembles a family, with people developing similar traits and qualities as performers.[158] Rice looks for playfulness and a lack of ego in her actors, a 'spirit' akin to the character, observing that 'the people that suit us are a little bit what I call "left-handed"'.[159] Many performers work repeatedly with Rice and are multi-skilled musicians, singers, dancers and actors. Some have day jobs, only performing with the company, as Rice enjoys seeing 'untrained bodies doing extraordinary things'.[160] As a result, her work challenges normative casting and situates itself on the margins through the way it celebrates what Braidotti refers to as the 'positivity of difference'.[161] Arendt's understanding of plurality as a way of allowing for individual uniqueness can usefully be applied as a means of appreciating this group dynamic.[162] Theatre critic Dominic Cavendish points to this when he comments, 'Few companies combine such ensemble zest with such individual truth'.[163] In this way the 'collective imagination' is simultaneously plural and unique.

Like Mitchell, Rice acknowledges her leadership within the theatre- making process where she carries the responsibility for the vision of the work, its quality and its potential for success. She explains 'the way I've been successful is when I've felt happy and confident, so I make every effort to find the best in everybody in the room'.[164] Rice achieves this by leading the process, so that the actors 'have the space to be free'[165] and her common agency as an actor gives her authority. Tristan Sturrock comments on her ability to work with 'the energies and the rhythms of how people work together and that's what creates a really exciting company'.[166] Enabling the 'best of everybody' requires playfulness and risk–taking, and Rice confronts fear, vulnerability and failure, repositioning them as strengths in the creative process. This way of learning is commented on by actor Lizzie Winkler: 'She often says, "Strong but wrong"! so I think, "I'm just going to give it a go"'.[167] This coupling of positive encouragement and direct critique has emerged as a trait of female directorial practice, which actor Tristan Sturrock described as being 'hard but soft'.[168] Affirmation and failure operate beside each other like a möbius strip. As a result, there is a re-orientation towards pleasure in the learning process. In Chapter 2, this is explained as a movement from the *via negativa* (learning through confronting blocks, which is the dominant form of learning Rice experienced with Gardzienice), to the *'via positiva'*[169] (learning through supported affirmation). Rice reflects:

> I think fear does work, but I think you need an awful lot of confidence to use that tactic and I don't have that … there are things that have to be found in the gap between me and an actor … I function better in a happy room.[170]

The means of achieving a 'happy room' are impossible to qualify, but a close consideration of the way that Rice negotiates this 'gap' between herself and her actors through the scaffolding of task and use of dialogue in rehearsal helps to illuminate her pedagogy in practice.

Play is a central way of learning and creating. In describing her Wise Children, Rice reflects 'We are, in many ways, professional children, and proud as punch to be so. And we are wise because we have to be. Whilst holding on to joy and a capacity for wonder, we also need to be clever and canny.'[171] Her practice generates two forms of play, identified by Kendrick in her interrogation of Callois' play theory – *ludus* (the structure of the game) and *paida* (the play instinct), which operate beside each other throughout the process.[172] It is through playing well together that the action, characters and eventually the text emerges. Rehearsals always begin with various games such as 'keepy uppy',[173] forms of volleyball, or grandmother's footsteps[174] and Rice will join in as a player and a referee. These games have been developed and the rules adulterated over the years to become part of a shared family shorthand. For example, when playing volleyball the third hit must be with an alternative body part; penalties are given for over aggressive playing, 'a wanker shot', 'double dibbs' or being 'too bad' and through this child-like game the group are bonded, alert and playfully competitive. Like Landon-Smith,[175] Rice reflects that she finds it easier to encourage males to be playful and that she sees this dispositional quality as gendered:

> I have a theory that boys are brought up to be greedy and to be naughty. You sort of say, 'He's a lad'! 'That's really funny'! and girls are brought up to be good and restrained and you're talking about your earliest blueprinting, 'Isn't she good'! 'Isn't she neat'! 'Isn't she polite'?[176]

**184** Considering Practice

She acknowledges that in her early career 'It was easier to pull the serious out of funny men than I have found to pull the funny out of serious women. It's a harder job'.[177] However, over the years she has developed this playful relationship with a group of 'top birds' including Annette McLoughlin, Dot Atkinson, Lizzie Winkler, Katy Owen and Tamzin Griffin. It is interesting to note this repeated reference to 'playing the fool' as a masculine trait and the comparative difficulty for females to access this.[178] Research suggests that a comparative lack of physical playfulness in girls is connected to issues around body confidence, which inhibit freedom in physical games and sports.[179]

At times, Rice's dialogic practice resembles the motivational speech of a sports coach. She side-coaches throughout rehearsal, which creates the dynamic of one continuous team game using phrases such as: 'Make me an offer'!; 'What don't we do? Show'!; 'Looking out! Always looking out'!; 'What should we do? We'll try it in, we'll try it out'!; 'What are we? We are strong and stable. We are bright and flexible'!; 'Stagecraft! Nothing to see! Nothing to see'!; 'Do it again, but be better'!; 'Strong but wrong'!.[180] Rice's dialogue is simultaneously playful and bonding, demanding and instructive. Shared responsibility through game playing continues into vocal warm-ups, led by one of the company, where the ensemble will practice tongue twisters and sing together. In all rehearsals, the musical director and musicians are working alongside the actors and any distinction is blurred as singing is a practice of the rehearsal room. This brings great unity to the group, as Rice notes 'Singing is a great leveler'.[181] The Balkan singing that she learnt with Gardzienice, collides with folk, punk and Ross's distinctive composition. The blended voices enable a strong sense of mutuality, allowing the ensemble to develop a polyphonic attention to each other and a shared rhythm. This relationality and generosity is evident in the physical warm-ups, led by Rice, which establish her as team leader, nourishing bodies with stretches, massages and stamina building exercises, whilst building the qualities of play and imagination.[182]

Rice explains the process of liberating actors within the terms of teaching:

> You teach the ensemble, you teach the team and then you go, 'Go! Be brilliant'! and the actors I work with, almost without fault, will be brilliant. If you hold them strongly and tightly and then you go, 'Your go'" they'll fly and spin and delight and it's a thing of great beauty of which I have no control over. What you've done is you've enabled and guided and suggested.[183]

Enabling, guiding and suggesting are the pedagogic strategies applied in the process. The starting point for developing work is always personal, responding to 'the itch'[184] that will lead her to work with a particular story, which resonates with an emotional memory and connects to her experience in some way.[185] She invites the company to find their own personal connections to the story, and to 'remember wrongly' as it is through the inaccuracy of remembering that one's unique vision is revealed.[186] Actors become invested through their personal connections to the material. In Rice's practice the ultimate authority is claimed by the story, which she explains, 'puts us all in our place because we all have the responsibility to tell it ... You take your bits, you take your turn, you support'.[187] Before working with actors, Rice explores the story with a composer and designer to find its palette, textures, colours, themes and emotions. She then harnesses 'the collective imagination' of the company to realise it. Shepherd explains that 'Emma demands that people work instinctively and make offers that she can then harvest, select, edit and craft'.[188] The play impulse, which has been developed through games and joint experimentation with the permission to try things out and to fail, underpins this process. Rice's use of questioning and instruction – 'Make me an offer'![189] – provokes the imagination of actor or musician to offer instinctive solutions to staging decisions that she will immediately accept, refuse or edit. Responses are recorded on big sheets of paper that remain in the rehearsal room, reminding everyone of their developing impressions, keeping them on track and documenting a shared ownership. Rice rarely gives actors research during the process as she feels it creates 'a school like attitude, where working harder automatically makes you work better, which isn't necessarily the case in a creative environment'.[190] This approach, physically and emotionally impulsive and free, stands in marked contrast to Mitchell's more cerebral and text-bound process.

The collective imagination is best illustrated in the way that Rice facilitates the construction of characters. Rather than the actor immediately taking responsibility for the development of their role, the ensemble share their descriptions, looking for contradictions or surprising interpretations and then collectively performing each one, observing each other's playing. Through this post-Brechtian approach, which starts with the actor's imagination, the potential of the characters to surprise and work against type is discovered.[191] Rice costumes each actor, moving through improvisation tasks, side-coaching and provoking with questions and tasks. Playing through mimetic improvisation enables a shared discovery of character and opens up choice for the actor. She describes this as a 'magical moment of alchemy ... of chemistry, when I know the heart of the person playing the character, and that will guide how that character sits within the structure of that work'.[192] This creation happens in the 'gap' between actor and director where the 'flights of fancy',[193] which Mitchell guards against, are actively encouraged as breaking rules; exaggeration and playfulness liberate imaginative possibilities.

By the second week of a five-week rehearsal the ensemble has started staging scenes and has already learnt a number of songs and choreographed sequences (dances or scene setting) and at that point the work builds quickly and the script is authored by Rice, sometimes in collaboration with writer(s).[194] Action choices come from the practical and logical staging of the story as opposed to fixing a psychological score. The actor may have to multi-role, play an instrument, dance, sing, set a scene or operate a puppet in any 10 minutes on stage and, whilst there may be attention given to the objective being played, it is always in the interest of sharpening and animating the story. The final stage of Rice's theatre-making is pinning down the script and working on the text. Rice's subversion of the text reflects a feminist practice that privileges emotional connection, impulse and somatic discovery. She explains:

> I work on the iceberg and the words are the sprinkle on top of the point. And I think that most theatre works the other way round – you work on the words and then you keep finding meaning. I would die a death working like that.[195]

In her adaptation practice Rice is not bound by fixed text, which must have been a restriction to her normal process at The Globe.[196] As Winkler points out, Rice's process isn't 'about the script, but the feeling and the flavours and the music and that feels quite unique'.[197]

## *Vital materialism and the 'feminine masquerade'*[198]

Drawing on Luce Irigaray's reading of 'feminine mimicry'[199] in relation to Elin Diamond's 'feminist gestic criticism'[200] allows us to consider Rice's approach to gender representation as a feature of her 'subversive populism'.[201] Thinking back to Chapter 1, and the intersections between techniques of gender and acting, Rice's approach can be viewed through the construct of the feminine masquerade. Joan Riviere's influential study identified womanliness as a mask, performed in response to male desires.[202] Following this precept, Luce Irigaray viewed the female masquerade negatively but developed a strategy of resistance through the construct of feminine mimicry.[203] Irigaray suggested that women, '[M]ust play with mimesis ... must assume the feminine role deliberately. Which means already to convert a form of subordination into an affirmation, and thus begin to thwart it'.[204] The excess of performed femininity turns masquerade into mimicry and so ironises the constructed feminine ideal. The deliberate acting out of prescribed femininity reveals its hidden mechanisms. Diamond explains this as a form of feminist gestic criticism in theatre-making. In Rice's pedagogy, a feminist acting approach emerges where feminine mimicry is played as an 'ironic disturbance' and constructions of gender are subversively critiqued.

In its content, Rice's work addresses repeated tropes of the oppressed female body: its vulnerability, objectification, sexual desire, social entrapment and emotional and physical transformation. Her protagonists 'explore female freedom ... the battle to walk your own path, to be in your own skin, to grab life'.[205] As with Mitchell, her actors collaborate in the feminist act to foreground women's stories and experiences. The vital materialism of the body and its ability to transform in its struggle to escape social inscriptions manifests itself repeatedly in physical mutilation: In *The Red Shoes* The Girl begs The Butcher to cut off her feet to stop her dancing; in *The Wild Bride*, her hands are cut off; *Rapunzel* loses her hair; in *The Wooden Frock,* The Girl is locked in the equivalent of chastity armour, to prevent her bereaved father from taking advantage of her. Rice's work highlights the value and sacrifice of the material body and how the transaction for freedom pivots on choice to present surprising images of shape shifting, stressing the hybridity of identity and states of becoming. In *The Wild Bride* The Girl is given mechanical hands, in *The Red Shoes* the protagonist has wooden feet and in *Nights at the Circus*, an adaptation of Angela Carter's novel, the protagonist Fevvers, an aerialist, has wings. Rice is drawn to folk stories of transformation such as selkies, seal women who shed their seal skin to marry a human and then end up returning to their instinctive self and the ocean, re-claiming their rightful skin and leaving human duty behind. She is fascinated with 'being in your own skin',[206] and what that might mean, and she resists stereo-typical casting. She comments: 'I love women to be beautiful for who they are. So I try very hard to portray women truthfully, so not turned out and not fully toned – all shapes and sizes and natural'.[207] She likes seeing skin on stage, its textures and imperfections. Rice's 'top birds' challenge normative representations of femininity through their physical body shapes, their height, strength, gangling clumsiness or unabashed exuberance.

The transgressive and unruly female body is a repeated thematic of 'the bad girl' plays, which include works like *Pandora's Box*,[208] *Bacchae* and *Rebecca*, where Rice poses the questions: 'What happens when you break the law and what stops you'?[209] This strand of work celebrates female sexual desire, with women as sirens, sexually empowered and defiant. In *Tristan and Yseult*, Yseult loves two people at the same time. *Pandora's Box,* an adaptation of Wedekind's *Lulu* plays, sees Lulu, as both femme fatale and victim, seduce and destroy countless lovers and husbands before she is finally murdered by Jack The Ripper. The idea of the female masquerade in theatrical and performative contexts is a recurring theme: *The Wah Wah Girls*, a collaboration with Tanika Gupta, explores the stories of Asian women who perform as Mujra dancers;[210] *Nights at the Circus* considers the ageing female circus performer.[211] Through twins, Dora and Nora in *Wise Children*, we re-visit a life-time of performing.[212] In *Rebecca,* 'a feminist work [where] all the characters explore different aspects of femininity',[213] Mrs De Winter, a dutiful young bride, casts off her naivety to discover her feminine power. In the last scene, as she performs a false fainting fit, she whispers to her husband, 'See what a fine little actress I've become'.[214] Hale, the actor who played the role, described the way that the character discovers her 'power' through learning how to perform her femininity.[215] Rice's actors bring the doubleness of the female condition, both being and being seen, and make it explicit through feminine mimicry.

Cross-gender casting is another way that Rice challenges constructs of re-presentation. In her early work with Kneehigh she experimented with drag, sometimes out of necessity in order to meet the demands of multi-role playing, but as her career developed she became more conscious of the ways that drag can operate on a knife-edge between critique and collusion. As Butler explains 'there is no guarantee that exposing the naturalised status of heterosexuality will lead to its subversion'.[216] The transgender community in the U.S. questioned the way Rice used drag for humour and, with greater awareness, she began to include female-to-male casting, as seen in *Rebecca* and *946*.[217] In this way Rice ironises inscribed gender constructions, delighting in the performativity of gender, and 'converting subordination into affirmation'.[218] Her insistence on 50/50 gender equality on the Globe stage, joking 'If anyone bended gender it was Shakespeare',[219] was an important move to re-figure representation through casting and deal with the stasis of gender equality from the eye of the storm.[220] As she explains: 'I don't like the terms "gender blind" or "colour blind" casting. When I cast, I am the opposite of blind: I have my eyes wide open and my mind is at its most alert, political and flexible'.[221] For Rice, in working with the story form through imagination 'there are no barriers to gender parity and diverse casting ... If I say a woman is a man, they [the audience] will believe it and if I cast a man and a woman from different cultural backgrounds as identical twins – no problem'.[222] In *Wise Children,* twins Dora and Nora were played at various times in their life by three sets of performers, the youngest incarnation were puppets and the oldest a female/male duo played by Etta Murfitt and Gareth Snook.[223] In Rice's work bodies are fluid, in relation with each other, with the audience and with objects. The audience can imagine a world where alternative states of being are possible.

### *Bric-a-brac, thing-ness and agential realism*

Working with objects, a feature of Kneehigh's creative practice, which Rice has developed, allows the company to explore their story-telling potential through props, set and costume from the first day of rehearsal. Matt Trueman, writing about Kneehigh's environment, observes how the 'bric-a brac on every surface – old props, puppets, bits of driftwood and string, shelves full of scripts, text-books and trashy thrillers', becomes 'a living Kneehigh museum'.[224] This produces a Kneehigh aesthetic in design terms as objects are re-used and modified for different shows. Rice continues to develop a way of working that gives agency to objects and in doing so blurs the divide between human and non-human in ways that, returning to Barad's concept, produce an agential realism. In rehearsal for *Rebecca* the dominance of objects was striking: musical instruments, items of costume, props, bits of set and puppets allowed the ensemble to transform time, space and character as they solved the problems of story-telling. It may seem obvious that what Jane Bennet terms 'thing-ness'[225] is an essential part of scenography in theatre but in Rice's work the way that the actors manipulate objects moment to moment, at one point setting up a scene, changing costume, operating a puppet or playing an instrument, is an essential feature of the form of the work. As with Mitchell's use of technology, Rice's actors animate the inanimate. Puppets, often animals (the cat in *946*, birds and the dog in *Rebecca*, birds in *Tristan and Ysault*), blur the edges between human and non-human to challenge anthropocentricism. Visual inventiveness departs from representation entirely when objects become other: umbrellas stand in for honking geese in *Wooden Frock* and sex is denoted by swinging on a chandelier in *Brief Encounter*. Using objects as agents to transform human action or to capture inner expression is most clearly seen through the repeated trope of lovers flying. In *Nights at the Circus* trapeze artist Fevvers soars aloft; in *Tristan and Ysault* the protagonist lovers are harnessed to bungy ropes, their weight held and balanced by other actors who pull them up, reaching, swooping and bounding above the stage. If Mitchell's use of technology can appear to make time seem thicker, Rice's use of apparatus can seem to alter gravitational forces. The object-focused orientation of Rice's practice presents actors with a range and diversity of challenges moment to moment and, when placed in conversation with Mitchell's very different aesthetic, offers another example of new feminist materialism, which re-positions and questions human autonomy.

In conclusion, although Rice and Mitchell's work are wholly distinct they tread common ground in various ways. Both directors have faced significant challenges in their careers, which have, in part, been problematised through gender. When we think about intersections between directing and teaching we can reconsider theatre-making processes as developmental pedagogies. Their respective practices illustrate the ways in which feminist directors, working in mainstream UK theatre, impact on the lifelong learning of actors, creative collaborators and audiences. A consideration of directing as a gendered practice draws attention to the ways that these practitioners, in their minoritarian position, enable choice for the actor to explore the possibilities of resistance in representation through critical acting pedagogies where the authority of teacher/director operates in subtle and complex ways: Mitchell leads from behind with her 'feminist method of physical action'; Rice leads from the front with her pedagogy for 'the collective imagination'. Their respective bodies of work, which push at boundaries and forms, can be usefully viewed through the lens of new feminist materialism to recognise the underlying bio-political theme, which fights matter with matter. Both practitioners examine female bodies that endure, transform, mutate, evolve, their unruliness standing in contrast to limiting ideas of representation and mimesis. In distinct and particular ways, they re-make mimesis through an agential realism. In Mitchell and Rice's work, the female ontology of acting examined in Chapter 1 can be seen to work beside the feminist interventions in acting pedagogies explored in Chapter 2. These director/pedagogues make ongoing and important contributions to UK acting pedagogies.

## Notes

1 Tracking statistical data through the ongoing research of Sphinx (formally the Women's Theatre Group) evidences little change in women's employment between the 1970s and 2000 with a stubborn 2:1 ratio across most sectors. https://sphinxtheatre.co.uk/ [accessed 20.06.20].Also, see Caroline Gardner, 'What Share of the Cake?' in Lizbeth Goodman with Jane de Gay (eds), *The Routledge Reader in Gender and Performance* (London & New York: Routledge, 1998) 97–102 and Jennie Long, 'What Share of the Cake Now?' 103–107.In the last decade media attention suggests a shifting cultural moment. Female directors include: Marianne Elliot (*War Horse*, 2011), Phyllida Lloyd (all female *Julius Ceasar*, 2012), Lyndsey Turner (*Chimerica*, 2013), Carrie Cracknell (*A Doll's House*, 2012). There has been a wave of female artistic director appointments that offer an optimistic shift in the landscape: Jude Kelly at the Southbank Centre since 2005; Josie Rourke at the Donmar in 2012; Indhu Rubasingham at Tricycle Theatre in 2012; Erica Whyman as Deputy Director of the RSC in 2012; Emma Rice at the Globe in 2016; and Vicky Featherstone at the Royal Court since 2012. Charlotte Higgins. 'Women in Theatre: Why Do So Few Make It to the Top?' *The Guardian* (10.12.12) http://www.theguardian.com/stage/2012/dec/10/women-in-theatre-glass-ceiling [accessed 11.11.13].
2 For example, Declan Donnellan, *The Actor and the Target* (London: Nick Hern Books, 2005).
3 Katie Mitchell *The Director's Craft: A Handbook for the Theatre* (New York & London: Routledge, 2009) is presented as a training guide for directors rather than actors.
4 Josette Feral, 'Building up the Muscle: An Interview with Ariane Mnouchkine', *TDR*, 33 (4), (1989): 88–97.
5 Ibid. 88.
6 Michelene Wandor, *Carry on Understudies: Theatre and Sexual Politics* (London: Routledge, 1981).
7 Alexandra Mermikides, *Negotiating Creativity: An Analytical Framework for the Study of Group Theatre-Making Processes*. Unpublished thesis. Goldsmiths College, University of London (2006) 86.
8 Feminist scholars such as Lizbeth Goodman (1996, 1998) and Elaine Aston (1995, 1999, 2007, 2008) have mapped some of the working methods and devising practices of feminist companies and this body of work provides frameworks for considering a female approach in theatre-making.
9 Anne Jellicoe, *Community Plays: How To Put Them On* (Methuen Publishing, 1987).
10 Michael Coveney, 'Annie Castledine Obituary', *The Guardian* (07.06.16) [accessed 17.06.16].
11 Staff writers, 'Obituary. Theatre's Defiant Genius', *BBC News* (21.09.02), http://news.bbc.co.uk/1/hi/uk/1628351.stm [accessed 02–16.13].
12 Manfull, xvii.
13 Clive Barker, 'Joan Littlewood' ed. Alison Hodge, *Twentieth Century Actor Training*. (London & New York: Routledge, 2000) 114.
14 Geoff Coleman, Head of Acting at RCSSD, acknowledges the significant disparity in the opportunities for challenging acting roles for female students and the problem of using plays driven by male narratives to train women. He states: 'The women were playing more maids than Lears'.Geoffrey Coleman speaking at The Young Vic (29.10.10), 'Creating the Roles and Expanding the Boundaries', *Vamps, Vixens and Feminists Fighting the Backlash*.http://www.sphinxtheatre.co.uk/resource.html [accessed 03.06.13].
15 Anon, 'Women in Theatre: How the '2:1 Problem Breaks Down', https://www.theguardian.com/news/datablog/2012/dec/10/women-in-theatre-research-full-results [accessed 20.06.20].

16 Alycia Smith-Howard, 'Knowing Her Place: Buzz Goodbody and The Other Place', *Early Modern Studies Journal*, 5 (2013): 78.
17 Interview with Deborah Warner. Glyndebourne, East Sussex (07.10.13).
18 Between 2012 and 2016 Phyllida Lloyd directed a trilogy of all-female Shakespeare: *Julius Caesar* in 2012, followed by *Henry IV* in 2015, and *The Tempest* in 2016. Sarah Frankcom's cross-gender casting of *Hamlet* at the Royal Exchange in 2014, with Maxime Peake in the title role, was the first female Hamlet for thirty-five years.
19 Mark Brown, 'The Globe's Emma Rice. "If Anyone Bended Gender It Was Shakespeare"', *The Guardian* (05.01.16) [accessed 08.03.16].
20 *Re-Naming the Director*. Rose Bruford College (05.05.12).
21 Ibid.
22 Katie Mitchell. *Women as Artists*. The Young Vic (02.03.15–06.03.15).
23 Ibid.
24 Phillip Oltermann, 'Katie Mitchell, British Theatre's True Auteur: On Being Embraced by Europe', *The Guardian* (9.02.14).
25 Charles Spencer, 'Women of Troy: Euripides All Roughed Up' (30.11.07) http://www.telegraph.co.uk/culture/theatre/drama/3669609/Women-of-Troy-Euripides-all-roughed-up.html [accessed 12.05.12].
26 Ibid. Libby Purvis, *The Times*.
27 Mitchell uses the term 'live cinema' as a generic description for this body of work.
28 Mitchell, *Women as Artists*, the Young Vic, London (02.03.15–06.03.15).
29 Ben Fowler, *Katie Mitchell: Beautiful Illogical Acts* (London & New York: Routledge, 2020)
30 Spencer, op.cit.
31 Ibid.
32 Both Di Trevis and Deborah Warner were interviewed for this study, and are referenced in Chapter 2. At the time I was not aware that Mitchell had assisted both of them.
33 Rebellato op.cit.
34 Interview with Katie Mitchell, the National Theatre (09.10.11).
35 Alison Hodge and Emma Rice were also influenced by Gardzienice.
36 In the 2014 retrospective for the National Theatre's 50th anniversary not a single female director was represented in the programme; the apparent blindness to this 'writing out' of women's contribution, despite Hytner's 2009 defence of female directors, shone a spotlight on the gendered bias in the industry. See Ottermann, op.cit.
37 Mitchell reflects on her own learning trajectory in three parts: the craft of acting and Stanislavski; the Golden Age of art history; and the feminist phase, which continues to search for new forms. Mitchell, 'Women as Artists', the Young Vic (02.03.15–06.03.15).
38 Mitchell, interviewed at the Young Vic (10.10.14).
39 Maria Shevstova, 'On Directing: A Conversation with Katie Mitchell', *New Theatre Quarterly*, 22(1), (2006) 17.
40 When an Austrian journalist commented that her work always explores women and death, Mitchell pointed to *Hamlet*, *Macbeth* and *King Lear* to posit, 'There just isn't a cannon of plays where women are constantly the protagonists and if you do tragedies people die!' Ibid.
41 Mitchell, Young Vic (10.10.14).
42 *The Forbidden Zone* (2014), commissioned by the Schaubühne Berlin to comemororate the centenary of the first world war, told the story of Clara Immerwah, the German chemist who committed suicide on the night of the first gas attack on the Russians.
43 *Fraülein Julie*, Schaubühne Berlin (2013).

44 Ibid.
45 'Women as Artists', op.cit.
46 This draws to mind Cole's comparison between the rehearsal room and the classroom. Johnathan Cole, 'Liberatory Pedagogy and Activated Directing: Restructuring the College Rehearsal Room', *Theatre Topics*, 18(2), 2008: 191–204.
47 Charlotte Higgins, 'Katie Mitchell, British Theatre's Queen in Exile' (14.01.16) https://www.theguardian.com/stage/2016/jan/14/british-theatre-queen-exile-katie-mitchell, [accessed 20.02.16].
48 Interview with Katie Mitchell, the National Theatre (09.10.11).
49 Mitchell, Young Vic (10.10.14).
50 Interview with Catrin Stewart, Natalie Klamar, Sarah Ridgeway, The Young Vic (23.09.14).
51 Interview with Esther McAuley, The National Theatre (14.05.12).
52 Interview with Sandy Mcdade, Hampstead Theatre (17.01.11).
53 While *The Director's Craft* targets directors, it might equally guide the actor in developing an approach to working on text.
54 I open up the various forms of critical pedagogy in Chapter 2. Paulo Freire is seen to have developed this approach. Paulo Freire, *Education for Critical Consciousness* (London & New York: Continuum, 1974) 44.
55 Mitchell, 'Women as Artists', the Young Vic (02.03.15–06.03.15).
56 Jonathan Pitches, *Russians in Britain* (London & New York: Routledge, 2012) 201.
57 'A Conversation About Making', Katie Mitchell in conversation with Paul Clarke and Siobhan Davies, July 2009. http://www.siobhandavies.com/conversations/events/mitchell-clark.php [accessed 29.12.14].
58 Ellen Donkin and Susan Clement, *Upstaging Big Daddy: Directing Theatre as if Gender and Race Matter* (USA: The University of Michigan Press,1993) 256.
59 Interview with Sarah Davey-Hull, Central School of Speech and Drama (17.11.11).
60 Mitchell, 'Women as Artists', the Young Vic (02.03.15–06.03.15).
61 Interview with Tristan Sturrock, Bristol (30.01.15).
62 Mitchell, The Young Vic (04.03.15).
63 Ibid.
64 Shvetsova, 17.
65 I go on to explain what Mitchell means by 'data'. Sociologist Bourdieu's examination of habitus is useful when thinking about Time and Place. Phillip Bourdieu, *The Logic of Practice* (UK: Polity Press, 1990).
66 *The Cherry Orchard* was performed at the Young Vic in October 2014.
67 There are two forms of action: the action of event, which changes the situation, e.g. a gunman enters the room; and the action of intention (or 'objective' or 'want'), which is played by each individual in response to that event until the next event. The intention is played to affect everyone else on the stage (e.g. I want to keep everyone safe), which ensures action is always relational. Some events can take place in one moment and some last for longer sections of time. For example, actors might identify the first intention to happen on the event and then, in what is termed a 'slow burn event', this might change and become a second intention. In this way the intentions are marked in the script as intention 'on the event' and intention 'in the event'. Also see Mitchell (2009) 64–65.
68 Rebecca Loukes in Phillip Zarrilli and Jerri Daboo, *Acting: Psychophysical Phenomenon and Process* (Basingstoke: Palgrave Macmillan, 2013) 46–63.
69 Interview with Sandy McDade, Hampstead Theatre (17.01.11).
70 Mitchell, 59.
71 Rebellato, 328.
72 Rebellato, 329.
73 Interview with Nick Fletcher and Esther Mcauley, The National Theatre (14.05.12).

74 Ibid.
75 *A Woman Killed with Kindness,* National Theatre (2011).
76 Interview with Kate Duchêne, The National Theatre (14.05.12).
77 Mitchell, Young Vic (10.10.14).
78 This was explained in Chapter 2. Andrea Milde, 'Linguistics in Drama Processes', *Working Papers in Urban Language & Literacies,* Paper 251, (2019) https://www.academia.edu/39625216/WP251_Milde_2019._Linguistics_in_drama_processes [accessed 25.07.19].
79 Ibid.
80 Elen and Robert Bowman set up Living Pictures in 1995 to provide training for directors. http://www.livingpictures.org.uk/.
81 Mitchell, The Young Vic (10.10.14).
82 Duchêne (14.05.12).
83 Elin Diamond, *Unmaking Mimesis* (London & New York: Routledge,1997).
84 Rosi Braidotti, *Nomadic Theory: The Portable Rosi Braidotti* (New York: Columbia University Press, 2011) 16.
85 Ibid.
86 Interview with Mitchell, National Theatre (09.10.11)
87 Observation of *The Cherry Orchard,* Young Vic (25.08.14–19.09.14).
88 Rhonda Blair, 'Reconsidering Stanislavski: Feeling, Feminism and the Actor', *Theatre Topics,* 12(2), (2002): 117–190.
89 Ibid., 185–188.
90 Ibid., 189.
91 Observation of *The Cherry Orchard,* Young Vic (25.08.14–19.09.14).
92 Mitchell (09.10.11).
93 Ibid.
94 Ibid.
95 *Small Hours,* Hampstead Theatre (2011).
96 Ibid.
97 Mitchell directed Sarah Kane's seminal 1998 play *Cleansed* at The National Theatre in 2016.
98 *The Forbidden Zone,* Barbican (2016).
99 *Ophelias Zimmer, Anatomy of a Suicide,* Royal Court (2016, 2017).
100 *Attempts on Her Life,* National Theatre (2007)
101 Maddy Costa, 'Alternative point of view: *The Malady of Death'*http://blog.barbican.org.uk/2018/05/alternative-point-of-view-the-malady-of-death/ [accessed 24.06.19].
102 Ibid.
103 Duchêne, op cit.
104 Interview with Duchêne, Young Vic (07.10.14).
105 Platform discussion with Katie Mitchell and Dan Rebellato, *Miss Julie,* The Barbican Centre (04.05.14).
106 Benjamin Fowler, *Creating Continuity out of Fragmentation: Katie Mitchell's Live Cinema Work.* (2015), unpublished PhD thesis, University of Warwick.
107 Mitchell, (10.10.14).
108 Six of the seven live cinema pieces made for theatre since 2006 have been set before 1950.
109 Mitchell cited by Jefferies (2011) 403.
110 Duchêne (07.10.14).
111 Louise Le Page, 'Posthuman Perspectives and Postdramatic Theatre: The Theory and Practice of Hybrid Ontology in Katie Mitchell's *Waves*', *Culture, Language and Representation,* 4(2008): 142.

## 194  Considering Practice

112  Ibid.
113  Ibid.
114  Mitchell explains: 'the actor is working with a double role. They have an additional character. They are not just themselves – that's a very subtle level of performance' Rebellato and Mitchell (04.05.14).
115  In her iconic 1975 essay, Laura Mulvey describes the way that film fetishises female representation and how 'the male gaze' becomes a form, of hegemonic control, denying the possibility of a female consciousness.Laura Mulvey, 'Visual Pleasure and Narrative Cinema', *Screen*, 16(3), (1975): 6–18.
116  Jane Bennet, *Vibrant Matter: A Political Ecology of Things* (Duke University Press, 2010).
117  Karen Barad, 'Posthumanist Performativity: Toward an Understanding of How Matter Comes to Matter', *Signs*, 28(3), (Spring, 2003).
118  *A Sorrow Beyond Dreams* premiered at Kasino Theatre, Vienna (2014).
119  Le Page, 149.
120  Donna Haraway, 'A Manifesto for Cyborgs: Science, Technology, and Socialist Feminism for the 1980s', *Socialist Review* 80, 15(2), (1985): 65–107.
121  Phelan (1993) 17.
122  Higgins, op.cit.
123  *The Bacchae* (2005), *Tristan and Yseult* (2006), The National Theatre.
124  *The Red Shoes* (2000), *The Wooden Frock* (2004), The National Theatre.
125  *Cymbeline* (2006) RSC, *A Midsummer Night's Dream,* The Globe (2017).
126  Emma Rice interviewed in Bristol (29.01.15).
127  I am particularly thinking of the reaction to *A Matter of Life and Death* (2011).
128  Lyn Gardner, 'We Like Our Plays to Be Foolish', *The Guardian* (19.07.04). https://www.theguardian.com/stage/2004/jul/19/theatre [accessed 02.06.15].
129  Duska Radoslavljevic in Liz Tomlin, *British Theatre Companies 1995–2014* (London, New York: Bloomsbury, 2015) 156, 158.
130  In 2014, I observed the rehearsal for the U.S. tour of *Tristan and Yseult* in London. In 2015, I observed the rehearsal for Rice's adaptation of Daphne du Maurier's *Rebecca* in Bristol, which toured the UK.
131  Hannah Furness, 'Noisy Audiences, Magical Forests and More Women in New-Look Shakespeare's Globe', *The Telegraph*. 05.01.16. http://www.telegraph.co.uk/news/celebritynews/12082858/Noisy-audiences-magical-forests-and-more-women-in-new-look-Shakespeares-Globe.html [accesses 14.05.16].
132  Lyn Gardner, 'As Emma Rice Departs, the Globe Has Egg on Its Face – and No Vision'. *The Guardian*. 25.10.16 https://www.theguardian.com/stage/theatreblog/2016/oct/25/shakespeares-globe-emma-rice-department-comment[accessed 04.08.19].
133  Kim Solga, 'Shakespeare's Property Ladder' in *The Oxford Handbook of Shakespeare and Performance,* ed. James C. Bulman (Oxford University Press, 2017).
134  Holly Williams, 'Emma Rice on Bouncing Back with Wise Children: 'This Show Has Been My Savior', i-news. 15.10.18. https://inews.co.uk/culture/arts/wise-children-emma-rice-interview-old-vic-globe/ [accessed 04.08.19].
135  Rice (29.01.15).
136  Ibid.
137  Ibid.
138  Ibid.
139  Ibid.
140  Ibid.
141  Ibid.
142  Ibid.
143  Whitney, op.cit.

144 Ibid.
145 *Rapunzel* (2006), *Brief Encounter* (2008), which transferred to Broadway, *Don Juan*, in collaboration with the RSC in (2008), *A Matter of Life and Death*, in collaboration with the National Theatre (2011), *The Wild Bride* (2011), *Midnight's Pumpkin*, with the BAC (2012), *Steptoe and Son* (2013), which toured nationally.
146 Total theatre is a term derived from Richard Wagner's concept of Gesamtkunstwerk, a total or unified work of art where movement, voice, music and spectacle work together.
147 Ibid.
148 Radoslavljevic, op.cit.
149 Ibid.
150 Mitchell (02.03.15–06.03.15).
151 Rice (29.01.15).
152 Shepherd (05.11.14).
153 Peggy Phelan, *Unmarked: The Politics of Performance* (London & New York: Routledge, 1993) 173.
154 Kneehigh occupy a number of barns on the cliffs of Goran Haven. The shared living rituals create the necessary conditions for a community, which as Rice explains, 'is when an ensemble takes on a life of its own', Radosavljevic (2013) 100.
155 Arendt, 244.
156 Maddy Costa, 'Troupe Therapy', *The Guardian* (01.12.15). https://www.theguardian.com/stage/2008/dec/01/kneehigh-theatre-cornwall-maddy-costa [accessed 08.02.16].
157 Ibid.
158 Rice (29.01.15).
159 Costa, op.cit.
160 Ibid.
161 Rosi Braidotti, *By way of Nomadism* (New York & Chichester: Colombia University Press, 1994) 161.
162 Arendt, op.cit.
163 Dominic Cavendish, 'A Shot in the Arm for the Junkie King', *The Telegraph* (26.09.06) http://www.telegraph.co.uk/culture/theatre/drama/3655572/A-shot-in-the-arm-from-the-junkie-king.html [accessed 01.06.15].
164 Emma Rice, Bristol (29.01.15).
165 Radosavljevic (2013) 101.
166 Tristan Sturrock, Bristol (30.01.15).
167 Lizzi Winkler, Bristol (30.01.15).
168 Sturrock, op.cit.
169 This is a gendered reworking of *the via negativa* that I explain in Chapter 2.
170 Emma Rice (29.01.15).
171 'The Wise Children Podcast with Emma Rice', Episode 2, 2–17 September 2018. Old Vic https://www.oldvictheatre.com/news/2018/09/the-wise-children-podcast-with-emma-rice [accessed 12.06.19].
172 Lynne Kendrick, 'A Paidic Aesthetic: An Analysis of Games in the Ludic Pedagogy of Philippe Gaullier', *Theatre, Dance and Performance Training*, 2(1), (2011): 72–85.
173 'Keepy uppy' is a ball game where the group work together to keep the ball up in the air.
174 'Grandmother's footsteps' is a playground game where one person turns their back and the group try to move towards them from a distance. When the player turns the group must freeze. Anyone spotted moving is sent back to the starting point.
175 Kristine Landon-Smith (07.03.13).
176 Emma Rice (29.01.15).
177 Ibid.

178 Landon-Smith suggests that males are more likely to perform 'playful' with a female director Landon-Smith, op.cit.
179 Iris Young, 'Throwing Like a Girl: Self-Objectification Predicts Adolescent Girls' Motor Performance', *Journal of Sport and Social Issues*, 29(79), (2005): 79–101.
180 Rice (04.08.14–06.09.14).
181 Rice (29.01.15).
182 Rice was movement director for Katie Mitchell on *A Women Killed with Kindness* (1992).
183 Ibid.
184 Emma Rice, *The Kneehigh Anthology: Volume 1* (London: Oberon Books, 2011) 9.
185 In interview she explains how the trajectory of the work maps her own experience: 'The only way that I can analyse them [the plays] is the way they reflect my development as a person. In the way that I am interested in the female condition, the human condition, at different parts of my life. So it is no mistake that *The Red Shoes*, which was all about freedom and personal freedom and the cost of freedom was at the time of my divorce. It's also when I started directing, so it was a great explosion of rage and upset and creativity and loss. Then you go onto *The Wooden Frock*, which was how do you heal? How do you armour yourself against what hurts you? And then *The Wild Bride* is how do you endure and mature?' Emma Rice (29.01.15).
186 Whitney, op.cit.
187 Emma Rice (29.01.15).
188 Mike Shepherd (05.11.14).
189 Observation notes *Rebecca* (28.01.15–30.01.15).
190 Theatre Royal. Haymarket. Masterclass (06. 02. 14).
191 Peter Thompson in Alison Hodge, *Twentieth Century Actor Training* (London & New York: Routledge, 2010) 125.
192 Radosavljevic, 102.
193 Mitchell, op.cit.
194 Rice has worked repeatedly with writers Carl Gosse and Anna Maria Murphy.
195 Duska Radosavljevic, 'Emma Rice in interview with Duska Radosavljevic', *Journal of Adaptation in Film and Performance*, 3(1), (2010): 93.
196 Pre Globe, her only foray into directing Shakespeare, *Cymbeline* at Stratford in 2006, used barely 200 lines of the original text and outraged purists Christian Billing, 'New Seed from Old Corn: Review of *Cymbeline* (directed by Emma Rice for Kneehigh Theatre) at the Swan, September 2006', *Shakespeare*, 3(2), (2007): 220–223.
197 Walker (30.01.15).
198 Joan Riviere, 'Womanliness as a Masquerade' in *Formations of Fantasy*, ed. Burgin, V., Donlad, J., Kaplan, C. (London & New York: Routledge, 1985) 33–45.
199 Luce Irigaray, *This Sex Which Is Not One* (USA: Cornell University Press, 1985) 77.
200 Diamond, 44–55.
201 Radosavljevic, op.cit.
202 Riviere, op.cit.
203 Diamond, op.cit.
204 Irigaray, 77.
205 Chloe Rickard, 'Kneehigh's Emma Rice on Directing *Steptoe and Son*' (04.04.13) http://community.nationaltheatrewales.org/profiles/blogs/kneehigh-s-emma-rice-on-directing-steptoe-and-son?xg_source=activity [accessed 04.06.15].
206 Rice, Bristol (29.01.15).
207 Ibid.
208 *Pandora's Box*, Newcastle (2002).
209 Ibid. Rice (29.01.15).
210 *The Wha! Wha! Girls,* Peacock, London (2012).
211 *Nights at the Circus,* Lyric Hammersmith, London (2006).

212 *Wise Children*, Old Vic, London (2018).
213 *Rebecca*. Education Pack. http://www.kneehigh.co.uk/show/rebecca.php [accessed 06.05.15].
214 Taken from observation notes, *Rebecca*, Bristol (28.01.15–30.01.15).
215 Interview with Imogen Hale, Bristol (30.01.15).
216 Judith Butler, *Bodies that Matter: On the Discursive Limits of Sex* (London: Routledge, 1993) 231.
217 *946*, The Asylum, Cornwall (2015).
218 Irigaray, op.cit.
219 Brown, op.cit.
220 'The Wise Children Podcast with Emma Rice', September 2018. Old Vic https://www.oldvictheatre.com/news/2018/09/the-wise-children-podcast-with-emma-rice [accessed 12.06.19].
221 Ibid.
222 Ibid.
223 Arifa Akbar, 'Wise Children Review. Emma Rice's Spectacular Carnival'. *The Guardian,* 19.10.18 https://www.theguardian.com/stage/2018/oct/19/wise-children-review-emma-rice-angela-carter-old-vic-london?utm_source=wordfly&utm_medium=email&utm_campaign[accessed 09.06.19].
224 Matt Trueman, 'The Church of the Lost Cause: Inside Kneehigh's wild Cornish home', *The Guardian*. 18.09.17. https://www.theguardian.com/stage/2017/sep/18/kneehigh-the-tin-drum-cornish-home-mike-shepherd [accessed 16.05.19].
225 Bennet, op.cit.

# CONCLUSION

In 2018, Madeleine Walker, following centuries of women before her, confronted the knotty problems for the feminist playing Kate in *Taming of the Shrew*. The play, a 'comedy', follows the pursuit, capture and submission of the outspoken Katherine by Petruchio, whose gaslighting tactics and domestic violence are distinctly unfunny in the twenty-first century. Kate's volte-face in Act V sc.ii, her admonishment to women that their 'lances are but straws' and to 'place your hands below your husband's foot',[1] presented Walker with a seemingly impossible challenge: how could she work from her feminist self when the role demands such subjugation? She reflects:

> I believe, in retrospect, that I was drawn to this research in my acting process because of the sheer abundance of situations (in the acting world as in life) where I have found the oppressive gender dynamics of a room forcing me to tame myself: laughing at an 'ironically' sexist joke in a rehearsal room; playing a part whose only access to power is through sexualisation; receiving direction that only seems to serve a male director or viewer's fantasy; keeping quiet about harassment or lower pay than male peers. These are situations women accept *all the time*, and I wanted to find out why.[2]

Through her training at RCSSD, Walker was alert to her gender as technique and encouraged by tutors to take more space, tap into her unruly self and work from her inner shrew. In facing up to the challenge she looked at past performances. How had female actors sought to 're-make' mimesis? In *Clamorous Voices: Shakespeare's Women Today*, Carol Rutter expands on this problem, interviewing successful British actors including Juliet Stevenson, Harriet Walters and Fiona Shaw about their portrayal of the role.[3] Female actors turn to different readings and strategies. Some, including Marie Pickford, in the first Shakespeare 'talkie' in 1929, adopt a Brechtian approach to subvert the scene by winking at the audience; some, including Elizabeth Taylor in 1967 and Meryl Streep in 1978, appear to sanction Kate's capitulation as evidence of deep passion and love;[4] Fiona Shaw played the scene as an extension of the private word-play shared with Petruchio in Act IV, suggesting that when you use words as dissembling armour you can maintain your inner shrew, whilst outwardly playing the game.[5] Similarly, Walker's interpretation wrangled with Kate accepting and performing the 'feminine masquerade'.[6] However, she was forced to concede that, in a #*Me Too* culture, the challenges that the play presents to feminists are perhaps insurmountable. She reflects:

> The question should be, rather than *how* the modern-day actor can survive a 'taming' narrative, *whether* they *should*. What if we refuse to be tamed? I want to be part of an industry that rewards and expects calls for fair ethics – regarding gender, race, sexuality, ability – and I have a feeling that the people who are going to make that happen are the shrews.[7]

Walker's training gave her space to consider these tensions, but female actors continue to be 'tamed' in training grounds, which according to Rosemary Malague, perpetuates females as 'victims and objects'.[8] Reflecting on U.S. practices, Malague points to deeply ingrained patriarchal structures, where 'females feel fearful' whilst 'males are feeling positive'.[9] In supporting young actors to deal with the inherent sexism in the industry, she urges that they become familiar with feminist thinking, work with plays that offer equal opportunities and apply rigorous script analysis. Whilst Walker's experience shows that such strategies do not necessarily solve the problem, it is vital that actors learn to recognise these walls when they see them and are equipped to start to dismantle them; not only the walls of sexism but the many barriers that stand in the way for minoritarian groups in acting. In this book, I've proposed a methodology to assess the critical potential (in this case feminist) of actor training pedagogies, looking to the practices of women working in training grounds and in the industry. This rethinks the broad curriculum of acting beyond a narrow idea of mimesis, to position it as a critical pedagogy, politically agile, which responds to these concerns. Working with approaches that equip actors with the personal and social knowledges, dispositional skills and techniques they need to reclaim their agency as cultural workers allows them to challenge normative appropriations. But how can we move beyond words to action and kickstart this re-construction? In this conclusion, I pull together the strands of thinking and practices explored in this book to think forward in a pragmatic way, addressing three questions: what needs to change in the culture of acting? What new theoretical constructs re-orientate ideologies in actor training? What pedagogical practices can we utilise?

## Changing the culture: A feminist manifesto for acting

'A manifesto: to make manifest'.[10] For feminists, manifestos expose what Ahmed terms 'the violence of the patriarchal order',[11] responding to the mechanisms of control in a particular time, place and location. I think of a manifesto as a provocation: drawing a line on the past, a statement of action in process, finessed and sharpened, a relational working document. Yvonne Rainer's 'No Manifesto' in 1965[12] captured the zeitgeist of change in post-modern performance and, returning to it in 2008, her additions and asides address the negative imperative in her earlier thinking. Perhaps Rainer had come to realise that working from an affirmative position might be more productive. As my project throughout has activated an affirmative politics, I'm drawn to a 'Yes Manifesto' that draws a line on the violence of the past and recognises the changes that are already starting to happen. Although a feminist manifesto for acting particularly responds to the position of women, in its desire to address oppressive systems, it includes all minoritarian groups marginalised due to age, sex, gender, race, class or ability.

How can a feminist manifesto for acting speak to the life-long learning of the actor, responsive to the ways that, at different times, she will face different types of walls? In the Introduction, I pointed to the ways that the female actor is marginalised and disadvantaged within training grounds and in the industry.[13] This manifesto steps backwards in time through the stages of an actor's career as a kind of systemic constellation, trying to map a more positive trajectory.[14] Let us imagine a manifesto that serves Walker as the actor she may become in later life, moving backwards through her late/mid/early career, backwards through training and backwards through school. What needs to happen, or continue to happen to develop sustainable training for the future that re-imagines the profession of acting? As the current global pandemic continues to teach us, any attempt to predict the future is perhaps futile and, as Braidotti cautions, we have to adapt to instability and change.[15] This manifesto offers jumping off points, directions of travel and ways of thinking, to hold on to as we keep our balance and journey forward.

### A Feminist Manifesto for Acting

- **Yes** to all actors receiving the National Minimum Wage
- **Yes** to equality in pay in every area of the industry
- **Yes** to ensuring that diverse stories are represented
- **Yes** to legislation that works towards equality in representation of sex, gender, race, class, age or ability in all fields of the creative arts
- **Yes** to working in a culture of zero tolerance to any form of harassment or abuse due to sex, gender, race, age, class or ability
- **Yes** to equality and safety in audition practices

- **Yes** to documenting women's work
- **Yes** to diversity at all levels of employment in training grounds with the urgent need for more BAME practitioner/academics
- **Yes** to ensuring diversity in recruitment of actors working with wider participation strategies
- **Yes** to a flat fee for drama school auditions
- **Yes** to more state-funded bursary grants to ensure inclusivity
- **Yes** to developing new approaches to training practices that reflect our changing world
- **Yes** to exploring the wider epistemic potential for acting and finding new ways to think through its practices
- **Yes** to more focused research into acting pedagogies
- **Yes** to more interdisciplinary initiatives and collaborations in research between drama schools and universities
- **Yes** to more interdisciplinary collaborations among training providers, professional practitioners and theatres
- **Yes** to ongoing work to decolonise the curriculum, in the structures of teaching and learning, the theories and practices examined and the play texts studied and performed
- **Yes** to rethinking the separatist and hierarchical approach in curriculum design, giving voice, movement and acting equal weight
- **Yes** to exploring new approaches to the showcase
- **Yes** to protecting and developing the study of Drama, Theatre and Performance in schools and colleges, lobbying that it be part of the Ebacc (English Baccaulareate)
- **Yes** to improving diversity in the study of Drama, Theatre and Performance at schools and colleges
- **Yes** to lobbying that the creative arts be part of the Primary National Curriculum

Why should this manifesto, hardly radical in its thinking, be difficult to achieve in the twenty-first century? Who/what are the walls that might block these initiatives? In order to action many of these factors, policy needs to change in the cultural industry, in training and in education. As a cultural industry, theatre presents itself as creative and progressive yet continues to exist in a state of 'organised forgetting', which perpetuates inequality whilst continuing to attract a female majority to train in the field.[16] However, recent initiatives indicate that the process of dismantling has started to gain traction. Ongoing efforts to push for gender equality by UK organisations like Equity and more recently Tonic Theatre's *Advance* move beyond debate and are starting to affect policies.[17] *Advance* has made headway over the last few years at a local level, supporting theatres to find their own ways to initiate moves towards gender equality, working with the particular context of that organisation.[18] More theatres are looking critically at what they can do to improve working conditions for women, such as gender equality in commissioning or programming writers, or ensuring gender balance in casting and directing across the season. There are a growing number of women in senior positions, whether producers or artistic directors, which indicates a sea change.[19] Sexual harassment and exploitative practices are being addressed through changes in policy and revised guidelines, such as Equity's 'Manifesto for Casting'.[20] Such changes, which have no doubt benefited from the momentum of the *Me Too* movement, could change the architecture of acting culture, but unconscious cultural bias is one wall that requires painstakingly slow unpicking. Changing the direction of funding takes time. Here we might look to the film industry in Sweden where funding structures regulate gender equality, ensuring that women's stories are represented on screen; or to developments in U.S. TV programming, where producers no longer see female-driven projects as a gamble, with increasing recognition that, as women are the primary consumers, programming must appeal to women.[21] The cultural psyche in the UK needs to embrace stories that have complex, flawed, failing and foolish female characters, allowing women to be other than 'victims and objects'.[22] Using the tools of feminist thinking to dismantle these structures seems to be vital.[23]

We are starting to see encouraging changes in institutional practices in training grounds, with gender balance in admissions at drama schools and an increasing sense that traditional notions of industry are no longer fit for purpose. There is more open discussion, acknowledging the paradox of training where, training the individual in personal and social knowledges as a potential agent of change happens *besides* teaching them to survive the industry. Research initiatives started by Drama UK (now The Federation of Drama Schools) continue to address the changing training landscape for actors, actioning policy around issues of consent in drama schools.[24] Training increasingly situates actors as creative artists, making their own work with politicised agency, as cultural workers and as entrepreneurs.[25] Initiatives, such as 'Acting Up' are addressing the lack of diversity in training grounds with a concerted effort to recruit more BAME practitioners at every level.[26] However, words like 'diversity' and 'inclusivity' can quickly lose traction, becoming catch-all terms that some BAME scholars and practitioners feel has muted the complex question of race.[27] There is a difference between gaining entry and being included. After the Black Lives Matter uprising in 2020, which led to accusations of systemic racism in UK drama schools, it is vital to bring these difficult questions of difference into the training ground, making pedagogical processes explicit and confronting problematic ethical questions at curriculum level.[28] The particular and unique bodymind should be acknowledged within a training approach, so that the positivity of difference might be mined and alternative ways of being examined. In this way, the question of *what acting is* in the twenty-first century can be interrogated, moving it beyond outmoded notions of mimesis to recognise acting as a critically engaged practice.

Conclusion **203**

This type of change is necessary for training grounds to re-shape the industry rather than being in perpetual service to it. MA Acting curriculums are increasingly working with progressive pedagogies that foreground identity politics.[29]

The phases of an actor's career are like stepping stones and, as with systemic constellations,[30] it is only by addressing the origin, in this case the early formative educational experience of theatre and drama, that sustainable change is made manifest. The decision to pursue an acting career can happen at an early age, often through attending extra-curricular drama clubs or theatre schools. Without ensuring the subject is fostered, developed and made accessible to all at primary school (ages 4–11) there is little chance of diversity at secondary school and beyond (ages 12–18). There is no separate strand for drama in the UK National Curriculum at primary (key stage 2) or at secondary level (key stage 3). Unless a head teacher recognises the creative arts as vital for a flourishing community, students may not experience drama, theatre or performance at all in school. Since the introduction of the Ebacc (English Baccalaureate) in 2011, there has been a significant fall in numbers of students studying the subject of Drama at GCSE (14–16) and at post-sixteen level in A Levels or Btec qualifications.[31] The Ebacc identifies five core subjects (English, mathematics, science, history or geography and a foreign language) and, as such, positions drama as a 'non-facilitating' subject. A 'facilitating subject' will help you gain entry into a high-ranking university. Although there have been recent moves to address the drop in students taking Drama and Theatre Studies at A Level, acting remains stymied by historical ideas of mimesis, its value as a technology of the self easily side-lined and passed over.[32] Without challenging perceptions in formative education we will continue to struggle to re-shape the landscape, enabling diversity and encouraging the political imperative of acting. We need to put pressure on governments to change educational policy, re-positioning creative arts subjects as part of the primary curriculum and the Ebacc. In the wake of the Covid-19 global pandemic, where the world has seen the importance of the arts in maintaining a sense of community, connecting, invigorating and reaching out across borders, it is time to re-think what is given value and why. In asserting the politics of acting we open up its potential, raise its status and arm ourselves for the challenges ahead.

## Theoretical underpinnings: A Critical Acting Pedagogy

*The future of our earth may depend on the ability of all women to identify and develop new definitions of power and new patterns of relating across difference.*
*Audre Lorde*[33]

Lorde's assertion speaks strongly to the ideas and practices explored in this book. As we consider new ways to think about acting pedagogy, the affirmative position offers an alternative to traditional male dominated training practices, where negation, without scaffolding the experience, can teeter precariously on the edge of abuse. Critical feminist theories, in particular new feminist materialisms, re-orientate perceptions around ways of learning and forms of identity, helping us to re-think the epistemic scope of acting and work from the positive imperative.[34] A Critical Acting Pedagogy is built on an ideological framework constructed through ideas of relationality: binary or dualistic constructs are reconceived through adopting a **thinking beside** position; bodies are both inscribed and inscribing, operating with a **vital materialism**; the **positivity of difference** is mined for its potential; **realism is agential**, created through diffraction in relation with human and non-human objects, where changing perspectives are inevitable as we exist in states of becoming. These four layers of critical thinking, considered in detail in Part One of this book and recognised throughout the varied practices in Part Two, challenge ideas of fixed identities, cultural inscriptions and reflective mimesis. In shifting our thinking about being in the world, we can re-think acting as a critically embodied process with the potential to shift culture.

Sedgwick's 'thinking beside' offers an alternative paradigm to the perpetual dualisms that dominate acting (mind/body, inner/outer, self/other).[35] Turning away from binaries to recognise constructs as existing in parallel, intra-active, we can see how, like a möbius strip, ideas are always *in relation with* each other. This book has pursued the value of considering acting pedagogy and women's practices *beside* each other. As examined in Chapter 1, the matter of acting comes into focus when considered beside particular constructs of female knowing: the in-between as a space of creative transformation; female visuality; force in vulnerability and constructs of doubling. Notions of doubling and the female body have preoccupied feminist thinking. Harris suggests that all women simultaneously exist in two states – the sexed female body and the socially inscribed body.[36] In the last decade, Marxist notions of the power constructions of the body have collided with phenomenological states of being and this reminds us of what Grosz referred to as the double body – the 'social' and the 'lived' body operating *beside* each other.[37] This doubling of the body, perceived as the state of female-ness, is the condition of acting. As such, the marginal position of being female can be seen to be a positive advantage in acquiring the types of knowledge necessary in acting.

Braidotti's consideration of 'vital materialism' situates the body in a continual state of becoming, able to re-configure inscriptions.[38] This position acknowledges advancements in science, where the body is plastic in its possibility to reform, adapt and be resilient. For acting pedagogy, this offers an alternative to fixed outlines that divide self and other. When we work from a new feminist materialist perspective, recognising that the self comes into being *in relation with* space, people, objects, in spontaneous constantly changing ways, we understand existence through relational notions of difference. So much of acting knowledge works in this space between, recognising and harnessing the transformational potential of the actor, always in process, moment to moment.

Braidotti's 'positivity of difference' seeks to establish an affirmative politics.[39] By viewing difference as liberating, enriching and politically productive we can find ways to move beyond notions of normativity. Braidotti points to 'joyful affirmation' as a way of reconfiguring the architecture of being together, as from this positive position we can operate in a more useful, productive and kinder way. Rather than accepting failure as negative and viewing anxiety or struggle as the most productive way to exert change, we might recognise the enhanced benefits of the positive position. Another alternative to the negative paranoid theories of affect is Sedgwick's reparative reading, which cautions that by constantly trying to avoid negative affects they become self-reinforcing.[40] It is easy to dismiss these theories as utopian, idealistic and antithetical to the practice of acting. Both Braidotti's 'affirmative' and Sedgwick's 'reparative' recognise the challenge and complexity in re-orientating away from the negative depressive position towards the positive. Hope and pleasure are seen as necessary productive and mobilising forces, which seems more important than ever as we seek alternatives to xenophobia, fear and revenge culture that seeps through the structures of advanced capitalism.

Karan Barad's 'agential realism' offers a way to recalibrate ideas of mimesis which, as feminists have argued, re-inscribe reductive representation. When we start from the premise that we are material *in relation with* other materials, a moving constellation of atoms, human beings come into being through dynamic co-constitutive emergence. For feminists, this allows us to re-make mimesis, not as reflection but as a diffraction, producing something new rather than replicating what has gone before as fact. This position has the potential to move beyond the Anthropocene towards an ecological perspective, where the non-human has as much agency as the human and we recognise the matter of other-than-human, or more-than-human, in constructing identity. Here, notions of fixed identity are replaced with the polymorphous or multiple body in constant flux.

These four layers of critical thinking from new feminist materialisms underpin an ideology for acting where questions of identity, so fundamental for the actor, are all-too-often neutered or avoided altogether. This builds an alternative topography, moving beyond phallogocentric constructions of self and other to give structure and shape to a Critical Acting Pedagogy. A training ground built on these principles could bring down some of the walls that stand in the way for Maddie as they re-orientate value systems. Rather than facing a future of playing victims and objects, she can see herself with the potential to re-shape culture. Three frameworks, examined in Chapter 2, and seen in the practices of Part Two, emerge as key strategies in pedagogic practice: *mimesis-as-play, jouissance, the via positiva.*

In turbulent times, as we struggle to keep our balance, we need to think in terms of process as opposed to product. Pedagogies are processes, actants of change, where *how* we learn is as important as *what* we learn. When we untie mimesis from its phallocentric fellers, recognising it as a process of learning through play, we can reclaim it as a feminist practice. As humans we make sense of the world through play-acting/acting-play, testing ideas, working with the imagination and exploring solutions to given circumstances. From the perspective of agential realism, mimesis can only ever be a diffraction, a way of reading insights *through* one another. As such, mimesis allows us to come into being through pleasure, through playful repetition, where the inevitable 'hiatus of iterability', offers the possibility for new formations.[41] This 're-making' of mimesis-as-play, is built on pleasure, which finds its transformative potential in *jouissance*. Although, as Gallop posits, this term might be seen to be 'beyond principle',[42] when used as a feminist material, *jouissance* is the pleasure of coming into being *in relation with* others, sharing the same liberating and potentially transgressive excess of pleasure.[43] Far from being a purely erotic pleasure *jouissance* unites body, psychology and spirituality to allow the matter of the body to shape-shift, to take more space, to change its materiality.

Through mimesis-as-play and *jouissance* an affirmative politics is produced, which, when guided and supported through the *via positiva*, enables the actor to experience the *potentia* in learning through failing.[44] The process of learning to act through the *via negativa* of male lineages has become synonymous with painful practices of learning through negation, and needs re-figuring for the contemporary moment. Rather than being allowed to experience the potentially damaging effects of learning through failure alone, this approach, whilst still enabling the actor to find their own solutions to their particular acting blocks, does so through support and kindness. This has emerged as a feature of feminist practice, which works with authority and power in a different way. Rather than working with a flattened hierarchy, feminist pedagogy passes power between teacher/director and actor, recognising and valuing the shared responsibility in the creative process of joint experimentation. The *via positiva* is an engaged pedagogy where learning is a positive exchange, mutually beneficial and potentially transformational.

I have observed these ideas enacted in the varied practices of the women in this study: Jane Boston and Nadine George (voice); Vanessa Ewan and Niamh Dowling (movement); Kristine Landon-Smith and Alison Hodge (acting); Katie Mitchell and Emma Rice (directing). They all place the vital materialism of the body at the heart of their work and foreground the positivity of difference, working with *via positiva*. Mimesis-as-play is a particular pedagogic feature in the work of Kristine Landon-Smith (Chapter 5) and Emma Rice (Chapter 6), where *jouissance* is an essential component. Some, like Alison Hodge (Chapter 5) and Katie Mitchell (Chapter 6) pursue an agential realism, where human and non-human come into being with and through each other. These ways of working are traits of female practice, not necessarily framed as feminist by the practitioners, but certainly located in feminist thinking. Critical pedagogies, which have developed from Freire's liberatory pedagogy, foreground choice and difference to empower and liberate the individual to take control of the productive processes of their learning.[45] A Critical Acting Pedagogy embraces feminist pedagogy, queer pedagogy or critical race pedagogy to recognise, in its scope and outlook, concern for *all* minoritarian positions, sex, gender, age, race, class, ability. This type of practice is emancipatory, allowing Maddie to playfully experiment, take risks and fail whilst being supported. In this way she shifts from passive servitude to cultural worker, working through a diffractive process to reflect the world back on itself in ways that might enable a more inclusive way of being.

## Pedagogical practices: Implementing a Critical Acting Pedagogy

What might a curriculum, shaped by this pedagogical ideology look like? In this section I offer a series of 'what ifs' to imagine a training ground built on the principles and practices that have emerged in this book; a female genealogy of practice as an alternative to traditional male dominated lineages and frameworks. I recognise that this is blue sky thinking, that ideas may not be financially viable, practical or too radical for institutions tasked to serve the industry. Some suggestions will, no doubt, provoke resistance and questions, some may already be happening, in discrete or explicit ways in practice. What if acting was perceived differently? What would be taught? Who would teach it and how? How would success be measured?

What if acting was re-conceived as a politically engaged practice, where the paradox of being a cultural worker, an agent of change, happened *beside* contributing to the industry and was seen to be a productive tension? Exploring acting as a technique of the body allows for more explicit consideration of identity politics. This doesn't mean that acting becomes 'academic'; it retains what it already does and *beside* practising skills actors explore their identity, in relation with being in the world, exploring what Ellen Margolis calls 'effective citizenship'.[46] This then empowers the actor as embodied and em-brained, introducing pedagogies that reflect those of progressive MA Acting curriculums. Learning would start with the particular lived body, enacted and enacting in response to the cultural moment and conversations around difference would be part of the interrogation of the craft. Acting practice could be experienced *beside* the contextual study of acting with universities working in collaboration with drama schools to develop different adjuncts to the curriculum, and tutors teaching across institutions.

Let's push this further. What if acting, like theatre, was seen to be a way of thinking? When acting agency shifts beyond mimesis to kinesis it can be perceived differently. When the personal and social knowledge of acting, the hidden curriculum, comes into vision its epistemic scope opens up. The field will become more diverse when people recognise themselves represented in a subject invested in questions of difference, concerned to find new ways of being in the world together. Schools might then re-consider the place of drama in the curriculum as a facilitating subject, where creative thinking is inherently political. Those working in this field already know this. The challenge lies in shifting understanding. Recognising the vital contribution that acting/theatre and performance make to cultural well-being could change funding mechanisms for training, enabling diversity. What if more people in power had drama backgrounds? What if more people in power were women?

What if the double-ness of every aspect of acting emerged as a 'beside knowledge' construction as the life body is explored alongside the social body? The actor works with a double gesture and a double vision that enables agency. This has emerged as a defining feature of feminist acting pedagogies. All the teacher/directors in this study make this explicit in specific ways. For the actor, already doubled as both object and subject, learning in this way reveals her choices as she comes to a greater knowledge of the inscriptions she is re-presenting, appropriating or resisting. This understanding comes from a heightened awareness of visuality, with looking-at-being-looked-at-ness examined as a feature of a female ontology of acting and seen in the work of Vanessa Ewan (Chapter 4), Alison Hodge (Chapter 5) and Katie Mitchell (Chapter 6). In this process actors come to recognise the performativity in their own behaviour patterns, so that they can self-reflexively check, monitor and consciously observe unconscious actions. This Critical Acting Pedagogy locates being in the space between (people, space, object), whilst simultaneously exploring the doubleness of acting (subject/object, inner/outer, reflexive/reflective). These constructs operate beside each other within a critically engaged learning process. This then extends our thinking about acting, beyond limiting ideas of mimesis, to attend to the politics of identity with the added benefit of potentially improving well-being for the actor.

What if acting pedagogy received significant investment in research? Developing as a field, intersecting social science, humanities and the sciences, acting as technique might impact across disciplines. What if it was commonplace in drama schools and rehearsal rooms for researchers to map practice, document hidden histories and investigate methods? Progressive collaborations between practitioners and researchers have been seen to be mutually beneficial; space is made to attend the complexities of pedagogy, work is documented and new ways of working are opened up.

What if acting curriculums could privilege process above product? What if actors and directors learnt beside each other, as they do in Russian training grounds? What if there were no showcases and agents engaged with students through work in progress showings, self-devised pieces or collaborative devised work. RADA's MA Theatre Laboratory starts with what the individual artist brings to the creative space, then discovers how individuals can work in plurality to make new work.[47] RCSDD's BA DATE (Devising And Theatre Education) similarly positions the actor as a creative artist with the focus on making collaborative work. What if this was the starting point for all acting courses? Alison Hodge's 'Relational Actor' (Chapter 5), Niamh Dowling's 'Nomadic Actor' (Chapter 4) or Jane Boston's 'Becoming Voice' (Chapter 2) might be the integrative strands of a developmental acting curriculum that looks beyond methodologies.

Indeed, what if, rather than continuing to build curriculums around the study of the methods of dead white males, a female genealogy framed learning to act? This genealogy would foreground the hidden curriculum and make it explicit in learning objectives. These might include: ability to work both individually and as an ensemble with impulse and instinct; ability to listen with the whole body; ability to work with relational awareness; ability to accept and give critique; ability to be reflective and reflexive; ability to work with discipline; ability to be self-motivated; ability to demonstrate empathy; ability to maintain self-care. Turning to Elin Margolis' list of essential competencies we might also add, 'recognising the contributions of team members with diverse backgrounds' and 'through devising work, encouraging themselves to love living with questions rather than valuing quick solutions'.[48] Without the expectation to work towards an end product, the showcase and the public production, the curriculum could find a different topography. A female genealogy is non-linear, fragmented and with a flattened hierarchy, forming a cartography of interconnecting and overlapping shapes. Catherine Alexander, who worked for many years with Simon McBurney as a member of Complicité, reflected on the shapes that each had drawn in order to illustrate their different approaches to theatre-making. McBurney's was a series of intricate lines, boxes and arrows, meticulous and detailed, moving forward in a linear sequence and direction. In contrast, Alexander described hers as resembling a circular, organic construction growing from a central point. She suggested that their responses were indicative of the difference between their sexed bodyminds, with her 'femaleness' more predisposed to resist linear and directional structures, but to work in spirals, circling, returning to the start and revealing the spaces between.[49] What if the curriculum was conceived as a spiral of re-learning and repetitions, exploring the infinite variety of choice and possibilities for the actor as creative artist?

What recurring themes, traits or qualities mark the interconnecting shapes of this genealogy and how might this work in practice? The power relations in women's work, either as teacher or director, operate more as a series of interconnecting shapes where each individual takes responsibility for his/her own role, as opposed to a top-down authority. Delegating and encouraging a reflexive and shared ownership of the creative learning process is embedded in critical pedagogic practices. A female genealogy would integrate and interconnect, finding the value in exploring these interconnections. What if, rather than building acting curriculums with separatist voice, movement and acting strands, which perpetuates a hierarchy of knowledge, these strands were given equal time, even taught beside each other? What if team teaching was possible or a particular skill/quality, 'readiness' for example, was explored by the voice teacher, the acting teacher and the movement teacher, investigating the ways that, from their different specialisms, they approach this acting challenge?[50] Could this allow the actor to synthesise and take more control of their process of learning? Re-visioning an integrated curriculum could place difference at its heart. For example, what if a text like Chekhov's *Three Sisters* was studied alongside the version by Mustapha Matura, by Tracy Letts or by feminist company Rash Dash, then re-imagined by the participant group? Could Kristine Landon-Smith's 'Intra-cultural Practice' (Chapter 5), Vanessa Ewan's 'Cultural Body' or Niamh Dowling's 'Ecological Body' (Chapter 3) form the backbone of a curriculum? Re-orientating perspectives about the underpinning ideology would sharpen the focus for the students. What if all actors had the opportunity to work cross gender? What might this open up in their technique beside their personal and social knowledge?

We can look to international directions to help us think outside traditional UK approaches to actor training when developing Critical Acting Pedagogy. 'The Whole Actor, Whole Person Training' (WAWPT) developed by Queensland University of Technology (QUT) offers an alternative model, which places the actor's well-being at the heart of the curriculum.[51] Responding to the Australian 'Actor's Well-Being Study', which identified high instances of mental health problems for actors,[52] a curriculum was developed, underpinned by twenty key elements, which placed the exploration of identity and agency beside knowledge and skills. Andrea Moor, commenting on the remodelled approach, notes:

> The adoption of these principles will hopefully flush out the kind of teaching that we now recognise as detrimental to the mental health and well-being of the actor. Processes that are shaming in nature or that make allegations of the students' ability without concise ways to remedy a problem have no place in a modern day drama school.[53]

Nationwide studies into well-being in UK drama schools might, as with the kickstart for diversity work prompted by the report 'Acting Up',[54] help to steer change.

How might a female genealogy of acting be recognised, nurtured and mined for its pedagogical value? What if the foundational ways that actors came to learn was through *via positiva* and *jouissance*? In this supported environment, through the dynamic of play and shared experimentation, there would be explicit dialogue about the choices being made through reflexive and diagnostic analysis. The actor becomes her own teacher with an orientation towards affirmation. What if the value of not knowing, of day-dreaming, of doing less was seen to be a strength? Where there is a shared, as opposed to equal, responsibility for the learning, enabling plurality and group responsibility, whilst recognising the distinct and particular contributions of individuals within the group; where a joint experimentation process is facilitated, with the teacher/director holding the authority but as an expert learner, working alongside the actor, as opposed to a master who holds all the answers. This facilitating authority would be created in diverse ways: through explicit and transparent explanations; through direct and honest interactions; through allowing people choice; through creating a dynamic where people are made to feel that they can take risks and fail, knowing that they will be supported; through delegation. This integrity and trust in the learning relationship enables practitioners to either lead from the front, like director Emma Rice, or from behind, like Katie Mitchell (Chapter 6).

What if, in rehearsal rooms, directors worked with 'a method of feminist action'? This approach offers an alternative to Diamond's feminist gestic criticism for acting, which utilised a Brechtian approach.[55] Playing on Stanislavski's method of physical action, Mitchell has developed an interpretation that foregrounds the politics of the body through rigorous textual analysis, whilst remaining in the realm of naturalism. Through the intense scrutiny of action choices, she enables actors to consider the ways that the body is inscribed by time and place and how events and intentions materialise through physical action. The negotiation of determining every action choice ensures that the double-ness of the gesture and visuality is built into this rigorous process. In this way the acting is authored through forensic realism as opposed to through Brechtian alienation. An alternative feminist acting approach can be seen in Emma Rice's 'feminine masquerade', where Rice explores what Irigaray terms 'the double gesture' through a form of mimicry. Through exaggerated appropriation the female actor subverts normative behaviour, pointing to the mask she wears. This approach examines femaleness in all its multiplicity. Like Nadine George's 'Queering Voice' (Chapter 3) Vanessa Ewan's 'Cultural Body' (Chapter 4) or Alison Hodge's 'Relational Actor', (Chapter 5), Rice and Mitchell enable a way of learning, which offers 'something particular' for women, allowing constructs of femaleness and femininity to become powerful sites of choice for the actor.[56] They resist representing females as victims or objects to present the sexed body as multiple, changing and powerfully complex. What if these approaches became common place in rehearsal rooms?

This book asks us to 'Act as a Feminist' and think about the ways that feminisms intersect with acting pedagogies. bell hooks maintains that advancing approaches to teaching and learning can 'create a new language, rupturing disciplinary boundaries, de-centering authority and rewriting institutions and discursive borderlands'.[57] Following this premise, this book has explored the ideologies of a female genealogy of acting intersecting with the pedagogies of women practitioners, to give shape to a Critical Acting Pedagogy. I hope that it contributes to the exciting and radical re-workings happening in the field at this time, as acting re-conditions itself to be fit for purpose in twenty-first century and beyond. Above all, I hope that this gives space to acknowledge the pioneering work of the women practitioners who have shaped the field of UK acting, inspiring future unruly women to take their space in this constellation.

## Notes

1 William Shakespeare, *The Taming of the Shrew*, ed. Barbara Hodgdon (The Arden Shakespeare Third Series: Bloomsbury, 2010), V.ii. 142–145.
2 Madeleine Walker, *The Taming of the Shrew: How Can the Modern-Day Actor Survive a 'Taming' Narrative?* (unpublished dissertation, MA Acting, RCSSD, 2018).
3 Carol Chillington Rutter, *Clamorous Voices: Shakespeare's Women Today* (The Women's Press, Re-print Edition, 1988).
4 Walker, 7.
5 Ibid., 8.
6 Joan Riviere, 'Womanliness as a Masquerade' in *Formations of Fantasy*, ed. Victor Burgin, James Donald, Cora Kaplan (London & New York: Routledge, 1986).
7 Walker, 15.
8 Rosemary Malague, RCSSD (15.03.16).
9 Ibid.
10 Sara Ahmed, *Living a Feminist Life* (Durham and London: Duke University Press, 2017) 252.
11 Ibid.
12 Yvonne Rainer, 'Some Retrospective Notes on a Dance for 10 People and 12 Mattresses called "Parts of Some Sextexts", Performed at the Wadsworth Atheneum, Hartford, Connecticut, and Judson Memorial Church, New York, in March 1965', *The Tulane Drama Review* (The MIT Press, 1965), 10(2): 168–178.
13 In the section 'Feminism: Where Are the Women?' I map the imaginary career of a female actor and consider the inequalities and marginalisation she will face in light of the data.
14 I refer to Systemic Constellation therapy in Chapter 4 'Women and the Matter of Movement' in the case study on Niamh Dowling.
15 Rosi Braidotti, *Nomadic Theory: The Portable Rosi Braidotti* (New York & Chichester: Colombia University Press, 2011).
16 Julie Wilkinson speaking at Advance (RCSSD), 2014. Platform transcript at Tonic Theatre. http://www.tonictheatre.co.uk [accessed 12.08.15].
17 Equity is the UK actor's union, which fights for fair terms and conditions in the workplace. https://www.equity.org.uk/about/. In 2017 they launched a 'Manifesto for Casting' to confront unfair and potentially exploitative casting processes. In 2018 the Casting Director's Guild responded with a new code of conduct.
18 Tonic Theatre's *Advance* programme confronts gender inequality in England's performing arts organisations. It was piloted in 2013, with a second series in 2016. 'Something prevented talented women from rising to the top. We wanted to understand why and do something to address it'. http://www.tonictheatre-advance.co.uk/about/.
19 Lauren Bell: *Women in Theatre: The Movers and Shakers*. http://www.atgtickets.com/blog/women-in-theatre/[accessed [07.08.14].This blog offers a roll call of names of women who have made a mark on the UK theatre landscape. She lists female playwrights who have won a host of awards including: Lucy Kirkwood, Lucy Prebble, Laura Wade, Nina Raine, Polly Stenham, Beth Steel, Anya Reiss. In 2005, Helen Edmundson's play *Coram* Boy was the first play by a woman to be performed on the Olivier stage at the National Theatre, followed by *Her Naked Skin* by Rebecca Lenkiewicz in 2008. Bell cites the increase in female producers: Sonia Friedman, Tali Pelman, Judy Craymer, Sally Greene, Nica Burns, Becky Barber, Rachel Williams, Rachel Tyson, Sarah Brocklehurst and Kate Pakenham. She also lists female critics: Libby Purvis, Lyn Gardner, Susanna Clap, Kate Basset. Female directors include: Marianne Elliot (*War Horse*, 2011), Phyllida Lloyd (all female *Julius Ceasar*, 2014), Lyndsey Turner (*Chimerica*, 2013), Carrie Cracknell (*A Doll's House*, 2012). However,

it is the wave of recent female artistic director appointments that offer the most optimistic shift in the landscape: Jude Kelly at the Southbank Centre since 2005; Josie Rourke at the Donmar in 2012; Indhu Rubasingham at Tricycle Theatre in 2012; Erica Whyman as Deputy Director of the RSC in 2012; Emma Rice at the Globe in 2016; and Vicky Featherstone at the Royal Court since 2012. Many believe that the last decade has shown a movement towards gender equality and one might assume that the 2010 equity legislation has started to take affect.

20 Equity 'Manifesto for Casting' https://www.equity.org.uk/getting-involved/campaigns/manifesto-for-casting/ [accessed 15.04.20].
21 Sarah Solemani, 'The TV and Film Industries Are Toxic – And It Starts in the Audition Room', (*The Guardian* 20.10.17) https://www.theguardian.com/film/2017/oct/20/tv-film-industries-toxic-starts-audition-room-harvey-weinstein [accessed 14.08.18].
22 Malague, op.cit.
23 I am referencing Audre Lorde, 'The Master's Tools Will Never Dismantle the Master's House'. in *Your Silence will Not Protect Me* (UK: Silver Press, 2017) 89–94.
24 In 2014, I attended 'The Changing Landscape', set up by Drama UK at Birkbeck University, (26.11.14). In 2018, the Federation of Drama Schools called for codes of conduct around consent in all UK drama schools. Georgia Snow, 'Drama Schools Commit to Ethical Guidelines to Tackle Sexual Harassment', *The Stage* (19.04.18) https://www.thestage.co.uk/news/2018/drama-schools-commit-ethical-guidelines-tack [accessed 15.04.20].
25 Catherine Alexander interviewed in London (15.07.15).
26 Tracy Brabin, Gloria De Piero, Sarah Coombes (2017) 'Acting Up Report: Labour's Inquiry into Access and Diversity in the Performing Arts', https://d3n8a8pro7vhmx.cloudfront.net/campaigncountdown/pages/1157/attachm [accessed 15.04.20].
27 'Twenty-First Century Acting Race and Inclusive Practice. What Next'?' Symposium at RCSSD, 12.09.19.
28 The murder of George Floyd by a white policeman on 25.05.20 ignited global support for Black Lives Matter. In response to messages of solidarity from UK drama schools, BAME students called out the systemic racism they had experienced.Lanre Bakara, 'Drama Schools Accused of Hypocrisy over Anti-Racism Statements', *The Guardian* (09.06.20) https://www.theguardian.com/stage/2020/jun/06/drama-schools-accused-of-hypocrisy-over-anti-racism-statements [accessed 17.06.20].
29 The Actor Training Roundtable, at RCSSD on 18 July 2019 gathered together nine MA Acting course leaders from the UK to discuss commonalities and differences in training actors in one year. Many courses foreground the politics of identity, looking at how the actor might be an 'agent for change' from inside the industry.
30 I explain the therapeutic practice of Systemic Constellations in Chapter 4 in relation to the movement training practices of Niamh Dowling.
31 Since 2010 the numbers of students taking Drama GCSE fell by 15.9% and the numbers taking A- Level Drama fell by 26.6%. 'Acting Up Report: Labour's inquiry into access and diversity in the performing arts'. https://d3n8a8pro7vhmx.cloudfront.net/campaigncountdown/pages/1157/attachm [accessed 15.04.20].
32 Between 2013 and 2019, The Russell Group, a group of high-ranking UK universities, offered support, 'Informed Choices' for those deciding what A Levels they choose in order to gain access to university. The facilitating subjects are: mathematics and further mathematics, English literature, physics, biology, chemistry, geography, history and languages (classical and modern). In 2019, after criticism that this list had relegated arts subject they revised 'Informed Choices' to scrap a list and to offer more personalised support. https://russellgroup.ac.uk/policy/publications/informed-choices/ [accessed 16.04.20].
33 Lorde, 105.
34 I theorise this movement in Part One of this book.

35 Eve Sedgwick, *Touching Feeling: Affect, Pedagogy, Performativity* (Durham & London: Duke University Press, 2003).
36 Geraldine Harris, *Staging Femininities: Performance and Performativity* (Manchester and New York: Manchester University Press, 1999) 17.
37 Elizabeth Grosz, *Volatile Bodies: Towards a Corporeal Feminism* (Indianapolis: Indiana University Press, 1994).
38 Braidotti, 161.
39 Ibid.
40 Sedgwick, 124–136.
41 Judith Butler, *Bodies that Matter: On the Discursive Limits of Sex* (London: Routledge, 1993) 234.
42 Jane Gallop, 'Beyond the Jouissance Principle', *Representations*, 7 (Summer, 1984): 110–115.
43 Kristi Lempiäinen, 'With You but Different: Jouissance and Feminist Writing', *Nora, Nordic Journal of Women's Studies*, 5(2), (1997): 105–118.
44 Foucault drew attention to the positive potential of power play when experienced as 'a sort of open-ended strategic game where the situation may be reversed is not evil', Michel Foucault, Power: *Essential works of Foucault 1954–1984. Volume 3* (London: Penguin, 1984) 298.
45 Paulo Freire, Pedagogy *of the Oppressed* (New York: Continuum, 2000).
46 Elin Margolis, 'An Eye on the Exit: Actor Training in a Liberal Arts Environment' in John Freeman (ed.), *Approaches to Actor Training: International Perspectives* (Macmillan International Higher Education, London & New York, 2019) 324.
47 RADA, MA Theatre Laboratory, https://www.rada.ac.uk/courses/ma-theatre-lab/.
48 Margolis, 245.
49 Catherine Alexander (15.07.15).
50 Sarah Davey-Hull, Morwenna Rowe, Anna Healey, 'The Interconnectedness of All Things ... Finding a Shared Language in Actor Training', workshop presented at *The International Platform for Performer Training*: 7th Edition, University of Kent, 9–12 January 2020.
51 Andrea L. Moor, 'Whole Actor, Whole Person Training: Designing a Holistic Actor Training Programme for Individual Career Longevity and Well Being', in John Freeman (ed.), *Approaches to Actor Training: International Perspectives* (London & New York: Macmillan International Higher Education, 2019) 26–43.
52 Ian Maxwell, Mark Seton and Marianna Dinyáné Szabó, *The Australian Actors' Wellbeing Study: A Preliminary Report* (2015), https://www.semanticscholar.org/paper/The-Australian-Actors'-Wellbeing-Study%3A [accessed 16.04.20].
53 Ibid. 42.
54 'Acting Up Report: Labour's Inquiry into Access and Diversity in the Performing Arts', https://d3n8a8pro7vhmx.cloudfront.net/campaigncountdown/pages/1157/attachm [accessed 15.04.20].
55 Elin Diamond, *Unmaking Mimesis* (London & New York: Routledge, 1997) x–xiii.
56 Alison Hodge (21.03.15).
57 bell hooks, *Teaching to Transgress* (London & New York: Routledge, 1994) 129.

# INDEX

Abbot, John 135
absence of women (in actor training) 11
acting: doubleness 207, 208; female connections to 32; as female ontology 26, 29–30, 37; as human science 46–7; inequality and oppression in learning 9–10; knowledge located within female domain 27; mythology of pain in learning 9; neutered pedagogies in 57–8; new paradigms for 25–6; observation as major part of 109–10; performance vs. 4–6; personal and social knowledge of 4–6; reconsideration of ideological foundations of 26; technique 4–6; as way of thinking 207–8
"Acting and Not Acting" (Kirby) 4
Acting BA degree 3
*Acting the First Six Lessons* (Boleslavski) 6
Acting Up initiative 202, 210
"Acting Up Report: Labour's Inquiry into Access and Diversity in the Performing Arts" 9
Action Theatre 103
active analysis 141–2
actor: challenges facing females 13–4; neutering of 12
actor and teacher/director interaction 46; female as joint learner 54; language in 47; reciprocity actions 47; verbal and non-verbal communication in 48–9; ways that facilitate learning 46–7
actor as cultural worker 6
*Actor Movement: Expression of the Physical Being* (Ewan & Green) 108
*An Actor Prepares* (Stanislavski) 6, 53
actor training methodologies 135–6
*The Actor Training Reader* 74, 134
*An Actress Prepares* (Malague) 12

Adler, Stella 11, 53, 134, 136
*Advance* programme on gender imbalances (Tonic Theatre) 201–2
Aeschylus 35
aesthetics 117
affinities 171, 172
affirmative learning 139
*Agamemnon* (Aeschylus) 35
agential realism 40, 82, 204, 205
Ahmed, Sarah 10, 11, 16
Alexander, Catherine 134, 209
Alexander, F.M. 101
Alexander, Gerda 103
Alexander Technique 51, 101, 103, 117, 119, 121, 124, 125
Alexandrowicz, Conrad 155
Alfreds, Mike 135
Allnutt, Wendy 100
American Method training 52, 53, 62
*Anatomy of a Suicide* (Birch) 175
anima/animus energies 30
apprenticeship model 53, 100
*Approaches to Actor Training: International Perspectives* (Freeman) 7
archetypes 61, 86, 144
Arden, Annabel 163
Arendt, Hannah 167, 182
Armstrong, Frankie 74
Arnold, Trish 100, 101, 102
*The Arrival* (Tan) 138, 142
*The Arrival of Sound* (Boston) 81–2
Aston, Elaine 12, 58, 61, 62
Atkindon, Dot 184
attention and attending 149
auditions 3, 9, 169, 200, 201
Auslander, Phillip 5
"The Australian Actor's Wellbeing Study: A Preliminary Report" (2010) 210

## Index

auteur (female) 165, 179

*The Bacchae* (Euripides) 179, 187
Bachelor of Arts degree in Acting 2, 76
Baker, Simon 182
Barad, Karen 38, 39, 48, 63, 82, 94, 146, 177, 205
Barba, Eugenio 30, 33, 101, 137
Barker, Clive 50, 163
Barker, Stu 182
Bartenieff, Irmgard 103
Bartenieff fundamentals 103
Barthes, Roland 107
Bassnett, Susan 11
Bates, Laura 13
Bausch, Pina 166
becoming voice 79–83, 94, 209
Bennet, Jane 38, 48, 63, 146, 188
Berger, John 33
Berry, Cicely 73, 74, 75, 85, 86
Best, David 117
Bharucha, Rustom 137, 138
bio-feminism 119
bio-literate feminism 38–9
biological determinism 31
Bird, Bonnie 108, 110
Black, Asian and Minority Ethic (BAME) 16, 137, 138, 140, 142, 202
black feminism 55–6
Black Lives Matter movement 9, 104, 202
*Black Watch* 87
Blair, Rhonda 35, 63, 64, 173
Boal, Augusto 60, 143
*Bodies That Matter: On the Discursive Limits of Sex* (Butler) 62, 143
body as matter 63
bodyworld 39, 48, 83, 147
Bogart, Anne 11, 101, 103, 117, 134, 136, 162
Bohr, Niels 39, 94
Boleslavski, Isaac 6
Boston, Jane 16, 39, 73, 74, 76–86, 87, 94, 140, 206, 209
Bowman, Ellen 172
Brahmachari, Sita 138
Braidotti, Rosi 12, 38, 48, 104, 107, 116, 139, 154, 173, 200, 204, 205
breath, exploration of 90, 151–3; tough and 90–1
Brecht, Bertolt 35, 40, 62, 63, 109, 153, 172, 173, 199, 211
Brener, Neil 173
British New Dance movement 102

Brook, Peter 137
Brown, Trisha 103
Bruford, Rose 135
Burton, Don 117
Bury, Margaret (Maggie) 108, 135
Butler, Judith 31, 37, 38, 39, 62, 107, 112, 113, 143, 188

Caillois, Roger 50, 183
Callery, Dymphna 101
Camilleri, Frank 7, 39, 48, 147
Campion, Jane 166
Cannon, Dee 136
Cannon, Doreen 136
capitalism 38, 80, 84, 89, 119, 147, 205
Carey, David 74
*Carry on Understudies: Theatre and Sexual Politics* (Wandor) 163
Carter, Angela 179, 187
Case, Sue Ellen 34
Casilda, Daniela García 146, 147
casting 9, 113, 143, 164, 179, 182, 187–8
casting couch 13
Castledine, Annie 163
Cavarero, Adriana 83, 141
Cavendish, Dominic 182
Chagrin, Claude 102
Chekhov, Anton 11, 210
*The Cherry Orchard* (Chekhov) 169, 170, 173, 174, 175
chora 83, 94
Chow, Broderick 59, 61
Christensen, Inger 167
Chubbuck, Ivana 136
Churcher, Mel 74
Churchill, Caryl 84, 85
Civil Rights Movement 77
Cixous, Hélène 31, 36, 107, 167, 176
Claid, Emily 102
*Clamorous Voices: Shakespeare's Women Today* (Rutter) 198
Clark, Gill 117
Clark-Carey, Rebecca 74
classical naturalism 171
*Cleansed* (Kane) 175
clown training 52, 53, 139
codes and keys 110–1
cognitive consciousness 146
collaborative performance making 54, 163
collective imagination 181, 182, 185, 189
commercialisation of training 134–5
community of practice 167, 168, 182
Complicité 134, 163, 209

# Index

Cone, Grace 135
Conference of Drama Schools (CDS) 1, 2
constructionist feminists 37
contemporary (women) practitioners 12
Conti, Ruth 135
continuum matrix 4
core as locus for feelings 148
*Core Training for the Relational Actor* (Hodge) 17, 145, 146, 152
Costa, Madda 182
critical acting pedagogy (CAP) 10, 109, 138, 148, 156, 169, 204; critique of power structures 59; feminist educational criticisms of 59–60; implementation of 207–11
critical performative pedagogy (CPP) 60, 61
cross-gender casting 187–8
cultural body 108, 109, 110–1, 210
cultural materialist camp of feminism 31
cultural sound house 76
Cumberbatch, Benedict 167, 168
*Cymbeline* (Shakespeare) 179

Damasio, Antonio 149
Dangerous Spaces 74
Davey-Hull, Sarah 169
de Beauvoir, Simone 31, 32, 83, 167
decolonisation of curriculum 16
Defoe, Willem 5
Dewey, John 46
dialogic scaffolding 110
Diamond, Elin 34, 35, 40, 62, 109, 111, 172, 186, 211
difference negotiation 58
Dineen, Molly 155
*The Director's Craft* (Mitchell) 168, 169
discovery process 110
diversity in actor training 16, 202
diversity in movement training 104
doing gender 113
doing intimacy 114–5
Dolan, Jill 34
Donnellan, Declan 135
Dostoyevsky, Fyodor 176
doubling strategy 15, 26, 29–37, 58, 94, 115, 176–7, 204
Dowling, Niamh 16, 34, 57, 101, 116–26, 206, 209, 210
drama and education (DIE) 58–9
drama schools 1, 2; affiliation to universities 2; compared to university drama education 2; practical and pragmatic differences to university drama education 3
Duchêne, Kate 172, 175, 176
du Maurier, Daphne 111, 179
Duncan, Lyndsey 164
Duppy, Dominique 89
Duprés, Maedée 102

Early, Fergus 102
East 15 drama school 2, 135, 136
*East is East* (Landon-Smith) 138
ecological body 39, 210
*écriture feminine* 176
educationalists 48
effective citizenship 207
"The Emotion Workshop" (Mitchell & Lythgoe, 2003) 174
empathy 45, 58, 119, 139, 147, 151, 155, 209
empowerment 8, 10, 38, 54, 59
epic theatre 102
*Escaped Alone* (Churchill) 84
ethical neglect (in actor training) 9–10
ethics of embodiment in acting 9
Euripides 35, 167
European naturalism 167
eutony 103
Evans, Mark 49, 101, 104, 105, 107, 108, 121
*Everyday Sexism Project* (Bates) 13
Ewan, Vanessa 15–6, 33, 39, 55, 57, 100, 101, 108–16, 126, 206, 208, 210, 211
Extemporary Dance Theatre 102

Featherstone, Vicky 14
The Federation of Drama Schools 9, 202
feeling body 149
Feldenkrais, Moshe 101
Feldenkrais technique 51, 101, 103, 119
female, state of being 12
female alienation 32
"The Female Role and Its Representation on Stage in Various Cultures" (ISTA conference) 30
female space 55
feminine, state of being 12, 31; mimicry 186; vulnerability and 36–7
feminine masquerade 211
femininity 146
feminism: acting pedagogies and 63, 64, 65; approaches to acting 34–5; explanations 10; hysteria and 36; intersectional 12; Lacan's key ideas towards shift in 31;

liberal 61; materialist 61; radical 61; second wave 31; theories of knowledge 27, 28; value of vulnerability 35
*Feminism and Theatre* (Case) 34
feminist acting technique 62–3, 175–6
feminist epistemologies 27
feminist gestic criticism for acting 211
feminist manifesto for acting in twenty-first century 17, 200–1
feminist materialisms 25, 37–8, 40, 48, 62–3, 77–8, 80, 119
feminist mimesis 34, 40
Feminists Improvising group (FIG) 74
*The Feminist Spectator as Critic* (Dolan) 34
"Feminist Transpositions" (Braidotti) 38
Fitzmaurice, Catherine 75
*The Fitzmaurice Voicework* 74–5
Fleming, Kate 74
Fletcher, Nick 171
Fogerty, Elsie 135
'follow me' methodology 49
*The Forbidden Zone* (Macmillan) 175
Foucault, Michel 8, 25, 39, 53
Foucauldian genealogy 8, 25
fourth-wall naturalism 180
Fowler, Ben 165
*Fräulein Julie* (Strindberg) 167
*Freeing the Natural Voice* (Linklater) 75
Freestone, Elizabeth 163
Freire, Paulo 8, 28, 46, 59, 207
Freud, Sigmund 5, 31, 32, 36
Froebel, Friedrich 49
*From Acting to Performance: Essays in Modernism and Post-Modernism* (Auslander) 5
Fulkerson, Mary 102
Furse, Anna 36

Gallop, Jane 107
game theory 50, 53, 184
Gardner, Lyn 6
Gardzienice (Poland) 29, 145, 146, 149, 166, 171, 180, 182, 183, 184
Gatens, Moira 32
Gaulier, Philippe 11, 50, 52, 138, 139
gender: embodied exploration of 80; formation as socio-psychological construction 31; intimacy and 16; Lacan's construction of 31–2; neuter of 25; as relational and contextual 38; as technique 198–9; terms of reference 11–2; in *via negativa* 52–3

"Gender and Theatre" report by Purple Seven 13
gender dysphoria 79
gendered cultural psyche 14
gendered implications 9
gendered power dynamic 11
gender equality in casting 179, 201–2
gender fluidity 12
Gender Identity Clinic, London 79
gender neutering 12
gender performativity 37
gender re-alignment 12
*Gender Trouble: Feminism and the Subversion of Identity* (Butler) 62
George, Nadine 16, 34, 37, 73, 74, 76, 86–94, 140, 206, 211
gestalt theory 117
gestic feminist critique 111
Gibson, Jane 100, 102
Gilman, Charlotte Perkins 167
Gilson, Erinn 36, 37, 153
Gindler, Elsa 103
*The Girl Child* (Dowling) 117
Giroux, Henry 28, 46
The Globe 100, 164, 179, 186, 188
*Going on the Stage: A Report to the Calouste Gulbenkian Foundation on professional training for drama* (1975) 1–2
Goodbody, Buzz 163, 164
Gorbatchevsky, Marie-Anne 87
Gotz, Elizabeth 31
Greek theatre 35–6, 153
Green, Debbie 108
Griffin, Tamzin 184
Grose, Carl 182
Grosz, Elizabeth 38, 48, 63, 105, 107, 204
Grotowski, Jerzy 11, 51, 52, 101, 137, 180
*Growing Voices: Nadine George Technique: The Evolution of Its Influences in Training and Performance* 86–7
Guilford School of Acting 2
Gupta, Tanika 187
gynocentric camp of feminism 31

habitual vulnerability 35
Hagen, Uta 53, 136
Hale, Imogen 109, 111
Hall, Sophie 145
Halpin, Anna 103
Handke, Peter 177
haptics 150, 151

Haraway, Donna 38, 48, 63, 178
Harris, Antonio 142, 204
Harris, Geraldine 12, 58, 62
Hart, Lindsay 34, 93
Hart, Roy 86
Harvey, Simon 182
Heath, Steven 32
Heidegger, Martin 150
Hellinger, Bert 120–1
*Henry IV* (Shakespeare) 164
hiatus of iterability 107
hidden curriculum 27, 28, 45, 58; in actor training 48–9; production of 46
hierarchical gendered system 118
Higher Education (HE) 2; gender impact in drama and acting in 57–8; loss of student discretionary grants for 2; SCUDD as representative of theatre arts in 6; student fee change in 2012 in 2
Higher Education Funding Council of England (HEFCE) 2
Hinduism 51
Hodge, Alison 11, 15, 16, 34, 37, 39, 63, 134, 145–56, 180, 206, 208, 209, 211
hooks, bel 46, 60, 211
Houseman, Barbara 74
*The House of Bernardo Alba* (Lorca) 154
Huizinger, Johan 50
Hulton, Peter 155
hyper-realism 174
hypnotherapy 123
hysteria 35, 36; as manifestation of social oppression 36

ideokenisis 103
*The Idiot* (Dostoyevsky) 176
improvisation 101–2, 141, 144, 172, 174, 185
inequities in actor training 13–4
Ingold, Timothy 149
*In Search of Our Mother's Garden* (Walker) 56
inter-medial form 176–7
International Centre of Voice, RSCCD 16
International Network for Voice Studies (INV) 76
The International Platform for Performer Training 7
International School of Theatre Anthropology (ISTA) 30
intimacy 16, 74, 91, 109, 111, 114–6
intra-cultural practice 137, 138, 210
*Iphigenia at Aulis* (Euripides) 174, 175

Irigaray, Luce 31, 57, 63, 82, 83, 85, 90, 91, 107, 151, 186, 211
Irving, Maggie 52, 53
Ivinson, Gabrielle 48

Jackson, Alecia Youngblood 48
Jaholkowski, Antoni 52
Jaker, Christian 149
Jamieson, Duncan 52
Jellicoe, Anne 163
Jerez, Marion 166
Johnson, Finlay 49
Johnstone, Keith 50
joint experimentation 55
*jouissance* (beyond pleasure) 107–8, 126, 205, 206, 210
Judson Dance Theatre 102, 103
Juelskjaer, Malou 48
*Julius Ceasar* (Shakespeare) 164
just lookingness 35

Kantor, Tadeusz 180
Kapsali, Maria 8
Karczag, Eva 117
Karnicke, Sharon 5
Kelley, Vic 27
Kendrick, Lynne 50, 52, 53, 183
kinetic awareness 103
Kirby, Michael 4, 5, 60
Klein, Melanie 55
Knebel, Maria 11, 134
Kneehigh 179, 181, 182, 187
knowledge: construction 46; as cyclical and repetitive 25; feminist theories of 26, 27, 28; reciprocal construction of 47; Western male theories of 26, 27
Kolb, David 46
Kristeva, Julia 32, 83, 107, 140

Laban, Rudolph 101, 108, 110, 135
Lacan, Jacques 5, 31, 32, 33, 34, 107, 113
Landau, Tina 136
Landon-Smith, Kristine 16, 63, 109, 137–44, 148, 155, 206, i, x, xii
Lanfang, Mei 153
Lang, Caroline 145
Lansley, Jackie 102
Lave, Jean 46, 47
Le, Jackie 142
LeCompte, Liz 166
Lecoq, Jacques 11, 50, 52, 101, 102, 105, 134
Lefton, Sue 100, 102

Lempiäinen, Kirstu 107
Le Page, Louis 176
lesbian, gay, bisexual or transgender, and people with gender expressions outside traditional norms (LGBT+) 12
Letts, Tracy 210
liberal feminism 61
liberatory pedagogy 172, 207
life is a journey 119
Linklater, Kristin 11, 73, 74, 75, 86, 134
Littlewood, Joan 11, 134, 135, 145, 163
live cinema 165, 169, 171, 176, 177
Lloyd, Phyllida 164
London Academy of Music and Dramatic Art (LAMDA) 74, 100, 102
Long, Diane 145
looking at being-looked-at-ness 109, 208
Lorde, Audre 58, 203
Louie, Annie 101
L.S.D. (The Wooster Group) 5
ludic performance theory 50, 53
Ludus Dance 102
*The Lulu Plays (Wedekind)* 187
Lythgoe, Mark 173, 174

MacDonald, Glynne 100
The Magdelena Project 11
*Making a Spectacle: Feminist Essays on Contemporary Women's Theatre* (ed. Hart) 34
Malague, Rosemary 12, 62, 199
"Manifesto for Casting" (Equity) 9, 202
marginal voices 76
Margolis, Ellen 7, 207
Marshall, Lorna 100, 101
Marx, Karl 38
Marxism 38, 164, 171, 173, 204
masks, use of 115
Master of Arts (MA) in actor training 8, 207
materialism 38, 61; of female bodies 175
materiality of bodies 104, 170
Matura, Mustapha 210
Mayröcker, Friederike 167
Mazeika, Krz 145
McAuley, Esther 168, 171
McBurney, Simon 209
McDade, Sandy 168, 171
McGilchrist, Ian 147
McLoughlin, Annette 184
mechanisms of power 1, 8, 34, 40, 59
*Medea* (Euripides) 35
Meerzon, Yana 5

Meisner, Sanford 11, 53, 134
melancholia from negativity 55
Merkimedes, Alex 163
Merleau-Ponty, Maurice 145
metaphorical language 123
method acting tradition 4
*Me Too* movement 13, 104, 199, 202
Meyer, Pippa 167
Meyerhold, Vsevolod 11
*A Midsummer Night's Dream* (Shakespeare) 179
Milano, Alyssa 13
Milde, Andrea 47, 48, 123, 172
Mills, Matthew 77, 79
mimesis-as-play 50, 60, 64, 205, 206
Mitchell, Bill 181
Mitchell, Juliet 36
Mitchell, Katie 16, 17, 35, 39, 40, 63, 64, 162, 164, 165–81, 185, 189, 206, 208, 211
Mitchell, Roanna 8
Mnouchkine, Arianne 11, 134, 162
monism 106
Moor, Andrea 210
Morris, Shona 55, 56, 100, 104, 118
Mortimer, Vicki 167–8
Moseley, Nick 135
movement: feminist position on training 104–6; inner/outer paradox in training 103–4; metaphorical language in training 123–4; misuse of power in training 104; women as dominant in field 100
Mulcahy, Betty 74
multiplicity of the self 16
Munk, Erica 30
Murfitt, Etta 182, 188
Murphy, Anna Maria 182
Murray, Simon 52

*The Nadine George Technique (NGT)* 74, 86
Nash, Jennifer 55, 56, 58
National Endowment for Science, Technology and the Arts (NESTA) 167
The National Theatre (NT) 73, 74, 76, 100, 102, 134, 166
Natural Dance Workshop 102
naturalism 5
Natural Voice Practitioners' Network (NVPN) 74
Neil, A. S 77
Nelson, Jeannette 74
neoliberalism 10

neuroscience 46
neutral/natural body 101, 105–6, 108
*New Dance* 102
Newlove, Jean 100, 101, 102, 108, 135
new materialism 48
Nietzsche, Friedrich 32
*Nights at the Circus* (Carter) 187, 189
*946: The Amazing Story of Adolphus Tips* (Morpurgo) 188, 189
nomadic paradigm 82, 107, 109, 117, 119, 126
"No Manifesto" (Rainer) 200
North, Marion 108

O'Brien, Ita 114
Oedipus complex 31, 32
The Old Vic 74, 100
Olivier, Laurence 4
*Ophelia's Zimmer* (Birch) 175
Overlie, Mary 101, 103, 136
Owen, Katy 184

Pagneux, Monika 11, 117, 134
*paida* (games) 138
paidic aesthetic 50
*Pandora's Box* (Wedekind) 187
Parowska, Dorota 145
Parrish, Sue 11
passive actor 8
patriarchal systems 10, 25, 30, 48, 61, 64, 76, 134, 164, 199
Paxton, Steve 102
pedagogical acting schools 5
pedagogy: in acting field 6–7; critical acting 10; diversity of learning prevents common 6–7; politics of 8; power and 8
pedagogy of the oppressed 27–8
*Pedagogy of the Oppressed* (Freire) 8
performance: acting *vs.* 4–6; exchange between actor and audience in 167, 176
*Performance Practice and Process* (Aston & Harris) 12
performance studies 2, 58; emergence of 3–4; as interdisciplinary approach 4; pedagogy and 60
performativity tool 26, 39
*Performer Training Reconfigured* (Camilleri) 7
Performing Arts Learning 7
performing the stereotype 143, 144
*Personal Safety in Movement* (Ewan) 114
*Phaedra* (Seneca) 35
phallocentric control systems 9
Phelan, Peggy 28, 33, 34, 54, 147, 152, 181

phenomenological theory of embodiment 38, 145, 173
Piaget, Jean 49
Pickford, Marie 199
Pineau, Elyse 46, 60, 143
Pisk, Liz 86, 100, 101
Pitches, Jonathan 11
Plato 82, 83
play as medium of learning 49–50, 183
play compared to games 50
play theory 183
pleasure and discipline 57
*The Politics of American Actor Training* (Margolis & Renaud) 7
porous body 149
positivity of difference 76, 88, 118, 204
post-Brechtian approach 174, 185
post-feminism 10, 13–4
post-modernism 144
post-psychophysical acting practice 25
post-Stanislavskian approach 173
post-structuralism 5, 38, 173; theories of identity 30
"Powerspeak: Women and Their Voices" (Rodenburg) 76
Practice as Research in Performance 7
pre-linguistic voice 81–2
Prestidge, Mary 102
Prior, Ross 7, 26, 27
psychoanalytic theories 5, 31, 39, 107; of identity 31
psychophysical acting blocks 51, 147
Puar, Jasbir 58
puppetry 188–9
pure movement 103, 105
Pursey, Elizabeth 74

racism 10, 16, 104, 202
radical feminism 61
Radoslavjevic, Duska 179
*Rainbow Reading Practice* (Fairbanks) 80–1
Rainer, Yvonne 200
realism 39
*Rebecca* (du Maurier) 111, 179, 187, 188, 189
Rebellato, Dan 171
Reby, David 77
reciprocal gaze 34, 147, 155, 178
*Reconsidering Stanislavski: Feeling, Feminism and the Actor* (Blair) 173
*The Red Shoes* (Andersen) 179, 181, 187
Reeve, Sandra 39, 110, 119, 122, 147
Rego, Paula 154

*The Rego Project* (Hodge) 153, 154–6
relational actor 209, 211, 145–9
remaking mimesis 40, 64, 177
*Renaming the Director (panel discussion,* Rose Bruford College, 2012) 164
Renaud, Lissa Tyler 7
reparative reading 205
*The Republic* (Plato) 82
revolutionary dance 102–3
Rice, Emma 17, 37, 39, 57, 63, 162, 164, 166, 181–9, 206, 211
*Richard II* (Shakespeare) 164
*The Right to Speak* (Rodenberg) 75
Ripman, Olive 135
Rippeth, Malcolm 182
Riviere, Joan 32, 112
Roach, Joseph 35
Rodenburg, Patsy 73, 75, 76, 80, 86, 88, 94, 102, 105
Rodowicz-Czechowska, Iga 145
Rose, Jacqueline 112, 113
Ross, Ian 182, 184
Roth, Gabrielle 101
Rousseau, Jean-Jacques 49
Royal Academy of the Dramatic Arts (RADA) 55, 74, 76, 86, 100, 101, 136, 208
The Royal Birmingham Conservatoire 2
Royal Central School of Speech and Drama (RCSSD) 2, 8, 16, 55, 73, 74, 76, 79, 86, 100, 102, 114, 145, 198
Royal Court Theatre, London 14, 84, 166
Royal Scottish Conservatoire 74, 86, 137
Royal Shakespeare Company (RSC) 73, 74, 86, 100, 164, 166
Roy Hart Theatre 86
RSVP Cycles 103
Rutter, Carol 198

Saint-Denis, Michel 101
scaffolding support (in teaching) 46, 53, 83, 90, 109, 120
Scaravelli yoga 145, 151
Schechner, Richard 3
Schenkar, Joan 54, 169
Schön, Donald 47, 49, 148
*The Second Sex* (de Beauvoir) 84
*The Second Text* (Boston) 84–5
Sedgwick, Eve 26, 39, 55, 89, 106, 150, 204, 205
seeing as knowing 33
self-objectification 155
Seneca 35

servitude of actors 8–9
Seton, Mark 9, 35
sexual harassment 13, 202
Shakespeare, William 91, 140, 163, 179, 188, 199
Shapiro, Sherry 33, 153
Shaw, Fiona 8, 54, 164, 199
Shepherd, Mike 179, 181, 185
*Sphinx (theatre company)* 11
*Small Hours* (Kirkwood & Hime) 174
Snook, Gareth 188
Snow, Jackie 100, 101, 105
social constructivist education 46
socio-scientific paradigms 146
somatics 103, 108, 140, 148, 156
*A Sorrow Beyond Dreams* (Handke) 175, 177
Spatz, Ben 11, 30, 33, 37, 61, 76, 116, 120
speech and language therapy 79
Spencer, Charles 165
Spicer, Tim 180
Spinoza, Baruch 106
The Standing Conference of University Drama Departments (SCUDD) 6, 7
Staniewski, Wlodimir 29, 30, 33, 101, 145, 153
Stanislavski, Konstantin 5, 6, 11, 53, 101, 134, 136, 140, 172, 173, 211
Stark Smith, Nancy 102
Steen, Ros 86, 87
Sterling, Fausto 38, 63
Stevenson, Juliet 164, 198
storytelling 178–9
Strasberg, Lee 11, 53
strategic essentialism 25
Strindberg, August 167
Stroppel, Elizabeth 62, 63
Sturrock, Tristan 54, 169, 182
subversive populism 179, 186
Summers, Elaine 103
Suzuki, Tadashi 101, 162
systemic constellation therapy 120–2

Tamasha 137, 138
*Taming of the Shrew* (Shakespeare) 198
Tan, Shaun 138
Tanner, Steve 182
Taylor, Calvin 28
Taylor, Carol 48
Taylor, Elizabeth 199
teacher/director role in actor training 162–3
*Teaching Actors: Knowledge Transfer in Actor Training* (Prior) 7, 26

Index  **223**

Teaching Innovation Network 7
Teatr Pieśń Kozla (Song of the Goat) 116
*The Tempest* (Shakespeare) 164
text-based acting 5, 8
*Theatre, Dance and Performance Training* 6, 7
theatre in education (TIE) 163
thinking-beside paradigm 38, 106–7, 204
thinking body 61
Thompson, Evan 147
Thorpe, Mark 46, 48
*Three Sisters* (adapted by Dowling) 117
*Three Sisters* (adapted by Letts) 210
*Three Sisters* (adapted by Matura) 210
*Three Sisters* (Chekhov) 210
*Throwing Like a Girl* (Young) 107
Thurburn, Gwynneth 86
*Titus Andronicus* (Shakespeare) 164
"To Begin with Breathing Anew" (Irigaray) 90, 151
Todd, Mabel Ellsworth 103
touch and sensation 149–50; female sensuality and 152–3
*Touching, Feeling: Affect, Pedagogy, Performativity* (Sedgwick) 150
Training and Performance Research Association (TAPRA) 83
Trevis, Di 73, 134
*Tristan and Yseult* 179, 189
Trueman, Matt 188
*Twentieth Century Actor Training* (Hodge) 11, 134, 145

uniqueness 88, 94, 119, 146, 182
university drama education 3; practical and pragmatic differences to drama schools 3
unlearning 51
*Unmaking Mimesis* (Diamond) 34, 62, 172

*via negativa* 49, 51, 52, 53, 54, 56, 109, 139, 148, 206; in Catholic doctrine 56; feminist perspective on 55–6; gender in 52–3
*via positiva* 57, 78, 107, 118, 126, 205, 206, 210
Viewpoints 103
vital materialism 204–5, 206
vocational actor training 1; blurring of providers 2–3; difference in funding 3
voice: healing 994; as primal energy 93–4; qualities of 91–3
*Voice* (Boston) 77
Voice Care Network 77
Voice Studio International 16

voice training 16, 73–5; theory and practice reconciliation difficulties 75–6; women in 74–5; women in compared to in actor training 135
*Volatile Bodies* (Grosz) 106
vulnerability 9, 26, 27, 28, 29–30, 35–7, 45, 49, 52, 54–6, 58, 60, 76, 79–80, 89, 153
Vygotsky, Lev 46, 49

*The Wah Wah Girls* (Gupta) 187
Walker, Alice 56
Walker, Madeleine 198
Wallace, John 86, 87
Walshe, David 88, 93
Walters, Harriet 164, 198
Wandor, Michélène 163
Warner, Deborah 164, 165
Warren, Iris 74
watchfulness 110
*Waves* (Mitchell) 176
*The Waves* (Woolf) 167
Weate, Catherine 74
Wedekind, Frank 187
Weiler, Katherine 46
Weinstein, Harvey 13
wellbeing 60, 119
Welton, Martin 150, 152
Wenger, Etienne 46, 47
*The Wild Bride* (Grose) 187
Winkler, Lizzie 183, 184, 186
Winslet, Kate 4
*Wise Children* (Carter) 179, 187, 188
Wolfsohn, Alfred 86, 93
woman, contingent term of 12; Greek theatre and 35–6; lack of work in actor training 134–6
womanism 56
*A Woman Killed With Kindness* (Heywood) 171
womb-cave 83
womb-theatre 82
"Women as Artists" (Katie Mitchell workshop, 2015) 164, 165
*Women of Troy* (Euripides) 174, 175
women's collaborative practice 54–5
women's liberation movement 163
The Women's Library, London School of Economics 11
Women's Movement 59
The Women's Theatre Collection, The University of Bristol 11
*The Wooden Frock* (Grose) 179, 187
Woodman, Francesca 166

Woolf, Virginia 167, 176
The Wooster Group 5, 176
working with time and
    space 149, 150–1
Wright, John 50, 135
Wright, Sarah 182

X6 Dance Collective 102, 117

Yaqini, Ysmahane 88

*The Yellow Wallpaper* (Gilman) 167
Young, Iris 107
The Young Vic 74, 168
*Your Voice and How to Use It* (Berry) 75

Zaporah, Ruth 103
Zone of Proximal Development (ZPD)
    46, 50
Zubryzcka, Anna 145